April 3rd.

VOICES
of WAR

Stories of Service from the Home Front and the Front Lines

Edited by Tom Wiener

LIBRARY OF CONGRESS VETERANS HISTORY PROJECT

WASHINGTON, D.C.

Page 1: John Enman (center), Canning Road Barracks, New Delhi, India, spring 1945.
Page 2: Army Guard *by Tracy Sugarman, watercolor, April 3, 1944.*

This 2012 edition printed for Barnes & Noble, Inc., by National Geographic Society.
ISBN: 978-1-4351-4194-0

Library of Congress Cataloging-in-Publication Data

Voices of war: stories of service from the home front and the front lines / the Library of
   Congress Veterans History Project.
      p.cm.
   Includes index.
   ISBN 0-7922-7838-0
      1. United States—Armed Forces—Biography. 2. Veterans—United States—Biography. 3.
   United States—History, Military—20th century. 4. Oral history. I. Veterans History Project
   (U.S.)

U52. V55 2004
355'.092'2—dc22
                                                                2004049986

Printed in China
12/RRDS/1

{ CONTENTS }

{ FOREWORD }

"No man and no force can abolish memory."

—FRANKLIN DELANO ROOSEVELT

AFTER FATHER'S DAY LUNCH IN 2000, I sat at a picnic table with my father and uncle as they recounted for the first time to me their experiences serving overseas during the Korean War and World War II. Realizing that my two sons were too young at the time to appreciate the stories, I picked up our family video camera and recorded their stories so that my sons would someday be able to hear their grandfather and great-uncle talk about their service to our country.

This simple experience gave me the idea to write the Veterans History Project Act in an attempt to get families across the country involved. I remain grateful to Congressman Amo Houghton, cosponsor of this legislation, who is himself a World War II veteran. Senators Max Cleland and Chuck Hagel, both Vietnam War veterans, carried the torch on the Senate side, and the bill passed quickly with bipartisan support. Almost four years after President Clinton signed the bill into law, the Veterans History Project has taken on a life of its own. Run by a small but dedicated staff of the Library of Congress, the project has collected thousands of stories from our nation's veterans and those who served with them, both on the home front and the war front.

Veterans are sharing their stories with families, friends, and students, who pass these memories on to the Library of Congress so we will have a large archive for future generations. Numerous civic organizations, including all of the veterans organizations, have become involved in this project. Under the leadership of my wife, Tawni, court reporters from across the country are volunteering their time to transcribe these oral histories for the Library of Congress. The Library is digitizing many of these tapes and making them available over the Internet. Imagine the powerful history lesson a hundred years from now when a student sitting at a computer in class can hear the account of a veteran who fought at the Battle of the Bulge or island-hopped the Pacific with General MacArthur. And perhaps that veteran is the student's ancestor! Historians will also be able to rely on thousands of firsthand accounts of our veterans years from now.

But the clock is ticking. Every day our nation loses approximately 1,700 veterans; with them go their unique stories, memories, and experiences. The work of collecting memories from these veterans is crucial. It not only allows us the opportunity to preserve an important part of American history; it also gives us the chance to say to these veterans what they deserve to hear: Thank you. More veterans every day are stepping forward to participate in the Veterans History Project. They are responding, once again, to one more request from a grateful nation. The Veterans History Project would not exist were it not for them. Their selfless service and timeless patriotism are lessons that must be preserved. This book is a tribute to them.

But we need help. Along with Congressman Houghton and Senators Hagel and Cleland, I urge all Americans to become involved in the program, to interview the veterans you know—your grandparents or parents, a neighbor, or a friend. The Veterans History Project can be seen as our veterans' link to immortality; it is a living legacy for our generation and a gift to future ones.

—U.S. Rep. Ron Kind
Washington, D.C., 2004

{ PROLOGUE }

What Did You Do in the War?

England: June 1944

They had so many ships loaded up to make the invasion you could practically walk from one ship to another to cross that bay. And at night a German plane came in and shook the land there, and an order come down: No cigarettes. No lights. No nothing. All they had to do was see one light and he would have had a lot of us there because the ships were so close together. We were in a house , and we could hear our planes going over to bomb Germany. And as they went over, a German plane came in under them and he was dropping bombs. He dropped 18 bombs in a row, and one was near a hospital, and blew all the windows out. If he had one more bomb, he would have got us, and I had to laugh. All the guys, they ran outside and they jumped into ditches and everything, and they didn't have clothes on or anything. It looked so comical I got to laughing, and then I could hear the bullets flying around there and I said, "This ain't no place for me."

We took off on the fifth, and then it got so rough they called us back. Then the order came on the sixth for us to go across the channel. I went across on an LST, with my crane and my dozer on there. I was a dozer operator. When we got out in the channel it got pretty rough, and I had to chain my dozer down because it was sliding down the deck. I was afraid it'd punch a hole in the side and we'd sink before we got there, and so many of the men on the boats were sick. It was a storm, really, when we was going over, and as we approached the coastline in the morning, the Navy was shelling the coast, and it was just like a fog. We were supposed to have been on the second wave, and I don't know what time we got in there and dropped the ramp, and the jeep that came off, the guy got wounded, and then the fire was so heavy that the ship's Captain backed us off and we went back out into the channel, and the jeep Captain, or the guy driving the jeep, they sent him back to the States, and he had a sister that lived in Ashtabula. He wrote his sister and told his sister about me, and she got a hold of my parents and told them where I was. They hadn't heard from me for so long and they didn't know that I was in the invasion on the French coast.

Not every veteran's story is as dramatic as Jay Adams's, but every veteran has a story to tell, as the selections in this book vividly reveal. From the first days of basic training to the indelible memories forged on and off the battlefield, military service covers a vast range of experiences and emotions. This book attempts to describe the experience of service from beginning to end: from anxious days of signing up to moments of courage, valor, and tragedy.

Voices of War tells the stories of more than 60 veterans and civilians whose lives were touched by the five major wars of the 20th century. *Voices of War* covers five wars, but it is not comprehensive in its detail. Significant battles and campaigns may be missing from these pages. World War II dominates this book, as it does the collections of the Veterans History Project; more than 50 percent of our stories are from that war, which involved 16 million men and women in uniform, far more than any other war in our nation's history. Our intention was not to cover every engagement in each war, but rather to offer an impressionistic and intensely felt portrait of the ground-level soldier, slogging through the mud of France, the jungles of the Pacific, or the desert of Kuwait. This is first-person history; the 60-plus contributors to this book report only what they saw. Their candor and their willingness to open up, whether in an interview or a series of letters or a journal, allow us to experience war unfiltered by ideology or political agendas.

—Tom Wiener
Washington, D.C., 2004

{ INTRODUCTION }

A Common Virtue

by Max Cleland

"WAR," observed the author of *All Quiet on the Western Front,* a German soldier's hair-raising autobiography of his experiences in World War I, "is not an adventure for those who are being shot at."

Indeed!

When one is shot at for the first time in combat and the fear and the rage about the meaninglessness of it all surface for the first time in your brain, war is no longer an adventure. It is a battle for survival. Many succeed at surviving on the battlefield only to bring home their grisly memories of the combat they endured. So many carry those ghostly thoughts to their grave.

Others thrive on the thrill of combat. It gets in their blood. Winston Churchill was a young British lieutenant engaged in the last cavalry charge on horseback in modern warfare. His exclamation became legend. "Nothing is so exhilarating," he quipped at his dinner table many years later, "as being shot at without result."

For most of us, however, it is a fearful thought that someone is actually trying to kill us. To go into harm's way under such conditions for days, months, and sometimes even years requires a special kind of valor. When Adm. Chester Nimitz witnessed the carnage among the U.S. Marines slaughtered on the beaches of Iwo Jima by the defending Japanese, he observed that on that tiny Pacific island, "uncommon valor was a common virtue."

Through the years I have talked to many veterans of military service. Regardless of their war, their generation, their branch of service, their rank, or how much action or lack of it they saw, they all had one thing in common: They

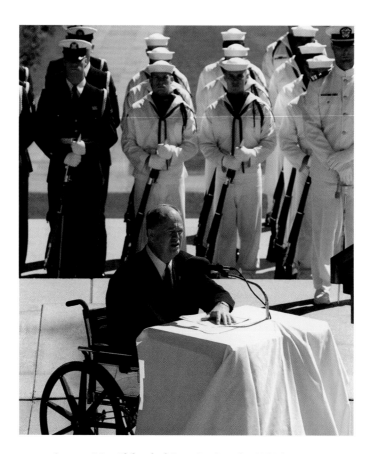

*Senator Max Cleland of Georgia gives the 1999 keynote
address at the National Prisoner of War/Missing in Action
Recognition Day ceremony at the Tomb of the Unknowns at
Arlington National Cemetery in Virginia.*

all thought of themselves as nothing special. Ironically, they all thought of themselves as basically common, just doing their jobs along with those thousands of others just doing their jobs, too.

But in this volume we see they were special. All of them! They exemplified uncommon valor. Their stories are captured here to remind us that when this nation goes to fight, it has within its ranks people of uncommon valor, people who rise heroically to the challenge of defending this nation but often feel that it is nothing special to do so. They continue to inspire us to rise and do the same.

—Max Cleland
Washington, D.C., 2004

{ CHAPTER ONE }

Answering the Call

Army Cpl. Vincent Reed, pictured here in a postcard portrait, was a postal worker in a small Missouri town when he was drafted for service in World War I in April 1918.

RAFAEL HIRTZ 1943

Rafael Hirtz, pictured here with his parents, Lucy and Paul,
was born in Buenos Aires; he became a naturalized U.S. citizen
in the 1930s when his family moved to the Los Angeles area.
Although eager to fight for his new country, he had to wait
until the United States entered World War II to enlist.

Deciding to Serve

"You want to be part of American history."

"I knew I had to go." *The words of Frederick Stilson, who volunteered for World War I in 1918, echo the words spoken by thousands of veterans. The sense of obligation, honestly and not grudgingly felt, is a thread running through many of the stories that follow, whether the soldier is off to fight in World War I, World War II, Korea, Vietnam, or the Persian Gulf.*

FREDERICK STILSON

World War I; Army; Memoir

When the United States entered the First World War in 1917, Stilson was working for the Interstate Commerce Commission in Indiana. Stilson's field crew worked on the main lines of the New York Central Railway.

After the declaration of war, the National Guard was immediately mobilized. I ran into them doing guard duty along the railway, especially where bridge structures were along the line. We were stopped before crossing the bridges and made to show an identification. They were afraid of sabotage, as some had occurred even before the war was declared.

I knew I had to go. I had registered for the draft, had been in the Illinois National Guard, and was an officer in the Washington State College Corps of Cadets while attending that institution. I wrote to several officers I knew, two in the regular Army. I asked them for recommendations to the first Officers Training Corps. I was ordered to report for physical examination in the early part of May 1917, and was successful in passing the examination.

I received orders to report to Fort Sheridan, Illinois, north of Chicago, to undergo training as a first lieutenant in the Corps of Engineers, U.S. Army. I packed my suitcase, said goodbye to the crew, and left for Chicago on May 15, 1917.

MALCOLM STILSON

World War II; Army Air Corps; Memoir
Frederick Stilson began a family tradition: His son Malcolm enlisted in World War II.

When the Japanese bombed Pearl Harbor on December 7, 1941, I was a freshman at the University of Southern California in Los Angeles. With all my classmates either being drafted or volunteering for the Army, Navy, Marines, etc., I quit USC in December 1942 and tried to enlist in a military service.

My father was a friend of Col. Bill Haigh at the Corps of Engineers, and, since I had worked on my father's surveying crew, I had the experience that the engineers could use. So Bill Haigh pulled some strings and got me assigned to a combat engineer battalion headed for the South Pacific. I flunked the physical, as the combat engineers didn't want to have someone with them whose eyes were 20/400.

I then walked into a Naval Recruiting Office. The officer in charge took one look at me and said, "Do those glasses mean anything?" And that was the end of that.

So I volunteered for the draft. I was called up shortly thereafter, took the physical, was classified limited service, and on December 11, 1942, was inducted into the Army. I had a week to settle my affairs, so I did not go on active service until Friday, December 18, 1942. I quote from my diary: "Today I entered the Army. We boarded the red cars for Los Angeles, and soon we were at the induction station waiting for the shipments to San Pedro."

CHUCK HAGEL

Vietnam War; Army; Interview

We were raised in little towns in Nebraska where the local American Legion club and the VFW were really the social centers of the universe. So we grew up with the blue Legion cap, with a sense of responsibility to this country. You didn't think about it. If the country was at war and had a need, you served.

I tried college—I tried three colleges, actually. It was not in the best interests of those academic institutions to keep me, nor in my best interest. I worked for radio stations, did various jobs in and out of school. And I was called at home one day by the draft board, who said, "Young man, you have six months to get back into college. We have levies, and they're big levies coming down." As you know, in '67, '68, the big buildup. And I sat before the draft board and said, "No, I think the best thing for me would be to go into the Army." It might not have been the best thing for the Army.

I was the oldest of four boys. My father had passed away, and my life was not coming together as it should. There was a war going on in Vietnam. I felt some sense of responsibility, so I volunteered for the draft and went in the Army.

I had the most famous of all MOS's [Military Occupational Specialty]—the infantry. And I didn't fight that—if you're going to be in the Army, you want to be a warrior. I didn't think it was very romantic or heroic to be a cook, although cooks are very important.

After AIT [Advanced Infantry Training] I was assigned to go to the then top-secret red-eyed missile gun course. This was the first shoulder-fired heat-seeking missile. And I was going to Germany after they trained us and moved into NATO units over there. But I volunteered to go to Vietnam. And all of my friends thought I was out of my mind. Nonetheless, I just felt it was the right thing to do. The war was going on, and they needed their best people, and I didn't want to be in Germany when a war was going on in Vietnam.

We were sent to Fort Dix, New Jersey, to process out to Germany. And that's where I took my orders down to the processing station and handed them in and said, "I'd like to go to Vietnam." At that point, there was a hush in the orderly room, and they said, "Young man, sit down," and a chaplain came out, a psychiatrist came out, two majors came out and they took me aside. Obviously they were concerned that I was running away from something. Obviously I don't think you'd find that many guys come in with orders to Germany and say, "I want to go to Vietnam." We talked for about three hours, about what my motives were. and they said, "All right, we'll take you off the manifest." I hung around Fort Dix for about two weeks while they reissued orders. They sent me back home to Nebraska for about five days, and we transitioned out through Oakland.

Max Cleland

Vietnam War; Army; Interview

On my father's side I was the fourth generation to be willing to serve our country in the military. My great-grandfather served in the 64th Georgia Volunteers under Robert E. Lee in the defense of Richmond and was wounded in the Battle of the Crater outside Petersburg, July 13, 1864. When I became secretary of state in Georgia, I went to Richmond and located the battle flag of the 64th Georgia Volunteers. It's now on display, shot full of holes, in the Georgia Capitol. My great-grandfather became a single-arm amputee. The calibers of the rounds in those days were so large that one shot could tear off an arm or just shred a bone. I just came across recently the draft registration for my grandfather on my father's side; he registered for the draft in 1918, and then the war was over. My father served in the United States Navy as an enlisted man, after the attack on Pearl Harbor. And I grew up with that legend, that incredible story of the attack and the response and Roosevelt and the day of infamy.

The draft hung over the head of every 18-year-old male in America in the 1960s, and you had to make a decision. I went to Stetson University in DeLand, Florida, for college. I had to make a quick decision: to join ROTC and see if I liked it and maybe graduate not only with a degree but with a second lieutenant commission, or graduate from college and go in as an enlisted man, which didn't seem too good an idea. Army ROTC was the only ROTC offered. Actually, my dream was to become a Navy pilot, but that didn't materialize. At one point I thought about being a helicopter pilot, but that didn't materialize. So eventually I was attracted to the First Air Cavalry Division, which was the first big unit sent to Vietnam by President Johnson. I volunteered for the Cav twice, once in '66, and got siphoned off to be an aide to a brigadier general. And in 1967, I volunteered again and got shipped off with the Air Cavalry Division.

I entered the Army on October 18, 1965. And no man or woman ever went on active duty with a greater sense of pride, of wanting to be there, of thank God I finally get my chance to make my mark in life, get out of the academic world. I'd had it with school. And a few days into being a young single officer at Fort Gordon, I said, "I'm going to tackle this thing called jump school." I knew I was crazy then, jumping out of a perfectly good airplane. But that was a great experience to survive and get my wings pinned upon my chest. Back in those days, that was what you were supposed to do. Keep in mind that in 1964, 1965, Barry Sadler's song "Ballad of the Green Berets" was the number one song in America. He was on *The Ed Sullivan Show*. Special Forces, Vietnam, Airborne, that was all de rigueur; that was all what was happening. And I was very much interested in the action.

I felt that I needed to take my place in the line. I didn't want to avoid the war of my generation. As a history major I knew these defining moments in history come along every now and then. And if you want to be part of American history

HUGH CLELAND 1940S   **MAX CLELAND** CA 1967

Military service is a Cleland family tradition. Max Cleland's father Hugh served in the Navy during World War II. Hugh Cleland's father served in World War I, and Hugh's grandfather fought for the Confederacy in the Civil War.

in the future, you better get in there so you can be a good leader afterward.

I chose Signal Corps because I wanted to be shot at every other day, not every day. I figured if I went infantry I'd be dead. I wanted to be part of the action, but I just didn't want to get killed being part of the action.

TRACY SUGARMAN

World War II; Navy; Interview

I was in Syracuse University in the College of Fine Arts. It was the middle of my junior year. I was at my fraternity house, and we were practicing a competitive choral sing on a Sunday morning. Someone came running into the fraternity house and said, "They've bombed Pearl Harbor!" And someone immediately said, "Who's Pearl Harbor?" Two days later, I joined the Naval Reserve. Went down to Buffalo, New York, on a train from Syracuse with a fraternity brother, Gene Berger, who ended up lost at sea in the Pacific. I went back, expecting to get called up anytime. And the other reserves kept getting called up. But the

Navy left me alone until I graduated. I graduated May 11, 1943, and on May 13th, I had to report to midshipman's school at Notre Dame University in Indiana. And when I went out there, I think it was the farthest away from home I'd ever been.

I think I was intrigued with the Navy simply because I had seen so little of it. I'd really never seen a ship up close. But it just seemed like exciting and adventurous duty. And sounded a hell of a lot better than walking. It never occurred to me to make it a career. You joined the reserves so you could serve during the war.

I knew there was a fleet out in the Pacific, but I knew zip about what was happening. I knew we had been having trouble with the Japanese diplomatically, but really, my attention, like most people's in the East, was focused on Europe. I was paying a lot of attention to Europe. Part of it perhaps was the fact that we were getting relatives showing up who were escaping Europe, relatives I didn't even know we had, coming from Germany, coming from Central Europe.

VIOLET ASKINS HILL GORDON
   World War II; Army Nurse Corps; Interview
I joined [in 1942] because my best friend, Mildred Osby, appeared at my house one day, all excited because she had learned that there was going to be organized a Women's Army Auxiliary Corps. She wanted very much to be part of it; and, as we were very close friends she thought it would be wonderful if I also was interested and would do so. At that time I was working in State Civil Service in Chicago; I was supervising a stenographic pool. I was not bored, but restless, kind of stuck, I guess. But I wasn't that excited about entering into anything that sounded as regimented as the Army. So I didn't pick up on it initially. She kept after me and after me, and I finally said, "Well, OK."

WALTER MORRIS
   World War II; Army; Interview
I was born in Waynesboro, Georgia, in 1921. My family migrated north to Newark, New Jersey, and I started my schooling in Newark. In 1937 my mother decided to send me back to my uncle in Waynesboro because of the bad influence I was getting in Newark with the street gangs and all. In 1939 I graduated from high school and started my apprenticeship as a bricklayer. Work was so scarce in 1940 that there was no work for bricklayers and certainly no work for apprentice bricklayers. The Army at that time was offering a one-year service to

anyone who wanted to volunteer for a year. And that was a godsend for me, because that allowed me to do something other than sit around all day. So I volunteered. In January 1941, I left Waynesboro for Fort Benning, Georgia, as an inductee.

RHONA KNOX PRESCOTT
Vietnam War; Army Nurse Corps; Interview
When I enlisted, I was living in New York City, where I was born and raised. I was in my last year of nursing school. And they recruited nurses then because the Vietnam War was escalating. I needed my senior year's tuition desperately. My cousin was in the military. Members of my family were military officers in the Army. My high school chums were in the military, a number of them were in Vietnam. It just seemed that all the time we were bombarded with the idea of war. I figured that since I was to be a nurse, an operating room nurse, that would be the best place to use my skills. Although all the branches were recruiting for nurses, the Army was the one that mostly guaranteed that you would go right to Vietnam.

ISABELLE CEDAR COOK
World War II; Army Nurse Corps; Interview
I was a young woman in New York City and had just graduated from Mount Sinai Hospital School of Nursing when war was declared in Europe. And pretty soon we were in the thick of it. The Army asked Mount Sinai Hospital to form a thousand-bed hospital for overseas service. They asked for volunteers, and since I was an unattached young lady, I felt that it was my duty to join the Army and to help soldiers overseas when they needed care. I didn't tell my family. I had a mother who was a widow with five children. I didn't tell her, I didn't ask her permission, I just signed right up. And then waited impatiently for them to call me for the service. Finally, in September of 1942, I got the call: "Proceed immediately to Camp Rucker, Alabama."

JEANNE URBIN MARKLE
Vietnam War; Army Nurse Corps; Interview
I come from a small town of about 100 people in northern Indiana. All teenagers want to leave small towns, so my aim was always to go out and see the world. I went to nurse's training at St. Elizabeth's Hospital in Lafayette, Indiana, and I graduated in 1965. While I was in nurse's training, my friends and I decided that

Recruitment posters for the armed forces reached their artistic peak during World War II. The posters cast a wide a net, encouraging men and women to serve in uniform and as civilians on the home front.

the best thing that we could do to get out of Indiana after we graduated was to have a plan where we would all go together. We wanted to go to Michael Reese Hospital in Chicago and live in the big city. During my junior year, Army, Navy, and Air Force recruiters came to the school. And I had already got the word from my mother that I was not going to Chicago. No child of hers was going to go up to Chicago, a strange place, the big city. So I showed her—I joined the Army!

And the only reason I picked the Army was because they would induct you as a PFC [Private First Class] immediately and pay you $335 a month. The Air Force and the Navy did nothing. They just had prettier uniforms. And so we joined the Army, two friends and I.

My whole senior year I got a check on the 30th of every month for $335, and that was the only tie I had to the United States Army. I was in the Army, I was a PFC, but I was still being trained as a nurse. But the minute you graduate, they come calling. We could not take our state boards until October, and then it takes forever to get the results. We were watching the mailbox every day, and were told that the envelope is big and thick if you get your license. One night, about two or three weeks after I'd taken my boards, my girlfriend called and said the captain had called from Indianapolis and said you had just passed your boards. And I said, "How does she know?" And she said, "The Army can find out anything." And so we three knew our results long before our classmates did. In December 1965, we went to downtown Indianapolis and were sworn into the Army as second lieutenants.

Rod Hinsch
Vietnam War; Army; Interview
Right out of high school, I didn't know what I wanted to be when I grew up, and I knew I didn't want to get married, so I decided to join the military. I had heard a lot about the paratroopers. When I was a kid, I had made a makeshift parachute out of an old linen tablecloth and jumped off the garage. Luckily, the garage wasn't very high and I didn't hurt myself too badly, but it didn't knock the want or the need out of me to actually do it properly.

Joanne Palella
Persian Gulf War; Army; Interview
I was in the suburbs of Chicago, Illinois, a suburb called Chambourg. I got in trouble in high school and had the option to leave or get kicked out, so I left. After that, I was working dead-end jobs and hanging around people that were

partying or getting high, and I wanted more out of life and military service was about the only way I could see to get out of that environment. I picked the Army because it gave the option of a job—MOS, it's called—that I wanted, and it also gave me more education benefits. I enlisted in October of '80.

NATHANIEL RALEY

World War II; Army Air Corps; Memoir

My father was chief of police [of Demopolis, Alabama] long before I was born. Early in elementary school, my parents bought me a set of encyclopedias, which included much about the Great War [World War I]. I became fascinated with the aircraft of that era. When I was about seven or eight years old, a barnstormer landed in a cow pasture at the edge of Demopolis. Daddy and I drove out to investigate conditions. Initially, no one seemed to want to pay his price to go for a ride. Finally, he said that he would take my father and me up for a free ride "just to get things started." (Being chief of police did have a few perks.) The airplane was a World War I biplane trainer called a Jenny. That did it for me; I wanted to be a pilot. That evolved into my wanting to be a military pilot, which was soon followed by my wanting to be a military fighter pilot. By the late 1930s that had further evolved into my wanting to be a pilot in combat.

I had planned to enter the University of Alabama to earn a degree in mechanical engineering. The war changed all that. I volunteered for pilot training (I had to obtain my mother's permission to volunteer) and, after many delays, I was sent to Santa Ana, California, for preflight training and classification in late July 1942.

DENTON CROCKER

World War II; Army; Memoir

Activities and concerns relating to the war began for me before induction into the Army. Starting, I think, in the summer of 1941, I became an airplane spotter. Whether there was some real concern for a possible German air attack on the East Coast, or whether it was a way of mobilizing people emotionally for the war effort I don't know, but for several hours on one or two nights a week, working together with another person, I climbed to the roof of the Swampscott, Massachusetts, high school, the highest building in town, and watched for planes. We telephoned each sighting to a report center giving altitude, distance, direction from us, and direction of flight. My draft number came up, I think in the fall or winter of 1941, but I obtained a deferment allowing me to finish my senior year and to graduate from Northeastern University in June 1942.

During my senior year I talked with my classmate friends about enlisting and which of the service branches was best, and I went with Bob Harrington to a Navy recruiting station to learn that my vision would prevent acceptance there. I also remember long talks with Dick Raymond about the rightness and the possibility of conscientious objection. I had heard of the exaggeration of German brutality in our U.S. propaganda during WWI, and was somewhat skeptical of the official line now. On the other hand, I had read Gregor Ziemer's *Education for Death* in an education course and had written a term paper on Nazi educational methods. I was of course appalled at the sort of brainwashing that was going on, and it put into question the whole Nazi system.

I believed, too, that regardless of what some thought were the excessive restrictions on Germany and the surrender terms at the end of WWI, the sweeping absorption of territory by a massive military effort had to be stopped. By the time June rolled around, I was ready to accept military service, but I was most hopeful that I might be assigned to the Medical Department, and so avoid the need to bear arms. I talked with Dad about this, and after the fact he told me that he had mentioned this desire to his friend Wenty (Wentworth) Williams, who was then a major at Fort Devens, the recruit reception center to which I was to be sent. I suppose that my unusually long wait for assignment once I was at Fort Devens was due to his intervention and to my therefore being held until a call for medical replacements was received.

SALLY HITCHCOCK PULLMAN
World War II; Army Nurse Corps; Memoir
June 1944 was a very tense time for the world and for my family. D-Day, June 6, 1944, had finally happened. My older brother John was a Navy pilot flying shore patrols in PB4Ys (Army B-24s) on antisubmarine duty out of England. We worried about him constantly, especially because we had had no news from him in many days.

I had graduated from Smith College three years before, with a major in geology and a minor in history. Thirty-six months later, I was newly graduated from Yale with a masters degree in Nursing. I had passed my physical exam for the Army Nurse Corps in the spring just before graduation.

In this tense time, I waited to be called to active duty. Despite my mother's horror at my wanting to serve, I felt compelled to go to help. My orders finally came.

And so it was, on June 21, 1944, I was on my way. My mom and dad borrowed gas coupons to drive me from Brattleboro to Greenfield, Massachusetts, where I boarded the train to Ayer, Massachusetts, the site of Fort Devens.

This was a highly significant time in my life. I was going to my very first job as a graduate nurse. I was twenty-five years old and had been in school for the past 19 years of my life. I was excited and determined to use all my training to help mend as many injured men and women as I could, and help them come home to their families and loved ones.

As I sat in that old railroad car (WWI vintage), with its green plush seats and no air-conditioning, I was terribly aware of how hard this leave-taking was for my mom and dad. My brother John was somewhere in Europe. I was going to be somewhere else. Neither of my parents was young anymore.

The train puffed along, and I kept saying to myself, in time to the clicking rails, "I want to go, I want to go." Whether I sat next to anyone else I can't recall, but I remember I tried to read *Taps for Private Tussie* [a popular novel in 1944]. I blotted my damp hands. I looked out at the bright, cloudless June day at the cozy farms and small houses. I said to myself, "Calm down, you sissy. Read your book and relax!"

JAMES WALSH

Korean War; Army; Memoir

James Walsh had a wrenching leave-taking when he set off to serve in the Korean War. In the summer of 1950, he finished his second year in the seminary, where he was studying to be a Roman Catholic priest. He was deferred from the draft and yet, as he stated in his memoir, motivated by, "teen-age hero worship of the men and women who'd lived in my Detroit neighborhood from 1943 to 1945 and had gone off to fight World War II in Europe and the Far East." Also, there was the example of his older brother Jack, who served in the U.S. Army of Occupation in Japan.

So at 19, he enlisted. His parents both objected.

Mom was succinct: "It's shameful throwing off black clerical garb for olive drab."

Dad's face reddened before words exploded from his lips. "You're daft, son, doubly so giving up both seminary and college deferments to fight in Harry Truman's Asian War. Living in a seminary was a life in a flower bowl; in the Army it's in a piranha-infested river. You'll be eaten alive! Why go from a philosophical library to a bunker, from prayers in the seminary's chapel to shell-pocked ridges?"

"It's my duty," I said, "to my country. For God, I'll fight the spread of atheistic communism."

Dad looked like the Archangel Michael about to slay the devil with a sword. "If it's a crusade for Country and God you're after, you'll find it in County Antrim in the

VIOLET ASKINS HILL GORDON 1942

Induction day for Mildred Osby, Sarah Emmet, Irma Cayton, and Violet Askins (far right). Soon after this photo was taken, Askins shipped out to Fort Des Moines in Iowa, where she was quartered in a segregated barracks.

north of Ireland in the Irish Republican Army against Plantation Loyalists from England, a crusade any Irishman named Walsh could sink his teeth into."

Instead, on February 6, 1951, I joined, and within a few days I'd bit into U.S. Army chow.

MARY SHELDON GILL

World War II; Women's Army Corps; Interview, Memoir

I was without doubt the first woman to join the newly formed Women's Army Corps (WACs) from Washington County in New York State. My home then was in the village of Greenwich, halfway between Albany and the Canadian border. I joined because I was patriotic and open to adventure after two boring years of New York State College for Teachers, which was like a glorified high school at that time.

When I first wrote my father that I was going to join the newly formed Women's Army Corps, he wrote back, "It will all be scum." I knew it would not be scum and went anyway. Later on he was proud of my decision among the townsfolk. I found a very dedicated middle-class group for the most part.

JOE BACA
Vietnam War; Army; Interview
The youngest child in a family of 15, Joe Baca was raised in the desert town of Barstow, California. His father had a third-grade education; his mother had never been to school. Baca had to learn English while attending elementary school.

A lot of what drew me to serve in the military had to do with my brother who served during the Korean War and seeing him come back wearing that uniform. And the influence by a person I worked with in the railroad, where I was working as a laborer. I had just graduated from high school. He was telling me about the military and about Airborne, and it was like a fantasy. You start listening to the good stories and the good times they had. And during that time we had the Vietnam War going on, so I volunteered for the draft.

There was a lot of pride in the community over my serving, but at the same time there was fear. My parents said, "Why don't you just go to school? Why do you have to go and volunteer and be in the military?" They were afraid. And they saw the changes in my brother from when he was in the Korean War and actually saw action. They had that fear for me.

JEANNE URBIN MARKLE
World War II; Army Nurse Corps; Interview
I had to go home and get my mom and dad to sign the papers after I enlisted. My dad was very proud, my mother was scared to death and not very receptive to the idea. She had lived through the Depression and, you'd think, the Victorian Age: Good girls did not join the service. But my father talked her into it.

JEANNE HOLM
World War II; Women's Army Corps; Interview
 After I graduated from high school in Portland, Oregon, I became a silversmith for a while, until the war started. It was 1942. Both my brothers were in the Navy, and I joined the first service that came along that accepted women, and that was the Army. I joined to serve my country, essentially. It never occurred to me to ask anyone. But my mother and grandmother were very enthusiastic about it. As a matter of fact, had they been young enough, they would have done it themselves.

VINCENT REED

World War I; Army; Memoir

I was deeply in love with Jo Glasscock, who lived in Rensselaer, Missouri. We became engaged in January 1918, and I was as proud a man as ever lived to know that such a splendid, sweet girl as Jo had so honored me as to promise to one day become my wife. Knowing I was soon to be called to service, she knit for me a sweater which I wore through all my Army life.

On April 20, I was ordered to report to our post office on April 29 for induction into the military service of the U.S. We reported on this date and were given our instructions and ordered to report the next morning at 6 A.M. I was placed in charge of the men.

That afternoon the clerks and carriers of the post office assembled around me and presented me with a wristwatch. I was deeply moved at the good wishes of my fellow workers and the thought that I might never take my place among them again. My last night at home I spent quietly with mother and wrote a last letter to my sweetheart.

I was up early the morning of the 30th of April, and after having breakfast, I gave my mother and Nell, my sister, one last farewell. As I was placed in charge of the men who were going to camp, I marched at the head of the group and we proceeded to the station. It has seemed a shame to me that Quincy could not provide a band for us that morning, and give us a good send-off. There was such a crowd at the depot that we could hardly make our way through.

At Carthage another bunch joined us. There was a big crowd at the depot and the band gave them a hearty farewell. At Burlington, we stayed about an hour. There was a band there also. As we crossed the streets, every one was crowded with people to see us leave.

STEVE BUYER

Persian Gulf War; Army; Interview

Steve Buyer shipped out to the Persian Gulf in mid-December 1990. At his send-off in Indianapolis, his father wore his department commander's Legion cap, saying good-bye to all the men in the unit that he could.

Later I asked Dad why he did that, and he said guilt from Vietnam. He wished he had done that then. I remember after saying good-bye to my family, I turned around and for whatever reason I felt this compulsion to go back to my father. I said, "Dad, I'm prepared for this, and he looked back at me and said, "You're the best I have to offer."

Basic Training

No matter which war, or which branch of service, the basic training experience is the same: disorienting, arbitrary, and physically punishing, even for those recruits who assume they are in shape. "It was quite a jolt," Helen Minor, a World War II WAC remembers, "not like home at all, or school, or anything." Every branch of the military understands that what lies ahead—the dangers and horrors of war for at least some of its recruits—can only be faced with a firm foundation of physical toughness, mental alertness, and a sense of duty not only to one's country but also to one's comrades in arms. Exercises are repeated over and over; kitchen or yard patrol requires spotlessness; there is classroom work for the officer candidates. These are the staples of the military menu, from prepping the doughboys for the trenches of World War I to anticipating the rigors of desert warfare in the Persian Gulf.

A soldier's basic gear is illustrated in the pages of John Enman's memoir. Enman, pictured in the photographs at right, served in the Army Air Corps during World War II, securing and processing aerial maps for Allied bombing runs in the China-Burma-India Theater.

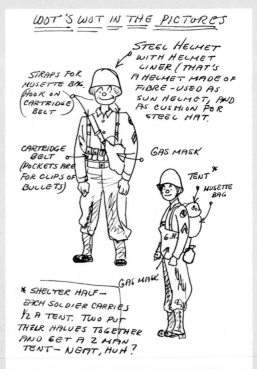

"The last man over" Wall scaling contest at Fort Leavenworth, Kansas. 4th of July, 1917

Co. B. 23rd. Engrs - On the march from Annapolis Md to Camp Meade. Md.

Frederick Stilson underwent training in the summer of 1917 at Camp Leavenworth, Kansas (top), and at Camp Meade, Maryland (bottom). Stilson's memoir, That Other War, *describes his World War I experiences in the Army Corps of Engineers.*

Letters Home, *Sally Hitchcock Pullman's memoir of her adventures as a nurse in the Pacific during World War II, includes this sketch of leaving home (above). A barracksmate of Marie Brand Voltzke finds a rare moment of respite (upper right), while Violet Askins Hill Gordon (second row, second from left) and her company drill at Fort Huachuca, Arizona, 1942.*

Guardian City, Saudi Arabia, 1990, from the Patricia Seawalt collection. For those like Seawalt, an Army officer called to serve in the Persian Gulf, training was an ongoing process, continuing even after arriving in the field.

Off to Field Duty

WACs, Daytona Beach, Florida, 1942

Mary Sheldon Gill, who donated the photo above, left a teachers'
college in upstate New York for a more exciting adventure when
she joined the WACs in 1942. Getting to train in sunny Florida
proved that life in uniform wasn't all blood, sweat, and tears.

A New Life at Arms

"You can imagine the culture shock."

The transition from civilian to military life, no matter what the era, is a jarring one. A long train or bus ride (sometimes one of each) lands new recruits at a location far from home. The climate and the surroundings are unfamiliar, and the uncertainty of what comes next is palpable. "We were all confused, we all felt stupid," *recalled Rod Hinsch of his first days in the service.* "They tear you down," *said Paul Steppe,* "and they wear you down, make you listen and learn."

ROD HINSCH
    Vietnam War; Army; Interview
I heard the strains of "Reveille." I was very dismayed to find out that it was recorded. I had always thought there was some guy standing out in front of the barracks, blowing "Reveille" on a bugle. And that made me very disappointed.

    You're eighteen years old, you just got out of high school, and you go into a situation where you're going to be disciplined heavily. There's going to be a lot expected of you, and this is something that most of us had not experienced. And so we're all confused, we all feel stupid, we all feel like we have left feet, we don't do anything right. It's a traumatic experience.

    I think everybody remembers their instructors, if not remembering their names, remembering little situations that happened with them. We had one black sergeant, a very good sergeant who would not let anything get by. I remember he had a big, booming bass voice that you could hear from a drill field away. You're walking along, thinking no one can see you, you've got your hands in your pockets, sauntering along—he'd catch you. His voice would carry all the way across, and he sounded like he was right in back of you: "GET YOUR HANDS OUT OF YOUR POCKETS!" He was somebody you would remember because when he yelled at you, your whole body vibrated. Your basic training people, you think about them, but the people in the advanced training courses who really teach you how to survive, those are the people you remember.

IRVING OBLAS

World War II; Navy; Letter to his wife, September 1943

We arrived [at Sampson Naval Training Station in New York] at 7:30 and were welcomed by a large number of sailors in dungarees who did nothing but kibbitz and yell, "You'll be sorry," etc., and warn of the tough days to come. The rest of the morning we were subjected to the usual indignities of a medical exam, worse than at Grand Central. The old-timers constantly tell us of all the trials we will face—some of them a good deal exaggerated—I'll describe them when they happen.

The C.P.O. [Chief Petty Officer] gave us a brief talk today, principally instructions on obeying orders. No "freedom" here—he cited a case of some fellows who wanted to sign a petition and were almost accused of mutiny—they didn't like the clerks of their company. One of the men in our company had an argument with a mess attendant and made derogatory remarks about the meat. His punishment followed: running around the mile track for some time carrying 100 pounds!

The Lt. gave a speech to the battalion in the afternoon—the volume of "don'ts" & prohibitions is astounding—there is a vigorous campaign against swearing—and there's plenty of swearing going on, too. Also, campaign on honesty and cleanliness. And he dwelt a good deal on the attitude of men who didn't want to be in the Navy—re: the sacrifices others have made, the need to adjust as long as we're in and can't get out, etc. A good many men frankly say they wish they were home and I've heard some say they'd do anything to get out. But that's to be expected at the beginning.

ISABELLE CEDAR COOK

World War II; Army Nurse Corps; Interview

Now you can imagine the culture shock, going from Manhattan down to Camp Rucker, Alabama, in Ozark, a tiny town of about 500 people. Real Southerners, and here are these Northern Yankees who came to invade the area.

And you can imagine civilians undergoing this basic training, when we marched and had backpacks and everything else. All the soldiers in the camp lined up to see the nurses marching by. And mis–marching most of the time.

BEN SNYDER
World War II; Army Air Corps; Journal; July 20, 1943

Mid-summer here in the heart of Texas leaves much to be desired. It is suffocatingly hot and humid. We are frequently marched back and forth. When "at ease" comes I pull out of my cap verses for memorization. It distracts the mind and helps to pass the time away.

CHUCK HAGEL
Vietnam War; Army; Interview

Those who have been through basic training know that it is a very unique experience. I was there in the summer of '67 at Fort Bliss, which, for those who are unaware of that garden spot, is in the desert right outside of El Paso, Texas. Oh, it was hot. Sand, desert, rocks.

I was in with a lot of kids who had never had any organization in their life. They were drafted from Navajo reservations; there were Hispanic kids. We had kids who had quit school in the seventh grade; we had some kids who had never worn boots, hardly shoes. Tough group. And of course, basic training is tough. They need to make you tough. And it was a survival issue for all of us. The drill sergeant would say, "Boy, I'm going teach you to be mean and tough, because if you're not mean and tough, you're going to get your head blown off in Vietnam."

I went down with five friends from Nebraska. We were inducted in Omaha and then took a train down to Fort Bliss. Got off that train at three o'clock in the morning. Hot, terrible, everybody was unsure of what was going to happen next, and you get a very abrupt awakening when the drill sergeant starts screaming at you. I was with one guy who was a dear, dear friend. He among other things was a drummer in a rock band, and so he had long hair and he had these wild bell-bottom pants on and a wild blue and white polka-dot shirt, with tennis shoes. These drill sergeants got us off that train at three o'clock in the morning and a new jarring gong of reality set in. And from that moment it was their world.

RON WINTER
Vietnam War; Marine Corps; Interview

I was going to college on a scholarship. I'd finished the first semester of my freshman year. Vietnam was starting to heat up; they'd already made the major landings there. And I was just looking around college and realized I didn't know what I was doing there or where I was going, and I left college after that first semester and joined the Marines. In the community I came from, the Marines were looked up to as the premier, elite service. And I figured if I was going to go, I wanted to be part of the best.

The boot camp experience is probably the most shocking thing a young person will ever encounter, going from the civilian world to the military. I met a lot of former Marines who gave me advice, but nobody can prepare you for the intensity of the shock when you get there, and you realize no one really cares who you are or what you did in the past, and they're not all that happy you're there.

I tell you, I can still remember the drill instructor getting on the bus, and it was like one o'clock in the morning in Parris Island, South Carolina, early January. Guy got on the bus with a Smokey the Bear hat and had a few nice words for the bus driver, and when he turned it was just this complete personality change. He's screaming at us, "You have ten seconds to get off this bus!" Well, there's maybe a hundred people on that bus, and he's saying, "Anybody that's left on this bus when I count down from ten is gonna die!" And all of a sudden you realized he wasn't kidding.

JOSEPH STEINBACHER

World War II; Army; Memoir

We were put on a troop train and began a trip to Camp Roberts, California, to begin basic training. I remember many hours of boredom on the train sitting and watching the countryside roll past. We did get good meals on the train in a dining car and went to sleep each evening in a Pullman berth made up by Negro porters. We arrived at Camp Roberts the end of June 1943 and it was very hot, very dry, and very dusty.

We picked up our luggage and all of us scrambled off the troop train, falling into two long, not very straight lines. A Chinese buck sergeant stood facing us. "Straighten out those lines and stand at attention," he shouted. "The soldier standing behind me is an officer. Whenever you address him you will stand at attention, you will salute, and you will say sir." Thus began my Army career, rapidly becoming a litany of shouted orders and close-order drill on a huge parade field of sticky asphalt, melting under the broiling sun. The company took long hikes under the same broiling sun with full field packs along rutted dirt roads where the dust was at least a foot deep and rose into the air in suffocating, choking clouds to settle thickly on everything.

Red Cross workers sew stripes on uniforms at Camp Patrick Henry, Virginia, 1944. Robert Lee Olen, a sergeant with the Army's Tenth Mountain Division, photographed Army life as a hobby while he served and later became a photojournalist.

JEANNE HOLM

World War II; Women's Army Auxiliary Corps; Interview

I went to Fort Des Moines, Iowa, for basic training. That was a new training center that they had opened in the summer of 1942 to train the women of the Women's Army Auxiliary Corps. Fort Des Moines was an old cavalry base— they had just taken the horses out. They turned the stables into huge dormitories for the enlisted women's basic training—two hundred women in one room. My first night in the barracks, I'm lying there looking up at the ceiling in my little bunk in the middle of the night, asking myself, "My God, what have I done?" But the next day, of course, when "Reveille" was blown on the bugle and a little Texas gal yelled, "All right, everybody hit the deck!" we were all up and so gung-ho you cannot believe it. We were so turned on by this experience.We felt like pioneers.

VIOLET ASKINS HILL GORDON

World War II; Women's Army Corps; Interview

I had never been at an Army camp; I don't think that any of us had. Fort Des Moines is an old, established camp. Of course, there had not been women there before, so they had to set up and establish housing and facilities for women. I do remember writing a letter home because officially we were dubbed "The Third

Platoon," referring to the platoon of women who were being trained as officers. We were housed in a separate barracks, an Army barracks, one long building. We all slept in this one long room with the cots, footlockers, and all of the Army paraphernalia. You have to remember that this was all before Truman truly desegregated the services.

STEVE BUYER
Persian Gulf War; Army; Interview
Steve Buyer's military training began at the Citadel, the prestigious military college in South Carolina that his father and brother attended before him.

What I recall most was a language I could not believe. I had never been called the names that I was called. And I couldn't figure out why they were treating me like that. The plebe system at the Citadel doesn't start until after the first three days, and when it starts you understand that there's going to be a militarization. I figured that out, but I was going to have fun with it. I was going to play a game with the system. I felt like I was one of the last to break. About December the system broke me. Then I realized today what this is. They break everybody. At some point, everybody breaks.

The intent is militarization. They're going to rebuild you. They're going to say, "Thank you, Mom and Dad. This child wasn't born with a set of instructions. You've done well, but we're going to polish this stone. And we're going to make sure that they are morally centered and that they will understand virtue is first, then values, and they will be steeped in character, and they will understand a true sense of honor." Before you lead, you better understand yourself and your depths of fear and your depths of courage.

I don't think America understands the militarization process, whether it's at our boot camps or at our military academies or the six military colleges. Our ROTCs do not have the rigor, nor the value added of a 24-hour military experience. I never would have believed what I just said had I not experienced it in the Gulf War itself. I saw some VMI officers, Norwich, North Georgia, Texas A&M, West Pointers, the Citadel: I saw these officers really rise above. I really hate to say it like that, because you had some good ROTC officers do well, too, but you could spot these academy grads or Citadel grads out of the group. You just could. It was their military bearing. When things got difficult, they weren't swayed at all by the emotions of the moment; they knew how to assimilate things well and keep focused. And by their bearing, they led.

PAUL STEPPE

Korean War; Marine Corps; Interview

Boot camp is an entirely different thing than most people think. They tear you down, and they wear you down, make you listen and learn. Discipline is a big thing in the Marine Corps. Some people cried. The ones that cried were the people who goofed up the most. If anyone goofed up, the whole platoon was punished. So you learn it's a buddy system, and you learn not to goof up anymore.

EDWARD SHROCK

Vietnam War; Navy; Interview

I was actually the first member of my family ever to go into the military. The day I graduated from college I got my draft notice in the mail. I applied to go to Officer Training School in the Air Force. And then, because the family that lived behind us had a son in the Navy, they talked me into applying for the Navy as well, and I did, and ended up choosing the Navy.

Officer Candidate School in Newport, Rhode Island, was a four-month training program. I arrived there on the 15th or 16th of May '64 and was commissioned on September 18, 1964.

How grueling it was. I had never been exposed to military training before, or the military. When our company first got there, we all thought, "My God, we'll never make this, no way we can ever survive this." But we decided to get together. We had a saying in our company; it was "Cooperate and graduate," that if we all helped one another, we could graduate. And we cooperated and every single one of us graduated. A lot of people washed out of that program, but in our particular company nobody did.

SIDNEY RICHES

World War II: Army; Memoir

Riches underwent basic training at Fort Benning, Georgia as part of a communications unit.

"Blood, sweat, and tears!" The blood came generally when you "burned a pole." Learning to climb a pole requires using lineman's spikes and belt. Up on the pole, if the spikes pull out, the hands are usually splintered attempting to halt the downward flight! The sweat—under a broiling Georgia summer sun, maneuvers, heavy construction, wire laying! The tears—receiving an "F" on a written exam!

STEVE BUYER 1991

Steve Buyer's reserve unit was called up to serve in the Persian Gulf War in 1990. Like his father and brother, he received his first military training at the Citadel.

DENTON CROCKER

World War II; Army; Memoir

The sergeant of the barracks I lived in was regular Army, and he knew from long experience how to shed work. He quickly noticed that I was familiar with the orderly forming of men into groups for roll call, marching somewhere, etc. (learned in Boy Scouts), and so very soon it was I who gave new batches of recruits instruction in Army style bedmaking and marched them to places for medical exams, to receive equipment, or to see the movie on venereal disease (no well-known star actors in this film). I suppose that I had to sit through that film a half dozen times. Its photos of disease-rotted faces and other anatomical parts should have converted one and all to celibacy.

PAUL STEPPE

Korean War; Marine Corps; Interview

The worst movie I watched was an operation on an infantryman's foot. He had frostbitten feet and gangrene had settled in his toes. A doctor took a pair of snips and cut the man's toes off and pus went everywhere. It was explained that the soldier had lost his foot at his ankle, for the gangrene had spread. The purpose of watching this was to make sure the Marines didn't let the same thing happen to them. Protect your feet and your weapon!

FREDERICK STILSON

World War I; Army; Interview

We were given a guided tour of the military penitentiary and also the Federal penitentiary during our stay in Leavenworth, Kansas, to impress us with the responsibilities of our job as Army officers, in case we should stray from the straight and narrow path, such as making away with government equipment, purloining government money, which we would be entrusted with, and disobeying the orders of our superiors. The interiors of these prisons were pretty grim, and some of the characters we saw therein didn't look too happy. We took the lessons to heart, and I never heard of any of our group trying to get away with anything.

NATHANIEL RALEY

World War II; Army Air Corps; Interview

In December 1942 Raley was sent to Basic Pilot Training School in Lemoore, California.

The decision was made that my entire class would be moved to the Basic School at Marana, Arizona. In early 1943, a roster was made of the remaining cadets in my class based on their physical height. We were rowed up in a single long line; I was 5'7" tall and placed toward the lower [shorter in stature] end of the line.

We were to be given a choice of single-engine fighter, twin-engine fighter, or bombers. The officer in charge began calling names, starting at the shorter end of the line. I was perhaps the sixth or seventh name called; all before me had chosen single-engine fighter. After a few more names were called, and all had chosen fighters, the officer in charge stated that the quota for fighters had been filled and that the rest would go to bombers. Sadly, I watched some grown men cry.

RAFAEL HIRTZ

World War II; Army; Interview

When World War II broke out, Rafael Hirtz was the 17-year-old son of a successful international businessman living in Los Angeles. Rafael, born in Buenos Aires, was raised in his father's native France, with French as his first language. The Hirtzes moved to America in the early 1930s, but Rafael's grandmother continued to live in France, and he visited her every summer. The Hirtzes were, he told an interviewer, a "very political family in the sense that we were always interested in what was going on in the world." *After the Germans invaded Poland in 1939, Rafael decided he wanted to join the fight against the Nazis. He tried to enlist in the Canadian Army but was told he would lose his naturalized citizenship if he did. He attended Pomona College for two years and then volunteered for the U.S. Army.* "They were rather shocked that anyone with any college education was going into the Army," *he recalled.* "Before the draft that just didn't happen."

Hirtz was chosen for Officer Candidate School and a specialty in communications.

One day in camp some officer came up to me and said, "Hey, you're wanted in that big tent down the road." And I said, "Fine. What's it all about?" And he said, "You'll know when you get there." So I went into this large tent; there must have been two or three hundred men in there when I entered. I went in, and the only place to sit was in the front row. Then this guy gets up on the stand and says, "Anybody who is not interested in a 50-50 chance of survival please leave now." Well, that was a rather astounding statement, but I didn't say anything. He told us that we had been picked because of our knowledge of language and our knowledge of the countries in Europe. I heard some rustling behind me but didn't turn around. Finally he made some remark, "Well, that doesn't leave too many," and I turned around and there were three of us left.

He explained that the United States was interested in forming an intelligence unit. Prior to this, there was none. I didn't know it at the time, but OSS, the Office of Strategic Services, had already been formed by President Roosevelt and General Donovan and a few British officers. They didn't want it known, because the military intelligence units of the Army and Navy and the FBI were very, very much against forming a U.S. secret service unit. Hoover, the director of the FBI, wanted to control all intelligence in the United States. He was very, very jealous of any other unit that was being planned. And he had no particular liking for Roosevelt anyway, and this was Roosevelt's baby.

They didn't know exactly what field I was going to go into. You had all types:

you had people who stayed in the background, worked in Washington; you had people in coding/decoding. Then there were people who went in behind the lines: people who went in singly that spoke French, German fluently and could not be mistaken for anything else.

Two days after I left this tent, I got my gear together and boarded a train and headed for Washington. I had to report first of all to the Navy Department in Washington. I went to that building and a naval officer said, "You're one of those." And I said, "One of those what?" He says, "Never mind; you report to Army headquarters," room so-and-so. I did that, and I think I got a shuttle around a section of Washington and finally ended up on F Street—there were some old buildings, and one of them was the headquarters of OSS, though no one knew it.

Then I was sent out to the Congressional Country Club for training. We had to go in a truck; we boarded it from the OSS headquarters, and they didn't blindfold us but they closed the truck so you couldn't see out. The next thing we knew we were out at Congressional Country Club, and we had no idea what it was. And we stayed there for three months without going out. The country club had changed. I mean, the golf course—you blew up things in sand traps.

We would go through testing where we would have to work very fast with our hands in building something. And we didn't know, of course, that there was always one person out of three that were working to build this in a race with somebody else, there was one who was really representing the training program. And just as you were ready and finished and thinking you could win, he would "accidentally" knock the whole thing over. Now if you reached back and punched him, you were out. But if you sat there and said, "Let's start all over again," you were fine. We would actually go into factories around the Washington area and we would have false identification and we would go in as if we worked there and we would take photographs and whatever we could. Set a plan about what we were going to blow up. And pretty successfully; only one or two of us were ever caught.

On the way ...

Junie darling,

How are you, sweetheart? I'm feeling wonderfully
well — and in spite of my deep rooted love of the soil
— especially that of New York and environs — (God
bless the pavement) I'm turning out to be
something of a sailor — not everything, mind you —
but something! Details of course will have to
wait until I see you again, sweetheart — but
it should be of no aid to those "krauts" to know
that I am extremely comfortable, deliciously fed,
and surprisingly enough am sharing the
general air of holiday spirit that's prevalent
aboard. That's one of the most surprising
features when I stop to think of it — but the
most typical words to describe the life and
attitude here are casual, unconcerned, remote.
You have to pinch yourself mentally several
times a day to realize that you are actually
going overseas; that you are actually in
some danger of attack; that all these guys
who you are sleeping, eating, playing
poker with are actually going to war! There

TRACY SUGARMAN 1942 *Letter to wife, June, while on transport to Europe*

Making the Adjustment

"Everything is based on survival."

So how did these new soldiers manage to accommodate themselves to a life they'd never known before? There is one theme common to every veteran's experience: a determination to see it through. Serving in wartime always involves a personal mission of some kind. It may be a yearning to succeed; it may also involve a quest to bring some clarity to an unfocused life. And for some recruits, determination may also be as simple as making the best out of a perplexing, frustrating, grueling, and sometimes discouraging experience.

BEN SNYDER

World War II; Army Air Corps; Journal; May 23, 1943

Now that we have been properly classified as to Military Occupational Speciality, the waiting begins. The first hurdle has been surmounted, friendships formed, and for we "feather merchants" there is a better sense of what we can expect in the military. There is a constant groping for identity, particularly for those of us who on our respective campuses were high profile. It requires an adjustment of consequence.

VIOLET ASKINS HILL GORDON

World War II; Women's Army Auxiliary Corps; Interview

It helped that we were young! I think that the thing that really sustained and enabled all of us was that underneath the adventurous aspect of it was a sense of duty; it was our country, that we were at war, and that there was a purpose to all of this. So there was excitement and fatigue. In the beginning it was mostly fatigue, because it was up at the crack of dawn and the day continued at such a pace until taps at night you were just exhausted.

BEN SNYDER
   World War II; Army Air Corps; Journal; August 29, 1943
My bunkmate is a long lean Texan from Beaumont named Franklin Dolan Smith. He nicely fits the image of a native son of the Lone Star State, laconic, affable, good-old-boy in the right sense of that term. Smitty is a treasure-house of rustic, homespun humor, a not inconsiderable talent when things become rough. We get along very nicely.

SALLY HITCHCOCK PULLMAN
   World War II; Army Nurse Corps; Memoir
There were wonderful women in this group of nurses. But five of us formed a special and lasting bond: Beulah "BC" Larsen, Elizabeth "Knowlsey" Knowles, Shirley Munson, Lillian "Mickey" McGuire, and me. BC, Shirl, and I still write. Knowlsey and Mickey are gone. Such a special bond is a rare and cherished thing.

MAX CLELAND
   Vietnam War; Army; Interview
My fellow second lieutenants? I found myself very much a part of them. I didn't know there were so many people like me. We weren't particularly hard-core West Point killer warriors, but we weren't particularly academicians out for a stroll in the sun, either. I think everybody had a sense of obligation, a sense of duty. We weren't fanatical, but we felt like we had to take our place in the line.

JOHN ENMAN
   World War II; Army; Memoir
My commitment to Uncle Sam "for the duration plus six months" began in the fall of 1942 when as a University of Maine senior I joined the Enlisted Reserve Corps. My call came in late winter 1943 and I wound up at Camp Upton, New York, made famous in World War I by Irving Berlin ("Oh, How I Hate to Get Up in the Morning").

   At Upton I was processed and was assigned to the Corps of Engineers for cartographic training because my college major was geology. Actual cartographic instruction came with my transfer to the Franklin Technical Institute in Boston

JOHN ENMAN 1944

En route to Canistel, Algeria. John Enman (back row, right end) joined the Enlisted Reserve Corps as a college senior and was called up in 1943. Assigned to the 2nd Photo Procurement Detachment, he shipped out to India in the spring of 1944.

for a 12-week program. We were quartered in a former warehouse cater-corner from Fenway Park, home of the Red Sox, and marched the streets to and from the school several miles away in South Boston. The unit sang as it marched, and it serenaded not only folks on the sidewalk and other service units, male and female, marching elsewhere, but also the women who worked at the large Salada Tea factory across from Boston Police headquarters. To the women we sang "Good morning, dear tea bags, good morning to you," and to the police, "Good morning, Dick Tracy." We shortly quit serenading the cops after they complained to our C.O., Captain Sargent, that our greeting was demeaning; so long as I was there, the women, contrariwise, leaned out their windows waving and cheering.

JEANNE URBIN MARKLE

Vietnam War; Army Nurse Corps; Interview

Our orders were to report on January 2, 1966, to Fort Sam Houston Army Hospital in San Antonio, Texas. My first airplane ride. I was 21. I didn't know anything. So naïve. Training lasted, I think, seven weeks, and the whole time I was there I was hearing snippets of "There's a war going on somewhere, somewhere over in the Pacific, I can't remember the name of the country. I don't think we'll go." I had never heard the name Vietnam; I couldn't have even found it on the map for you. I was having too good of a time; it was a wonderful time. There were 70 nurses and 200 doctors. We had a good time.

JOANNE PALELLA

Persian Gulf War; Army; Interview

I was in basic training with a whole company of females. It was a truck company. They wanted to prove that we could be as tough as the males, so they worked us pretty hard. But I remember actually enjoying it and learning a bit of respect for hard work. It was the end of January, the beginning of February in Fort Dix, New Jersey. It was very cold. I remember sleeping outside in bivouac time in a half-tent, and you get together with someone else with another half-tent, and there's no floor and you have to dig a trench around it—lots different than regular camping. It was hard, but I think I earned some respect for myself and others.

I got through those early days first out of cockiness, then fear, and later out of wanting to succeed, wanting to do everything I was capable of doing.

RON WINTER

Vietnam War; Marine Corps; Interview

I second-guessed myself after about 12 hours in Parris Island when I had a moment to myself to think. As the weeks went by, I started to realize there was a purpose: They immediately strip you of everything that you've known and were comfortable with in civilian life, because you were about to become a Marine, and it's an entirely different world with an entirely different set of standards and requirements.

CHUCK HAGEL

Vietnam War; Army; Interview

You don't have many privileges as a private, and you expect that. You are handled in a way—and I think it's different today, and it should be—that you don't ever know anything, you're never told anything, nothing is ever explained, you do what you're told and be damned glad of it, and everything is based on survival. And you better listen carefully. We're going to say it one time: "This could be the difference between coming back on your feet and your coming back in a body bag."

Marie Brand Voltzke
World War II; Navy Women's Reserve (WAVES); Interview
Voltzke trained at Oklahoma A&M College in Stillwater, Oklahoma.
Our quarters were conducted as if they were a ship. We requested permission to go ashore when leaving the premises, and to come aboard upon return. Rules of discipline and the line of authority were strict in adherence. We stood four-hour watches on night duty. We patrolled with flashlight, listening and looking for unusual sights and sounds. I dreaded the trips, but more so if time remained to sit at the desk. We were cautioned that sailors caught asleep on watch were subject to being shot.

Malcolm Stilson
World War II; Army; Letter to his parents, January 4, 1943
There is one thing the Army is teaching me, that is, freedom is really something worthwhile. I like this life, but I will be glad to return to an unregimented existence.

Donald Spencer
World War II; Army Air Corps; Letter to his parents, May 28, 1943
Spencer trained at Keesler Field in Biloxi, Mississippi.
The country down here is really pretty, except that it is hotter than hell. It is so hot that I take a shower every chance I get and that doesn't seem to be enough.

They have really been working us the past few days. We took another physical today, it was really rough, but I passed and that is what counts. This is a pretty camp, but the part we are in is new and we are about a mile from the mess halls, and just about as far from the latrines.

We live in what they call huts and that name really fits them. They are just temporary barracks and thrown together. We sleep on cots and they are really hard. The only things I really hate are those darn G.I. shoes. I have blisters all over the bottom of my feet and my toes.

Please do not worry about me because it is not as bad as I made it sound. Tell all hello for me and tell them to write. This letter is probably all mixed up, but with all the noise in this hut it is kind of hard to concentrate on a letter.

{ ONE MAN'S STORY }

Warren Tsuneishi

"I always thought of myself as American."

Born on the Fourth of July, named after an American President, raised by his immigrant parents to believe that he was truly an American, Warren Tsuneishi had so many reasons to answer the call when the United States entered World War II. There was, on the other hand, the matter of where his family would be spending the war: in an internment camp 870 miles away from their home.

Tsuneishi's parents emigrated from Japan to Los Angeles, his father arriving in 1907, his mother in 1915. His father hoped to study for the ministry at the University of Southern California, but illness and family obligations forced him to alter his career plans. He became a truck farmer in Duarte, California, specializing in berry crops, and in his spare time he wrote haiku and published a poetry magazine for Japanese immigrants. The Tsuneishis had ten children; their fifth was born on July 4, 1921, and they named him after the country's new president, Warren G. Harding. Warren Tsuneishi and his siblings attended public school in Duarte where, he told an interviewer, "we became thoroughly Americanized"— although his parents sent him to Japanese language school as well.

He graduated from Monrovia–Arcadia–Duarte High School in 1939 at the top of his class, but a counselor discouraged him from attending college because of the scarcity of job opportunities for Japanese Americans. Urged on by his parents, Tsuneishi applied to UCLA and was accepted. Even with ten children, the family could afford his education; UCLA charged no tuition for California residents and only $27 a semester in student fees.

In September 1941, Tsuneishi transferred to the University of California in Berkeley. Three months later, the Japanese attacked Pearl Harbor, and as he

WARREN TSUNEISHI 1944

Tsuneishi (left) with a buddy in the Philippines, where they served as translators for U.S. military intelligence. Tsuneishi followed the advice of his older brother to volunteer for this work rather than serve in a Japanese-American combat unit.

would later tell an interviewer, "I could see nothing but bad things happening to me in the future." Executive Order 9066, signed by Franklin Roosevelt in February 1942, began a shameful chapter in American history, as the Tsuneishis and thousands of Japanese Americans living in the three Pacific Coast states were ordered to move inland to relocation camps. Warren and his family, allowed to take only what they could carry, were evacuated in May, first to the Tanforan Assembly Center in Manzanar, a small town in the high desert country of California, and then to Heart Mountain Relocation Center near Cody, Wyoming. This was to be the Tsuneishi family home for the duration of World War II.

"The one thing I missed most was my freedom," Tsuneishi wrote in a letter to the Veterans History Project. Also, he was broke. "I went into camp with $15 in my pocket and lost that learning to play poker." So when recruiters for sugar beet farmers in Idaho came offering jobs, Tsuneishi was "one of 12 to volunteer

"Serving Our Country" read the banners held by Warren Tsuneishi's mother, Sho Murakami Tsuneishi (above, left), and a friend, Shima Yamaguchi Takata, at Heart Mountain Relocation Center near Cody, Wyoming, where Japanese Americans were confined during the war. Each woman had four sons serving in the U.S. Army, as symbolized by the stars on their In Service flags. In the photo at right, Warren visits Heart Mountain in the uniform of the U.S. Army, winter 1942-1943. It was, he recalled, "a Kafkaesque kind of situation."

for stoop labor." After the summer, he was returned to Heart Mountain, only to catch a real break: "With the assistance of the American Friends Service Committee [a Quaker organization], I was permitted to enter Syracuse University in January 1942 to complete my college education."

In September 1941, the Army had started a program, the Fourth Army Intelligence School, to train Japanese language specialists. Warren's older brother Hughes, drafted before Pearl Harbor, wound up in that school, located in the Presidio Army complex in San Francisco. After December 7, the school was deactivated and was placed under the jurisdiction of the War Department, which relocated it to Camp Savage, a former Civilian Conservation Corps facility near St. Paul, Minnesota. It was now dubbed the Military Intelligence Service Language School. In April 1942 Hughes wrote to Warren, urging him to apply for the MISLS and not enlist in the infantry, where he would become, as Warren recalled, "useless cannon fodder." Warren did want to finish his education at Syracuse, and the school offered him a speeded-up program, which allowed him to graduate that August.

He was accepted by the MISLS and, after a brief stay at Long Island's Camp Upton, reported to Camp Savage for what he called "one of those total immersion courses in military Japanese." The goal of the school was to train teams of translators who could decipher captured Japanese military documents and give the U.S. forces a distinct advantage in the brutal war in the Pacific. Ironically, Tsuneishi found himself regretting his experiences at the Japanese language school back in Duarte, where "I had not been a very good student."

Before he shipped out, Tsuneishi was granted a leave of absence. He took a train to Heart Mountain, and when he walked up to the gate in full uniform, the sentry who checked him in "didn't even blink an eye." It was, as he said in an interview, "a Kafkaesque kind of situation." With two sons in the U.S. Army, "my mother was quite anxious about me. She's Japanese. She has Japanese feelings. She's not necessarily for U.S. victory in World War II, a war against her own country."

"In my heart," Warren Tsuneishi said in an interview, "I always thought of myself as American." But he admits that his "emotional makeup" was Japanese; "instead of resisting unconstitutional acts of the government against me, I took it without fighting, and to that extent I guess I was more Japanese than American—if that stereotype is true."

{ CHAPTER TWO }

A Day in the Life

A deck of cards and a little floor space are all the members of the Army's 10th Mountain Division needed for a spirited game aboard a troop ship in this 1945 photo by Robert Lee Olen.

MARY SHELDON GILL 1944

Mary Sheldon Gill's collection includes this photo of a company of WACs lined up for drill at Moore General Hospital in Asheville, North Carolina. Gill performed clerical work at this Army hospital, where WACs encountered both resistance and acceptance.

Close Quarters: The Daily Routine

"The barracks are not home sweet home,
but a place for rest from exhaustion."

It is the inescapable experience of every GI's life, no matter what era, no matter what branch of service. Sharing living quarters with scores of total strangers, with little chance for privacy, let alone peace and quiet, is the biggest adjustment any civilian faces after entering the military. Everything is done in public, from rinsing out your underwear to reading a Dear John letter from your now ex-sweetheart. Barracks life is part of subsuming your individual identity to the collective will of the military, to be willing to be part of a group effort to fight a war, to prepare yourself for even greater sacrifices ahead.

IRVING OBLAS
  World War II; Navy; Letter to his wife, September 23, 1943
Oblas was stationed at the U.S. Naval Training Station, Sampson, New York.
  As I sat down in the barracks tonight to write this letter, a gob came over followed by a riotous mob and put down a big box of candy, which he was doling out. What a madhouse! I came in lucky for a bar of chocolate and piece of hard candy. You see, all food has to be finished immediately—it's against rules to keep anything like that in the lockers.
  Where do you think I was tonight? I decided to see the movies and get a little relaxation from the constant rush and activity and milling mob. For instance, right now, there are about a dozen conversations going on in a loud and vociferous manner so that you can't help hearing all of it at the same time you are doing something else. Gad, how I long for the peace of our homestead where I could read while the radio was going full blast!

BEN SNYDER

World War II; Army Air Corps; Big Spring, Texas, 1943; Memoir

All of us have now become part of our surroundings. The barracks are of Nashville tar paper, beaver board variety with the only difference coming from the stove pipes which raise their pointed heads above the roofs like the minarets of some Islamic city. They are of the worst GI variety, in sharp contrast to the permanent base quality of aristocratic Ellington [his previous base]. We live primitively. Our quarters are hot, difficult to clean, crowded, and below standard. There are double-decker bunks with footlockers at each end and not much else. Being roused in total darkness and run mercilessly through our paces day after day, the barracks are not home sweet home, but a place for rest-from-exhaustion.

MARIE BRAND VOLTZKE

World War II; WAVES; Interview

Voltzke arrived for duty in Washington, D.C., where 33 barracks housed 4,000 WAVES— the largest WAVE quarters in the world.

To compensate for having the lower bunk, I permitted my bunkmate to hang her weekly washed hose by hangers from the springs of her bunk. Passersby shook their heads in disbelief.

Rita, from the Bronx, patiently taught me how to knit. I learned to roll my hair in pin curls, and was told to wear a girdle. Oh, they were all helpful, teaching me not to "catch a streetcar," and many other proper phrases that corrected a West Virginia "hillbilly." I made many dear friends and continue to correspond with them at Christmas.

CHARLES RESTIFO

World War II; Army; Fort Benning, Georgia; Memoir

At times some GIs would try practical jokes to release tension in camp, like nailing down a guy's boots after he continuously took other fellows' boots. One night we dressed a goat in a GI uniform and put the goat on the bed of one of the men who was always playing jokes on others. Someone poured beer on the bed, and of course the fellow thought the wet was from the goat. Another soldier had false teeth and would pop them out at breakfast while he was eating cereal. It was disgusting. Finally, one day, the teeth disappeared and he could not eat his steak at night. He finally had them returned after several days of begging and never did pop his teeth again.

MALCOLM STILSON
World War II; Army Air Corps; Memoir
The CQ (Charge of Quarters) personnel go on duty at 4:30 in the afternoon. There are passes to be given out, errands to run, gig-lists to pull, and jobs to find for those who were gigged (for "gig," read punishment for minor infractions of military life).

As the sun sinks slowly into its bed of night, from afar is heard the song of the sleepy camp in the form of "Taps." As the squadron sinks into sleep the CQ's "day" has started, and he settles down to his routine job that occurs night after night throughout the year. (Though not the same personnel every night.)

We sit up all night awaiting calls that never come. If they do come, they are either good or bad, signifying the arrival of babies or the death of some loved one in the family. Mostly the job is dully routine, broken only by the curses of some newly awakened KP or the sodden humor of a drunk coming in after hours, and who has to be helped to bed.

Bed check is always a dreaded task. Slamming into the slumbering barracks, taking the names of those that have to go to the latrine for a last-minute relief job, or who are too sick from drink to stay in the hutments. Jones is absent. Green is gone. Smith is AWOL. Call the OD (Officer of the Day).

Bugs creep and crawl over us and further increase our misery. Four o'clock and the KPs have to be awakened. After much sweat and strain, pounding this man awake and that man into semiconsciousness, we herd the unwilling to the mess hall and turn them over to the grim and forbidding KP pusher.

Finally the time passes and morning rolls around. First call is sounded, while the sun still sleeps behind the far horizon, and then reveille is called. With much clinking and clanking of mess kits, the sleepy GIs fall into their ranks and stagger off to breakfast. Then the CQ's day is almost over, and the sun comes up in golden glory singing a paean of praise for the new day in the making. The weary CQ staggers off to his hut and drops heavily into his bunk, thankful that another night is gone and that a day-and-a-half vacation is before him.

FREDERICK STILSON
World War I; Army; Fort Leavenworth, Kansas; Memoir
The entire regiment had to march to mess across the quadrangle to a gigantic mess hall, gym, and armory where we were assigned places at long tables. Ours was near an entrance, so we got in first and out first. The food was prepared by contractors, and during the seven weeks we were there, the food was not very

good, and sometimes downright rotten. Being on contract to the government, the men couldn't do much about it, but there was many a breakfast that all I could eat was oatmeal mush with a slice of bread and coffee to wash it down.

JAMES BAROSS

World War II; Army Air Corps, New Guinea; Memoir

I can recall best our dinner entrees. We would stand in a long wavering line with our mess kits firmly in hand, and as we approached the mess tent, men there with cleavers hacked off the tops of cans of salmon, which they then inverted and shook, and shook, and shook over our mess kits until, with a sucking, wet, schlushy sound the contents of the can would come sliding out, at which time another man would cover the salmon with a large chunk of bread.

At one place in the camp was a large 16-foot-square pyramidal tent, guarded by two armed GIs during the day and the night. We became fascinated by what the tent might contain, checked a bit, and sure enough, found that it contained cases, cases, and cases stacked to the top of prepared fruits from Tasmania. Peaches, apricots, pears, apples, all sorts of fruits grown on that productive island were there, in number-ten-sized cans, just sitting. None of the fruit was being served to us, certainly not to the enlisted personnel for sure.

Hope springs eternal among restless, hungry troops, and we devised a plan. We had a couple of our bunch spend some time in intense conversation with the guards at the front of the tent, while others of us cut into the tent from behind and removed cases and cases and cases of peaches, apricots, pears, apples, and whatever other fruits were available.

From that evening on we did not stand in a wavering line with our mess kits in hand waiting for our dinner of canned salmon. We had one or more of our group get enough bread to occupy our left hands while we partook of various fruits. True, a diet of fruit only can become a bit of a drag, but we managed. I, to this day, cannot eat canned apricots without thinking fondly of my dinners at Port Moresby.

JOHN ENMAN

World War II; Army, India; Memoir

At our New Delhi mess hall, most food was quite palatable, although for me there were a few exceptions. The oatmeal, which I liked, appeared to be rather liberally sprinkled with small raisins, which did indeed turn out to be organic, except they were weevils, tasteless, but I presumed, nutritious. The powdered eggs, powdered milk, dehydrated potatoes, and Australian butter were awful.

No reminiscence of wartime service is complete without a description of GI food. Robert Lee Olen snapped this chow-line photo aboard a troop ship in 1945. Opinions about military food are surprisingly varied, but no one ever mistook it for home cooking.

The latter came in large tins, guaranteed not to melt in the searing Indian heat, and it didn't, but it had the look, feel, and consistency of yellow axle grease. On Thanksgiving and Christmas the cooks went all out as we had the traditional turkey and "all the fixings." It is too bad those feasts are not farther apart, as one could then better enjoy the second. Between Christmas and Thanksgiving culinary talents were bent upon still more ways to prepare Spam.

VINCENT REED
World War I; Army; Aboard ship to France; Memoir
Our meals consisted mostly of goat meat made into a thin watery stew, strong orange marmalade, and a poor grade of bread. It made me furious to think that the English were getting well paid for transporting us and yet they could not serve us any better food. There was a large vat of small potatoes on deck, and when we became too hungry, we would peel some of those and eat them raw.

JOANNE PALELLA
Persian Gulf War; Army; Interview
When we arrived we were given MREs—Meals Ready to Eat— twice a day. We were also brought a hot meal by the Saudis that worked out there. My first sergeant was in the Vietnam War and he refused to eat the hot food, stating that we

BILL VICARS 1965

*Bill Vicars gives a buddy a haircut at Bien Hoa Air Force Base,
Vietnam. Vicars was in the 173rd Airborne, among the first
Army units involved with fighting the Vietnam War. He served
a second tour of duty four years later.*

don't know if it could be poisoned, and we don't know if they're Saudis or Iraqis,
and that would be a great way to get a group of people. And then a lot of us just
stuck to eating MREs.

JAMES BAROSS

World War II; Army Air Corps; Memoir

Several buddies had devised a delicious drink. One of them had become friendly with the flight surgeon who had access to hospital alcohol, a pure, clear liquid
of great potency.

A canteen cup, about a pint, with the powder from the lemon drink from K
rations, a quantity of water with an equal quantity of hospital alcohol, and just
a pinch of salt, was delicious.

In comparison with what was available in the States perhaps it was nothing much, but what we had we had and were not the least bit critical of it. Sitting around the perimeter of a tent, the filled canteen cup would be passed from hand to hand, each man taking a drink. A neat, orderly procedure.

When the cup was emptied, it would be refilled, no big bother, and a few refills would be sufficient to carry through an evening of chatting about the events of the day.

I was there one evening and thoroughly enjoyed the discussions. At some late hour I decided to go home, that is, go to my tent, the fifth up the row just across the road, and go to sleep. But when I attempted to get up and walk, I found I couldn't. I was perfectly sober, could think rationally, and remember events to this day, but I could not stand up and walk! No way could I stand up!

There were no offers of assistance as most of the others were strangely afflicted with the same malady, so I was on my own to get home. But I made it!

I recall so well crawling, hands and knees, over the gritty ground, foot by foot toward my tent, and laughing all the way. I felt so foolish, so silly, crawling, but that was the only way to get there, and get there I did.

DENTON CROCKER
World War II; Army; Memoir
I served on KP [Kitchen Patrol] several times and was assigned to various work details (unloading trucks, etc.). KP was an eye-widening exposure to institutional cooking. I remember opening 20+ very large cans of spinach, and in the classic image of KP I peeled mountains of potatoes. In later weeks a machine did the "peeling," removing the skins by abrasion, but just cutting out the eyes of so many potatoes was an exquisitely refined monotony, which I remember clearly 50 years later.

HELEN MINOR
World War II; Women's Army Corps; Interview
KP could be anything. I well remember my day behind the mess hall. There were great barrels where they threw the garbage. One barrel was definitely for fats and oils and things of that nature, another one was for vegetation, and another one was for just any old thing. And somebody had dumped them all in together and they had to be separated. I'm out there in the pouring rain separating garbage with my bare hands. I well remember the menu that day; it was oatmeal and grapes. I still remember that menu. And it was just miserable out there. But I got through it; what else do you do?

IRVING OBLAS

World War II; Navy; Letter to his wife

The chow really isn't too bad. When you consider the magnitude of the problem of feeding 5,000 men three times a day, they handle the situation very well. Still, I can't eat beans for breakfast—and most of us can't diagnose most of the concoctions fed us.

JAMES BAROSS

World War II; Army Air Corps; Memoir

When one goes into the military service, he is all eyes and ears as there is so much to learn. One thing I was advised to do, among numerous other things, was, when I was in the chow line and bread was available: Always take two slices or chunks.

When I showed some doubt as to the wisdom of the advice, I was told, "It just makes sense. You take one to eat and the other to wipe your hands on."

MALCOLM STILSON

World War II; Army Air Corps; Memoir

While in the mess hall one day, I found some graffiti on the wall that helped to while away the time while standing in line. Some wit wrote it while he was standing in line waiting for the delicious meal ahead. "Food will win the war, but how are we going to get the enemy to eat here?"

JOHN BUTLER

Vietnam War; Marine Corps; Interview

Basically, you lived in the ground. Every man carried a poncho liner and a poncho, and you would wrap up in that at night, having dug a hole, and that's where you lived. We were always short of water. This area is not mountainous at all. It's all plains and rice fields. There are very few streams, and because of the pollution and the habit of using human and animal feces to fertilize the fields, none of the water was potable. So we had to pump our own water and then get water where we were re-supplied. I carried five canteens and used water very sparingly. You didn't wash. You didn't hardly even brush your teeth. Water was used strictly for drinking. And then you had C-rations, which were metal cans with food. Not unlike the MREs of today.

In your pack you carried everything on your back, basically, that you lived with. Which was your C-rations, your water, your ammunition, your poncho, and poncho liner. You put that on your back every morning and you started walking. And you walked till you reached a point where your mission was accomplished or where you'd contacted the enemy and then dealt with them. And at night you'd form a perimeter, a circle, everybody'd dig a hole, usually four —two to four men in a hole. Eat whatever you felt you could eat that was in your pack, drink a little water, and then stand watch off and on—obviously with some time in there for sleep—until the next morning. And then basically the routine started all over again

KEVIN ROY LEE

Persian Gulf War; Army; Interview
Lee was in the Army Reserves in November 1990 when his transportation company was called up to serve in the Persian Gulf War.

The previous commander told us, "We're going to the desert. You don't need to take your cold weather equipment, you don't need to take your heaters; leave all that back in Chattanooga. It's the desert; it's hot. But when you get to the desert, at night it's cold. So we were really missing our heaters and things like that. We went to Log Base Echo in the southern part of Iraq. It was just a flat place out in the middle of nowhere, no landmarks, no nothing. In order to move out there, we had to move an engineering unit with us. That was a big mission in itself: setting up concertina wire, building up berms, setting up tents, make all your new supply connections, whether it's for getting food or getting showers.

You're battling with sand everywhere. That tractor trailer wasn't really meant to be an off-road vehicle. We're talking about nuts and bolts shearing off from the sheer vibration of the equipment, tires going flat. That was a big commodity, trying to find replacement parts, to keep things rolling. You're trying to keep 85 percent of your tractor trailers operational. We had to do an awful lot of scavenging and bartering, taking stuff off one truck to keep another truck running.

We figured out a way to get hot showers by getting an immersion heater, which is what you would use to clean up your utensils that you use for a kitchen. Further down the road, there weren't even showers. One of the most wonderful purchases I made before I went to Saudi Arabia was a bag that you could use as a shower. I hung it up in the gooseneck part of the truck. It held about two gallons of water, and I could have a shave and shower in about two gallons of water. It was nice about every two days to fill that up and leave it out in the sun. It would be fairly warm by the time night would fall, and you could get a fairly decent shower.

Samuel Boylston's witty illustrations of the frustrations and occasional joys of everyday life in the service decorated the letters Gerald Duquette sent home to his wife during World War II. Boylston and Duquette served in the Pacific Theater with the Army Air Force. Boylston's collection in the Veterans History Project includes 60 samples of his charming envelope art.

Word from Home: Mail Call

"Our mail is the only thing that keeps our hearts
and our chins way up there."

It may be difficult to recall, in these days of instant messaging and e-mail, that hand-written letters once carried many a soldier, sailor, or marine through the tough days from training camp to the battlefield. The most eagerly consumed piece of mail was (and continues to be) the package, sure to draw a crowd, especially if it contained the promise of homemade food. The mail wasn't just a matter of keeping in touch; for some, it was also a vehicle for expressing romantic notions that would either cement a newly formed marriage or build the foundation for a postwar union.

MALCOLM STILSON
   World War II; Army Air Corps; Memoir
I always looked forward to receiving letters from home and friends. The mail orderly would come into the barracks and shout, "Maillll Callll!" in an exceedingly loud, sharp, and irritating voice. Anyone standing or sitting in the main aisle of the barracks at this time should duck out of the way or start running, too, as a bedlam of shouting, crashing, running, and pushing breaks forth. The man with the mail throws up his arms to protect himself, and then he is suddenly obscured by a group of shouting, gesticulating creatures who bear little resemblance to soldiers. Suddenly someone with a loud voice shouts, "At ease!" and there is a sudden hush in the barracks. Tense excitement grips everyone as the names of the lucky mail receivers are shouted out. The men fortunate enough to have letters return to their bunks with happy faces and singing hearts, while the other unfortunates droop down the aisle, hopes shattered, morale broken, with nothing to live for. I know it ruined my morale not to receive mail for a while.

PAUL STEPPE

Korean War; Marine Corps; Memoir

Sometimes mail did not reach us, which can be expected. There could be any number of reasons other than warfare for these delays, and many never question "why," and others grumble and complain for hours. Mail and packages from home were very important to everyone, especially packages, and in particular, large, nice ones regardless of their condition when received, squashed or otherwise. The receiver of the package becomes the most popular fellow in the squad, and as you open your package, you notice that there are people waiting in line that you have never seen before. Where did they come from? Everyone waiting for handouts! The vagabonds took anything you gave them, but if what they saw didn't appeal to them, they fled like flies and the line dispersed as quickly as it formed. Canned spam was one of our favorite items to receive and to disperse to our bunker buddies. Two cans could feed six buddies for a good evening meal and breakfast. Everyone in our squad shared what they received, even if it was just a single cookie.

DENTON CROCKER

World War II; Army; Memoir

There is constant reference in my letters to who sent what items of food, candy, clothing, personal items, etc. Although I thanked one and all, Mother especially wanted to be aware so that she could thank them, too. While it is true that some of these items were a real pleasure to have, it is also true that the Army supplied us with all our necessities, and oftentimes I would reply to a suggestion that, well, it might be nice to have it, but it is easiest to travel light. The relationship, Army food = bad food, just wasn't so in my case and I gorged on it. But the myth persisted and fortunately my relatives never fully accepted my protestations.

VINCENT REED

Word War I; Army; Memoir

I wrote almost daily to Jo [his fiancée] and mother. One of the brightest sides of my Army life was the mail. I never failed to get regular letters from Jo and mother, then a few others from friends of mine. They were a great source of comfort to me.

DONALD SPENCER

World War II; Army Air Corps; Letter from his mother, April 11, 1944

Received a letter from Dick tonight. [Richard Spencer, Don's older brother, was serving in the Army Air Force in Europe.] The cussed censors had cut it all to pieces. There was about three inches of the front page left, one third of the second page left, and only about half of the third. It made me so damn mad I called them everything under the sun. Dick has been so careful, always. It had to be some cussed particular censor. Just like some Army Air Force inspectors. Ha!

FREDERICK STILSON
  World War I; Army of the Occupation; Memoir
Due to the censorship order, I was supposed to read every letter written by the men in the outfit to their families, girlfriends, etc. As there would be hundreds dumped into the office mailbag unsealed, I would read one at random and order the mail orderly to seal them up. The officers were evidently trusted, and only two of my letters were ever opened, as we were allowed to seal ours up. Finally, toward the end of operations, I just let all the outfit seal their own and the censor's stamp was applied. I was too busy to attend to such details.

The yearning for something solid, something pure, something positive in wartime led inevitably to infatuations and hasty marriage proposals, as well as lifelong romances. We've already seen how the mail was one way to nurture affection and commitment, but fraternization became more and more common with the World War II-era entry of women into uniform. And as Jeanne Urbin Markle's Vietnam War account demonstrates, there is nothing like orders to ship out to war to bring off a marriage, even if one of the partners is unaware of those orders.

DENTON CROCKER
  World War II; Army; Memoir
This is not an especially notable letter, but on this day, Dec. 6, 1942, I initiate something that will change my life forever. I write my first letter to Jean-Marie. We had gone out to eat and to the movies a couple of times before I entered the service, and we got together at least once while I was at Devens.... I had been fascinated by her and suddenly I knew that I had to know her better and not let her get away. The letter is five pages in which I review my Army history to date. The salutation is to "Jean" and I sign off, "Sincerely, Denton." I record here the end of the next-to-last paragraph and all of the last one:
  "Taking it all in I enjoy my work, am learning much, am sleeping and eating well, and am thoroughly satisfied with my lot.

"I would like very much to hear from you, know how your work at Simmons is progressing, how many stories you have written—did you get any done this last summer?—and to find out what is new in the vicinity of Beach Bluff. Also, if any of those pictures your Mother took came out at all well, I'd like to see one."

So began in earnest what was common in wartime, a courtship, largely by letter, but punctuated by intense times together. Even now, 50 years later, I fill with emotion thinking of the building fire of it. I wonder too if it might have gone less well had I not gained enormously in confidence through the Army experience.

Jean-Marie apparently has kept all of my letters to her and there were not many initially, the first one which is quoted from above bears the date Dec. 6, 1942, and the next is dated March 25, 1943, but the contents of that second letter make it clear that the intervening time, which included a furlough, was productive:

"The 'day' we spent together was one of the happiest of my life and I will treasure the memory of it always. Every time I see you and thus come to know you better, the more I want to see you again. It is a vicious circle and I am delightedly trapped in it. It is very likely that you will notice a decided increase in correspondence from me for I'm not going to let you forget me.

"When I got home after leaving you, my mother was reading in bed so I went in to say goodnight to her. When I went back into my room my mirror showed you, beautiful, had deposited a certain red substance around my mouth. I felt that my mother showed great wisdom by saying nothing. However, should I by some queer trick of fate (of course it wouldn't be by design!) have the opportunity to kiss you goodnight again sometime—a gentle reminder concerning this matter would be greatly appreciated."

A P.S. says, "I am still smelling carnation," a reference to JM's perfume, the scent of which became a fixation for me.

MARY SHELDON GILL

World War II; Women's Army Corps; Memoir

Two of my close friends went overseas, to the South Pacific. Kay met and married her true love; the chaplain who married them lent them his hut for their wedding night. Kay made a wedding gown and nightie out of a parachute. They later returned to the states and were divorced as he "ran around," Kay wrote me.

JEAN-MARIE JENSEN AND DENTON CROCKER 1943

In March 1942 Denton Crocker began writing to Jean-Marie Jensen back home in Massachusetts. While home on furlough in November 1943 he asked her to marry him.

BEN SNYDER

World War II; Army Air Corps; Memoir, 1944

Snyder was stationed at David-Monthan Field in Tucson, Arizona.

My good friend and bunkmate, Franklin Smith, was married quietly on Saturday night. As luck would have it, I could only be best man in absentia. We landed at 6:30 P.M. and I rushed into the church at precisely 8:35 P.M., seconds after the vows were exchanged. But no matter. The newlyweds are comfortably situated in a cottage on Warren Street where they share the amenities with a rotund, spinster landlady and three nondescript cats. C'est la guerre and the housing shortage.

Incidentally, more and more of the brethren are approaching the altar as our lives in the States diminish. There were three from our class last week and two more in prospect this weekend.

It is highly unlikely that I will join the stampede to matrimony. However, after writing those lines, there suddenly is a girl who has come closer to claiming my heart than anyone since Chapel Hill.

Her name is Rosemary Pickens, a coed at the University of Utah, who comes from nearby Ogden. She is Mormon, of course, but of the soft-shell variety (or whatever it is properly called). She is musically inclined, fun to be with, game for whatever might prove interesting, and very good company.

The fact that she is inclined to come to Tucson on her spring break suggests that this is becoming a relationship of substance. Wartime travel is no picnic under any circumstances and her willingness to put up with "whatever" and come down here by bus says a great deal. Needless to say, her being with me will be more than welcome.

TRACY SUGARMAN

World War II; Navy; Letter to his wife

How I miss the fun of having you with me, Junie! So often I feel like sharing something new with you—rumpling your hair—walking with you, holding you close to me. We'll spend our lives making up for this mess, darling—and I'm going to take you with me even if it's to the corner grocery for asparagus! I'm bursting to know what you've been doing with yourself—what you're thinking— where you've been going. Just take care my darling, for nothing is so important as your staying well and happy—'cuz it's going to be my best guarantee of keeping my own perspective healthy and our values as they were.

Pooch, please have a picture taken. I haven't <u>any</u> since you're Mrs. Sugarman—might even get married wid ja when this goddam war's over! Time to kiss you g'nite sweetheart....

ARNOLD ROBBINS

World War II; Army; Letters

Arnold Robbins, a heavy equipment operator stationed in Iceland spotted Anne Hass in a group photograph a buddy had received from home. He prevailed on his pal to encourage Anne to write to him.

Dear Arnold,

You don't know me but I have heard a friend rave about his buddies & have seen your picture among these buddies. I decided I should like to write to you, & if you wish, I shall be your home front reporter. That is, if you don't already have one.

My description is average. Nothing exceptional. 5'4" in height, 122 lbs., black hair & black eyes (not rings, I mean eyes). I reached my 23rd birthday in the hot month of July. Isn't it awful! But our consolation is that no one believes it. That's good! No one has even come up to 20th as a guess. But I had a grand 23 yrs. I hope it will continue. And that you & all the boys will come home victoriously & continue from where you all left off.

I while away my hours at the Red Cross Blood Bank, with a small salary. But its a life-line job & I want to be part of it. If everyone did his or her bit, victory will be ours, for no matter how bad things look at times; where there's life, there's hope, happiness & success. I have found it to be so. I hope you'll write & tell me about yourself & perhaps we can enjoy a grand correspondence.

With Best Regards I hope to be your friend,

Anne

Dear Anne,

I just finished a long letter to you, Anne, and now I'm writing you a quicky to kind of prepare you for it. I was so darned glad to get your letter, Anne, and it made me feel kind of warm inside. I am hoping that you will be my home front reporter because I don't have any.

That same friend has told me so much about you Anne that I feel as tho we are old pals, and I have been trying to get up enough nerve to write to you but now, Anne, I am going to really start writing to you. Congratulations on your birthday Anne, many happy returns of the day, and Anne, I hope you have a million more of these. What day in July was your birthday? I wish you wouldn't have seen that picture of me, Anne, because it was lousy. I never could take a good picture and that one was among the worst. I am getting some taken in town tomorrow, Anne, so a good one (I hope) will be on its way to you. Will you send me one of yourself, Anne? Sammy sends his regards. Thank you Anne with all my heart for your friendship. I will try my darndist to be really worthy of it.

So long for now, Anne.

DONALD SPENCER

World War II; Army Air Corps; Letter to his parents, October 29, 1943

It must be nice to have a girlfriend back home, that you think is waiting for you, but I am afraid I am not quite that lucky. I guess my girl, Janice, has forgotten that I even exist. I have not heard from her in months, and it does not look like I

FREDERICK STILSON CA 1918

"One day's mail from the States." reads the caption in this photograph from Frederick Stilson's memoir of life in the Army Corps of Engineers during World War I.

ever will. I wrote her again several weeks ago trying to find out what the matter was, but she never answers my letters....

[*A note written on the back of the envelope*] Guess I talked too soon, I just received a letter from Janice. Ha!

MARIE BRAND VOLTZKE

World War II; WAVES; Interview

Many girls had and kept a sense of humor. All was not fun, however, and heartache was not relegated to men only. There were "Dear Jane" as well as "Dear John" letters.

JEANNE URBIN MARKLE

Vietnam War; Army Nurse Corps; Interview

After completing her Army nurses' training, Markle was stationed at Fort Carson, Colorado.

I became an Army nurse in a big Army hospital. Most of my time spent there was going from ward to ward and learning how to take care of different people, even officers' wives. I met Brian [Markle, a doctor at the hospital] and got engaged in the summer, and we decided to get married. We got married on August the 6th [1966]. I flew home to Indiana during an airplane strike. He drove home, and we got married and we left immediately for Denver. He had not told me before he left—because I told him while I was home that week if he had orders for Vietnam that I was not getting married, I was canceling the wedding—he didn't tell, but he'd already received orders. He had orders for Vietnam and he said, "Do you want to go with me?" and I said, "No, I do not want to go with you. I'm going to stay here."

I got sick and was put in the hospital. On the second day, my boss, who was the chief nurse, Colonel McCormick, came into the room and said, "Jeanne, I just got a telex from Fifth Army headquarters in Chicago wanting to know why you haven't sent in your papers to go to Vietnam." And I'm sick in the hospital, and I said, "I didn't send in any papers. I'm not going to Vietnam." And she said, "Well, what's it all about, because they got a telex from Washington, D.C., wanting to know why you hadn't signed up. They're waiting to assign you a day." I said, "Call Brian." And as it had happened, the general's son was a friend of ours at Fort Carson, Colorado, and he was a lieutenant, and Brian had just mentioned, "Gee, I wonder if Jeanne could go with me, if she wanted to." And unbeknownst to us, the lieutenant called his dad in Washington, D.C., and he arranged it.

And so I said, no, I didn't want to go. My colonel explained to me that I was going to go some time and that if I didn't go this time, I might meet Brian on the airplane, passing him in the night, and we'd be separated two years possibly instead of going together. So I signed the papers, and they telexed Washington, D.C., and they sent me my orders, and we were both going to Vietnam.

Picturing War

Most of the collections in the Veterans History Project depend on words to tell their stories. The letters, diaries, journals, and spoken reminiscences of thousands of veterans of five wars tell unforgettable stories. A number of collections contain illustrative material, usually photographs, which adds to the historical record. And in a few cases, the veteran was a professional photographer or artist who recorded impressions and events.

Tracy Sugarman was one of those veterans. A fine arts student at Syracuse University in December 1941, he enlisted in the Naval Reserves two days after Pearl Harbor. Sugarman and his college sweetheart, June, were married on September 24, 1943, and shortly thereafter Sugarman shipped out to England. He was to command an LST craft in support of the Normandy invasion, but first came months of training exercises in England—and waiting for the orders to come down for World War II's biggest operation.

Sugarman was never too busy not to do two things on a regular basis: sketch scenes of GI life and write to his new bride. It's difficult to select which is the more eloquent: his visual impressions of men in uniform or his heartfelt letters to his "Junie." In 2000, Sugarman published a generous selection of both in a book, *My War.*

Sugarman says he saw each drawing as "a kind of dialogue between the sailor and me

or between the event and me. All I was trying to do was capture some moments so that I could send them home to my bride so that she could get a sense of what these moments were like." Sugarman added modestly, "They were never meant to be seen by anybody but my wife." Fortunately, she saved them, and his 34 watercolors and 35 black-and-white drawings are now part of his collection at the Library of Congress, along with over 270 letters to June.

"I had learned how to draw, how to paint at Syracuse," Sugarman said in his Veterans History Project interview, "but I don't think I really learned why until I went to war and I found those media were the way I could come to terms with getting through a bad time. If I put it on paper, I could deal with it." During his postwar career as a nationally renowned commercial artist, Sugarman says, "That has been a guiding principle to my art over the years. I think the best work I have done has been spontaneous, on the spot, responding to a moment."

An art student at Syracuse when the U.S. entered World War II, naval officer Tracy Sugarman sketched and painted throughout his hitch. "Fog In the Morning Off France," watercolor, August 12, 1944 (opposite). "Crew Off Duty," watercolor and graphite, 1944 (above).

Sugarman saw each drawing as "a kind of dialogue between the sailor and me or between the event and me." He drew spontaneously, only rarely from memory of a subject. He intended the artwork to supplement his letters home to his wife June, whom he had married shortly before shipping out. "Cutting Spuds for Chow," watercolor, 1944 (top). "Fowey Poker," watercolor and graphite, 1944 (middle). The only time Sugarman got seasick during the war was just after he'd won a big poker pot; he threw up all over his winnings. "Fowey Doughnut Wagon," pencil, no date (below, left). Fowey refers to an English port where Sugarman's ship docked. "Bunking Down," oil, 1944 (opposite).

Oil Quickie
-November aboard an LCI - Normandy, France.

"USO show—
honest!"
march 1 st (?)

"USO Entertainer," watercolor and graphite (opposite), 1944. "Rough Water in the Channel," watercolor, (above) 1944. Sugarman was part of the D-Day invasion, commanding a small group of landing craft on June 6, 1944. Details of what happened to him on that day can be found in Chapter 3. He spent several months afterward stationed on the beach at Normandy, helping to coordinate the massive landings of men and matériel.

A Matter of Rank:
Officers and Enlisted Men

"They are perfect and we are scum."

As long as there are titles and ranks and stars and bars and stripes, there will be friction in the military. But the enlisted men aren't the only ones with complaints, as Lt. (jg.) Tracy Sugarman points out in a letter to his wife. And not every enlisted man assumed every officer was unfeeling, selfish, and incompetent. Witness John Wister's passionate defense of his own commanding officer, a man willing to admit his imperfections to the men under him. That trait would make all the difference in a key moment when the order is given and soldiers are expected to respond without a second thought.

TRACY SUGARMAN
      World War II; Navy; Letter to his wife, May 17, 1944
I'm not being paid to enjoy this job—just to do it. Like everything else in this world you have to pay for what you get—and for the thrill of putting on this uniform for the first time back at Notre Dame, being a naval officer and your husband all at once—for the pride and the satisfaction of being an officer—you pay and pay and pay in inconvenience, drudgery, repetition, and responsibility. It's strangely enough a debt that never gets paid but daily becomes more and more demanding of your time and energies. Your satisfaction must come from within if it comes at all. Commendation from your superiors is as rare as thanks from your inferiors—and there is a hell of a tendency so often to let down. But you don't because you know that someone <u>has</u> to do the job. You hope for the respect of your superiors and the affection of your men—but after a while you get to the point where the job itself is the important thing—and if you're not being appreciated it's just too bad.

IRVING OBLAS

World War II; Army; Letter to his wife, January 28, 1944

El commando has been on a rampage for the past week or two. The only thing that relieves the strain is when we get out of the office and are able to chuckle over the incidents that occur. Some of them are hilarious to us, though in cold black and white they may not be quite the same. The latest scuttlebutt is that he's been recommended for sea duty—which, despite his previous stand on that matter, seemed to annoy him no end. In fact, he found several occasions to berate the boys for not fully appreciating their soft jobs, telling us we'll never be killed sitting in the office. This outburst was partly due to a memo from the Exec. Office, requesting all those who wanted sea duty to submit their names. He misunderstood the wording of the notice and insisted that each of us sign under one of two columns: "I desire to go to sea" and "I do not desire" etc. Nobody was anxious to commit himself and we, therefore, all signed under a 3rd column, "No preference."

DONALD SPENCER

World War II; Army Air Corps; Letter to his family, October 9, 1943
Spencer was stationed at Lowry Field, Denver, Colorado.

This place sure has changed out here as far as the way it is run since Dick [his older brother] was here. We go to school six days a week, and only get one day off. There is a new Commanding Officer, a one star General, and he is one hell of a guy. He was the one who thought up all this stuff, just to make it look as if he is doing good here. He was one of the Generals who was at Pearl Harbor when it was attacked, and was broken from a Major General to his present rank for that. He is up for another court-martial and we are hoping that he gets busted again, so we can get a new commanding officer.

JOHN WISTER

World War I; Army; Memoir

When I was moved to the Chateauroux Hospital in early April, a man in the bed next to me said that if he ever had a chance to shoot his commanding officer he would do so, and he was offering to bet that this officer would be shot by one of his men before the first charge he was in was over. When opinion is as unanimous as that, I think there is no doubt that the right is on the side of the men and that they would be justified. For whatever bad habits the American soldier may have, I have found him quick to appreciate a good officer, and where I have heard one case of threat I have usually heard many cases of loyalty. The way a good officer inspires a man is truly marvelous, and is one of the compensations of war. Nobody could treat us better than our major here, and in return the men are loyal. It is true he makes mistakes, which are irritating if they mean extra labor for the men, and they make criticism at that time. It is true he makes too much emphasis on military form and dress, which in a working organization where our fifty men have often had to do the work when they should have many more helpers, we have felt to be foolish. But we remember that he has a tremendous burden on his shoulders, and he is learning by his mistakes, and is sometimes man enough to admit them himself, which proves to me that he is a splendid type of man because that is difficult to do in an Army as strong for making a god out of the officers as ours is. They are perfect and we are scum. And scum we are, for anything lower than the enlisted men I met in two hospitals I cannot imagine.

DENTON CROCKER

World War II; Army; Letter to his parents, November 22, 1942
Crocker sent this letter from Camp Pickett, Blackstone, Virginia

I have been instructing my squad in drill and have given several of the talks during class hours in the platoon. I think I have told you that the men in this group are much older than those with whom I trained. One man has two daughters and a son. He cannot read or write and since he is in my squad I have written some letters for him and I read his mail for him when it comes in. Another man was a machine gunner in the German army during the last war. Being older men they learn less quickly and it is difficult to make them adopt that military bearing which is a sign of a well-trained soldier.

One night last week a fellow named Martzel—he is about forty—got a phone call at about 10:45. I went to the company office with him. He got word that his wife, who was in an institution, had just died. He told me it was probably due to her receiving news of his being in the Army since she had a nervous disease. When you become a leader of such a group of men as these and they come to you with their problems and troubles, you begin to realize what a lot of pathos is existent among them.

MARY SHELDON GILL

World War II; Women's Army Corps; Memoir

Most of our female officers and non-coms were fair and I had no negative

Robert Lee Olen photographed these soldiers from the 10th Mountain Division in their sleeping quarters, ca 1944. In wartime, the needs of the individual are secondary to building a sense of mission among the group.

experiences with them. The GIs who worked with us at processing were specially picked: one a retirement-age man with a wife and two gentlemen who were engaged to be married.

I always did my duty but never buttered up. One non-com did not recommend me for Sgt.'s stripes there, but I did a few weeks' duty as assistant to the processing director when my roommate went on furlough, and she intervened and saw to it I got stripes as was fair, as I was a conscientious worker if not a butter-up.

I went before the board for Officer Candidate School and they liked everything about me except for my too soft and diffident voice. They asked me to work on my voice and come back again, which I did. I still could not speak up confidently to the board, so I was rejected.

They were right; at that time I did not have the ego strength required to be an officer although I was very competent about drilling troops during our weekly practice. Now I could make a good officer, but not then.

We didn't have it all rosy at first. Before we arrived at Moore General Hospital in North Carolina, the camp commandant told his men that we were little better than prostitutes, and we had to come and go through a separate gate. However, three weeks after we arrived, that all changed and we were readily accepted as a vital part of the camp life and work.

JAMES BAROSS

World War II; Army Air Corps; Memoir

Rank was of little importance. While officers wore their bars and leaves and eagles on their shirts, and took rank more seriously, enlisted men rarely had any mark of rank on their clothing. It was unimportant and just too much of a bother.

There was a definite difference in the food and sleeping quarters for officers, but rank was relatively unimportant otherwise and no saluting of superior officers was done or expected.

One day a new officer came into the squadron area. Finding himself somewhat ignored by those of lesser rank and not being saluted, he complained to the commanding officer, who told him quite emphatically that when he had been overseas as long and had done as much as those around him, maybe then he could come back and register his complaint once again. He didn't.

Balancing the interests of the group against the desire for individual freedom and expression wasn't easy for some men in uniform. Tensions often erupted and punishment was doled out, as the accounts reveal.

SIDNEY RICHES

World War II; Army; Memoir

Each incoming group of new trainees developed (at first) unruly personages. It was my policy at the time to let the individual platoon sergeants handle any minor breaches of discipline, of which there seemed to be a plethora. It was nothing less than amazing how these characters straightened themselves out in such a short time! One farm boy was out and out rebellious. For two weeks we tried to get through to instill in him the basics of military functions but without success. One Monday morning he appeared at roll call all slick and shiny and was a model trainee until graduation. I've always suspected that he was a victim of "barracks" punishment.

FREDERICK STILSON

World War I; Army; Memoir

I got mine a couple of times when I stepped out of line and had to police the barracks and grounds, being confined to the post a couple of weekends for some infractions of the rules. Our punishment was generally picking up cigarette butts and bits of paper from the front lawn of the barracks, or doing menial work inside, besides our regular assignments. I didn't lose very much time off, though.

MALCOLM STILSON

World War II: Army Air Corps; Memoir

Warren [his younger brother] was assigned to the Army Student Training Unit at Montana State College. They marched every place on campus, that is, from class to class and to chow, which must have added up to several miles a day. In gym, after their calisthenics, they ran the 2.2-mile run, a cross-country race. He ran it in 18 minutes, 13 seconds. It was the farthest he had ever run for time, and it did not bother him, much to his surprise. Somebody cussed out the captain, which brought about a restriction. So, instead of going to town, the group put on their comfortable hiking shoes and were led on a 12-mile march, which brought them onto campus at about midnight. Warren felt sorry for the fellows who had dates in town that night.

BEN SNYDER

World War II; Army Air Corps; Ellington Field, Houston, Texas; Memoir

As we prepare to depart, our tactical officers have instituted a Reign of Terror, which has stretched us to the breaking point. It began about ten days ago when six of our squadron slept through reveille. Excessive punishment became the norm, a kind of oppressive send-off before we leave to try our luck in the wild blue yonder.

On Saturday came the payoff. Knowing that we would be figuratively drawn and quartered if we so much as left a strand of cobweb lurking in an obscure corner, we scrubbed and swept and dusted until we considered our quarters letter perfect. It was playing a game against a more skillful opponent. The defense was prepared (we thought) for the weekly standby inspection.

When the imperious Lt. Fogg came wheeling into the barracks, we thought we had him. Minutely inspecting every possibility, he sought the weak link in our chain and was stopped at every turn. Our smug smiles of satisfaction must have antagonized him, for in a burst of fiendish ingenuity, we were nailed with but a single stroke. Lying on his back on the floor, he peered underneath our blanket rolls. If a streak of white sheet was evident under the springs, we were his!

The result could have been foreseen. With about half of the squadron, we walked "tours." In our case it was three hours, back and forth, white gloved, stiff and straight in the heat of a late summer Texas sun. Trudging solemnly around a rectangle a hundred yards long and twenty-five yards wide, we were contributing in a curious way to the war effort. How painfully absurd!

BEN SNYDER 1945

Taking advantage of a leave pass, Ben Snyder, a bombardier, and his navigator buddy Hal Ellison (left), stroll through Sydney, Australia. In his memoir, Snyder writes eloquently of "down" time while flying missions in the Pacific Theater.

Taking a Break: Recreation and Leave

"The uniform seemed to impress people."

After all the marching and drills and KP, after all the bad chow and the days when the mail brought nothing from home or sweetheart, there was the promise of some downtime. It could be a movie viewed sitting out in the rain on a South Pacific island, or it could be a weekend furlough to fly halfway across the country on a military transport plane. There were even GIs, like Captain John Earle, who was specifically charged with providing diversions, supplying the troops with luxury items as basic as candy bars or cigarettes or playing cards that would keep up their spirits.

JOHN EARLE

World War II; Army; Letter to his family, March 25, 1944
As a Special Services officer, Earle had duties that included doing everything possible to improve the morale of the 4,000 men in his regiment. In addition, any job that came up that was not covered by Army regulations came under Special Services.

After the 19 days were up they had to march 20 miles back over the mountains with all their equipment to reach their rest camp. They got in about 10 o'clock at night and they sure were bushed. We had the PX and a movie going but most of them were too tired to come to them. They hadn't been paid in a month-and-a-half and most of them were too broke to buy anything, so I just issued every man a beer, a pack of cigarettes, and three candy bars. It came to $800, and as my fund only had $250 in it, I had to do some fast talking to raise the money. I went over to see the adjutant and told him that his fund had about $3,000 in it and that it would be a good idea for him to pay the bill. He was too tired to think properly or give me an argument so we went over and woke up the colonel to get his permission. He rolled over, said yes, and went back to sleep. I've found that is the only way to spend Army funds, for if you let them think about it, the answer is sure to be no.

JAMES BAROSS

World War II; Army Air Corps; Memoir; Biak Island, New Guinea

Just up the road from our squadron area movies were shown. When a new movie arrived we all attended the showing that night. Showings were on a screen stretched between two palm trees and we sat on the ground. On the ground, that is, unless it was raining, which it did about half of the time.

When it rained, we sat on our helmets and draped our ponchos over our heads with the hole, through which the head was supposed to go, right in front of our eyes. It made for dry watching of the movie.

Coconuts grew all over the islands of the Pacific and they fell, when ripe, causing us to attempt to avoid them when possible. However, the movie showing area was in a coconut grove and all during the movie we would hear plop! plop! plop! as they fell.

The same movie would be shown for as long as we had it, usually a couple of weeks. Boredom caused many of us to attend night after night until we could narrate the actors' lines along with them.

FREDERICK STILSON

World War I; Army; Memoir

Our training ended August 11, 1917, and those of us who didn't have commissions already received ours on the 14th of August. During the two months at Leavenworth, those of us who could play musical instruments formed a regimental orchestra. I happened to play the mandolin since my college days, so got in on that. We gave a concert a few evenings before we all left the post, which was attended by most of the "brass" and their wives and families. We spent considerable spare time in practice. This group played both popular and classical music. There were about 75 in the orchestra with a conductor and an arranger, all volunteers.

JAMES BAROSS

World War II; Army Air Corps; Memoir

One of the more colorful ground people in our squadron was an Indian named Sam

Keeps the Mountain. He was a member of some tribe from one of the western states, and oil in great quantities has been discovered on land belonging to the tribe.

Each month Sam would receive, in the mail, a check from one of the oil companies that handled the drilling and gathering of the oil. The amount of the check was enormous in our eyes, amounting to several thousands of dollars, and Sam could dominate any poker game that went on in the squadron, which he did. He was not a great poker player, but he was a great source of income for those who played.

BEN SNYDER
World War II; Army Air Corps; Letter, October 7, 1944; Kauai, Hawaii
Much of our marking time here is devoted to sport, but increasingly card games (considerable money changing hands) with the consumption of vast quantities of beer. I'm an occasional participant but more inclined to dig deeper in *The Oxford Anthology of American Literature*. Dad, I'm beginning to appreciate the value of a college education.

HELEN MINOR
World War II; Women's Army Corps; Interview
I got transferred to Fort Leonard Wood, Missouri. And that, oh gosh, is way out in the country, way out in the woods. It was awful. The closest town was six miles away, and none of the women were allowed in the town. You couldn't go to town. It was a tough town.

So every women's barracks had a mail catalog, and if you needed or wanted anything or wanted a gift to send home to somebody, you would order it out of the catalog. We didn't get off the base. We had movies—10 cents, if you didn't know how to sneak in. You have your friends taking tickets. Well, I mean, in enlistment, we got $50 a month. Of course, everything, room and board, was provided, your clothing. But if you wanted to buy anything at all, like candy, you didn't have room to put it, unless you ate it. And so there wasn't too much activity. They had some NCO clubs on the base, which were for non-commissioned officers. Well, the key word was "officer," and we were not officers, we were privates, so we didn't go to those. We just didn't do much, really. By the time you got through with a day's work you were glad to go back to your barracks and rest.

HELEN MINOR

World War II; Women's Army Corps; Interview

Minor was stationed at William Beaumont Hospital, El Paso, Texas.

We would get three-day passes once a month, maybe, but you had to be back right at the end of that weekend. I took a three-day pass once and I went to Los Angeles because I'd never been to California before. I just wanted to see what it was like. I went down to the airfield, I think it was Fort Bliss Airfield. You could get a free plane ride any time you wanted to. There were planes coming and going all the time and they were going all over the United States, and you'd just go in and sign up. They'd say, "Where do you want to go?" We tell them our final destination. They'd say, "Well, we don't have any going right there, but you can go here or there." Sometimes we'd go just to go. And I went to Los Angeles. I was so worried about the return trip I took a train back so I would be back on time. They had weather planes, too, that went out every day to certain areas.

Every place you'd go, it was really neat because you'd go to the airfield, and they'd say, "Check your chute out." You always had to check out a parachute. The planes were very crude; they were C-47s, which means they were transport planes and there were just two rows of metal seats down each side of the interior and noisy, awful noisy. And then you get an Army truck or some kind of transportation in to the closest base and just go to the headquarters and say you want to spend the night. They issue you some bedding and tell you where to go to sleep. And you could go to that area mess hall so it didn't cost you a thing when you're there.

IRVING OBLAS

World War II; Navy; Letter to his wife, October 26, 1943

I notice you are counting the days [until his furlough]. This morning everyone was exclaiming: only a week from today. These chaps count the days with the same fervor the Rikers inmates do. Now, tonight it's less than a week to go; in fact at this time next week I should be home.

Don't concern yourself with meeting me on the street. With the slow trains we will have, the chances are we won't reach New York until at least six and maybe later. Don't worry if I am overdue.

SIDNEY RICHES

World War II; Army; Fort Benning, Georgia; Memoir

But then we had our sometimes nights and weekends of R and R. I became acquainted with a lieutenant from Virginia who had a car (a rarity) so we could

John Enman, who was stationed in India as a cartographer with the Army Air Corps, received this enlisted man's pass in October 1944 to visit the town of Agra. Enman spent much of his free time touring the countryside.

visit Columbus for some good food and femininity. Occasionally, but not often, we'd cross the river into Phenix City, Alabama. "Sin City" it was called then but I learned years later that the town had been cleaned up.

BEN SNYDER

World War II; Army Air Corps; Letter sent from Big Spring, Texas

Either I have an innate talent for finding hospitable families close by or I am just lucky. It was the Duckworths of Houston and now the Inkmans of Big Spring. In the first case, there was an attractive daughter, Florence, who quickly departed for New York to study ballet. In the second, there is Camille, still a senior in high school, with whom I have developed a relationship. There is a reservoir of good will to be tapped in these communities. One need only seek and it can be found.

I suppose there are various venues for "finding," depending upon what one might be looking for. In my own case, the after-church-services social hour is the most likely source of new friendship. There are other options, of course: bars, bowling alleys, drug stores, or wherever young people congregate. The fact that we are on Main Street for a common purpose gives us a certain legitimacy whatever our differences in origin, background, or section of the country.

IRVING OBLAS

World War II; Navy; Letter to his wife, January 30, 1944

Just back from my weekend in Ithaca. And I've heeded your warning and

MARIE BRAND VOLTZKE CA 1944

*Stationed in Washington, D.C., during World War II, WAVE
Marie Brand (left) took advantage of her leave time to visit the
city's tourist attractions, including its fabled cherry trees.*

watched out for the co-eds—tho, for part of the sightseeing tour of Cornell I had
the company of two other girls, besides [his cousin] Johanna.

Spent Sat. eve in the town, ate a good meal, had a haircut and went to see a
movie. Ithaca was jammed with soldiers and sailors who attend special schools
at Cornell. The "Y" had no accommodations and I had to stay over at a tourist
house—a comfortable room.

I had a good breakfast—orange juice, fried eggs, and coffee: $.50!—and
then went to stand on a corner, waiting for a bus. A car pulled up and an elderly woman driving it asked me if I wanted a lift. The power of the uniform! I was
taken aback and a bit embarrassed but she was so gracious that I accepted and
she drove me up the hill to the university; after which I finally succeeded in
locating Jo's residence.

I didn't know whether I'd recognize her, but when she came down the hall she looked a great deal like Ma except that she's not as tall as I had expected. As you will note from the enclosed program I had to attend services (which is meant for all faiths) because Jo sings in the choir. I was agreeably surprised to hear a liberal sermon against discrimination. The chapel was well attended— soldiers, sailors, students, women, and visitors.

Later, Jo and I had dinner at a restaurant in one of the buildings of the college. Lamb chops for me—delicious, to boot. And the rest of the afternoon, we toured the campus accompanied by two of Jo's friends—"torch bearers," i.e., girls who don't accept dates with other boys because their own b.f.'s are away in the services.

FREDERICK STILSON

World War II; Army; Memoir

During my five weeks at Fort Sheridan in Illinois, I made two weekend trips down to see Essie at Peoria, Illinois, as I was entitled to a weekend pass every other weekend. We discussed our marriage plans and set our date at about August 15th, as soon as I was commissioned and could get my 15-day leave before being assigned to duty with some regiment. We enjoyed our weekends together going up to Galesburg to my folks, too. I met people on the street who stopped us and shook hands as though I was a long-lost son or brother. The uniform seemed to impress people, or so I thought. War was a new thing to them. All they remembered was the appearance of the G.A.R. (Grand Army of the Republic) veterans of the Civil War. Even the Spanish-American War Veterans had faded out of sight by this time.

JOANNE PALELLA

Persian Gulf War; Army; Interview

I didn't get leave while I was out in the desert. But leave while I was stationed in Europe was wonderful. I've been able to backpack and travel. I've been to 19 different countries and most of them were on a mountain bike with a backpack. And that's the way I usually took my leave; I knew I could never afford it on my own otherwise. If I went to Belgium or Holland or Italy I could stay in the military barracks if they had an extra bed or cot, and eat military food—that was a cheap way to go. I would buy my food from bakers and backpack all my food and wine, travel that way.

MARIE BRAND VOLTZKE

World War II; WAVES; Interview

Being stationed in D.C. gave many exciting outlets that compensated. Day shift permitted time in the evening to attend the *Washington Post's* Starlight Concerts at Meridian Park, the most memorable being the Von Trapp Family Singers, who had fled Austria to evade Hitler's onslaught. I saw my first ballet, I attended stage plays, Navy, Army, Marine band concerts. I am so grateful for the exposure to many forms of art. All of this entertainment was free for service personnel.

Afternoon shift permitted free mornings to visit and sit in on discussions in Congress, attending and witnessing military funerals at Arlington National Cemetery. I attended the parade when General Eisenhower came home after V-E Day, visited the art museum and the national monuments; my favorite was the Lincoln Memorial.

Coming off midnight shift, I had 72 glorious hours for exploration. All I needed was a signed permit to leave a forty-mile radius of Washington, D.C. My friends and I took a tour of New York City, staying at the Taft Hotel. Guy Lombardo was playing in the dining room. He came to our table and sang "Irish Blue Eyes" to me, a great moment! Visiting the Luray Caverns in Virginia, we stayed at the Mimslyn Inn, my first stay at a luxury hotel, listed as one of distinction, with marigolds in the finger bowls, no less.

JOE BACA

Vietnam War; Army; Interview

It was a great experience taking my MOS at Aberdeen Proving Grounds in Maryland. But then, I also learned a lot. I hung around with a lot of African Americans, a lot of athletes. We came into Washington, D.C. We were at a local bar or nightclub in the evening, and we were asked to leave. And it was really upsetting to me. Here we are, serving our country, and we're not being served. It was race. I don't think it had to do with us being soldiers, because outside of that one place people appreciated the fact that we served in the military, just as when I was stationed at Fort Campbell, Kentucky.

"Hurry up and wait," is the service expression universally understood as the experience of being told to get ready for your next assignment, then being told to hold in place as the days and weeks pass. Denton Crocker was a scientist assigned during World War II to an anti-malarial unit in the South Pacific. Crocker and his fellow scientists were extensively trained to study the mosquitoes that were giving

the U.S. military fits, and to offer advice on how to combat a disease that was competing with the Japanese as America's worst enemy in the Pacific Theater. In an appendix to his memoir, My War on Mosquitoes, 1942-1945, *Crocker quantifies the quintessential GI experience.*

DENTON CROCKER
  World War II; Army; Memoir
Of my three-and-a-half years in the army (1,272 days), I was productive for only 768 days (60%). This productive time was spent as follows: instructing/training (232 days, 18% of total days of service) and doing the job I was trained to do (536 days, 42% of total days of service). The remaining 40% of my time was spent: 1. being trained (121 days, 10% of total), 2. in travel related to my duties, not counting furlough travel (88 days, 7% of total), 3. on furlough (65 days, 5% of total), and 4. waiting (230 days, 18%).

Training time seems reasonable given the need for basic military training as well as for training in my sanitation specialty and the malaria survey sub-specialty. Considering the distances of our training and work sites from home and from each other, travel time is understandable, as is the average of one day in 20 for furlough. The waiting is harder to understand. I have given a possible reason for the 10-week delay at Devens, the reception center, but the totally unproductive 7 weeks at Jackson Barracks, our second location in New Orleans (a staging area for embarkation) seemed at the time unreasonable stagnation. Here, waiting for shipment overseas, our mail was censored and no furloughs were allowed. With our unit equipment packed for transport, there was no chance to engage in any productive work. We were allowed occasional passes to go into town, but Bob Roecker and I, in desperation to escape the awful boredom, developed a ruse to get away more often still. Assuming the guards at the compound gate were poorly trained to spot transgressors such as we, we walked nonchalantly past them, flashing our open Medical Department identification cards at them. These cards were rather official-looking documents, with a stamp, a fingerprint, and a signature. We did this several times and were never challenged. Whether the guards were fooled or simply played along with us I don't know.

{ ONE MAN'S STORY }

Irving Oblas

"Who knows where I'd be better off?"

Among the most thoroughly documented collections in the Veterans History Project are those featuring correspondents like Irving Oblas. In September 1943, he enlisted in the Navy and was assigned to the U.S. Naval Training Center in Sampson, New York, 300 miles from his home in New York City. Irving was separated from his wife Lilyan and their infant daughter Rema for the next 11 months, during which he wrote to Lilyan almost daily. In August 1944, the family was reunited when Lil and Rema moved to Geneva, New York, and the Oblases moved into off-base housing.

Oblas's letters are filled with the details of the life of an enlisted man, a regular guy who's trying to adjust to barracks life, who eagerly awaits the mail (his collection unfortunately includes only a few letters from Lil), gripes about his mercurial commanding officer, and tells tales of taking leave, either to nearby towns or home to New York City. In effect, writing to Lil was his way of keeping a diary, though his letters are generally less reflective than anecdotal.

"Everything has been hectic," he wrote to Lil on September 15, 1943, "starting, of course, with the train ride—there was no sleeper & no reclining seats." Later, he notes, "At present, it is very difficult to write—emotionally, I mean. Right now, I wish I were home. However, in retrospect, it probably won't seem so bad—I'm sure in a few days I'll be more adjusted. Truth to tell, every one of the new recruits seems to be in a fog—that's the typical reaction."

Oblas's letters are full of complaints: about the noise in the barracks, the lack of privacy, the rudeness of some of his fellow recruits—but surprisingly, not about the food, which he generally accepts as second-rate without dismissing it

*Irving and Lilyan Oblas, 1944, and a letter from Lil with news that
their daughter Rema had spoken her first words. Irv wrote Lil
almost daily between September 1943 and August 1944, when she
and Rema were able to move to Navy housing near his duty station.*

as inedible. Much of his serious complaining relates to his boss. Oblas was a court stenographer in civilian life, and he managed to land the same duties in the Navy, though he was often confined to an office, doing clerical work. The climate in that office was determined by an officer Oblas sarcastically referred to as "El commando." He was, at least according to Oblas, a man of many moods, most of them foul. In January 1944, when Irving wrote to Lil, "El commando has been on a rampage for the past week or two," he details the man's pettiness and obtuseness, allowing that he and his buddies were at least able to laugh about Harris away from the office.

As a court reporter, Oblas had a unique view of the Navy and its more troubled characters. "Attended a court martial today," he wrote Lil on May 25, 1944. "One of the men accused is the father of five children; he claimed his wife and two children were sick so he went AWOL. That's the second man with 5 children who has been up for court martial. Looks like other people have their troubles, too."

Oblas kept his ear cocked for rumors. Two months after arriving at Sampson, he almost shipped out. He wrote Lil on November 12, 1943, "Last night a friend told me my name was on a list posted in another barracks. I investigated & found it to be so, instructing me to report for an examination — physical. I went up there & was told my name was on the list for draft to go to L.I. [Long Island] but that it had been scratched off. So I remarked maybe I would have been better off there. To which a chap present said that it was for sea duty!"

He was apprehensive about being shipped to another location farther from Lil and Rema, but he was also ambitious enough to want a better posting. In February, when a female civilian employee joined his office, he found himself with less work to do and time to think about his niche in the Navy. "I'm tempted to ask [El commando] for a transfer to another department at the station," he wrote Lil on February 2, 1944, but he never got around to it.

Five days later, he wrote, "Another surprise—and a disappointment, too! This morning, while on the breakfast chow line, I spied a familiar face—a former student at the Hunter Shorthand class, Bob Cole, who was writing 200 while I was struggling for my 175 words per minute. According to him, he is scheduled to be sent to the Bklyn. Navy Yard as the court-martial reporter—the job that I had applied for! Such are the vicissitudes of life."

In March 1944, Oblas did enjoy a small moment of triumph. "Big News!" he wrote Lil on March 27. "The Legal Office has had a momentous revolution—and I think I am still flabbergasted from the effects of the upset. Do you remember that I told you Lt. Commander Van Brunt was to be transferred from Sampson last weekend? That was the original order but instead, El commando was substituted—and he is no longer here! He was given two days' notice (the office staff presented him with a bouquet of flowers for which I owe fifty cents) and off he went on Friday to a shore station in South Carolina."

Nothing was more important to Irving Oblas—even getting rid of his nemesis—than a reunion with his family. Oblas's letters are filled with plans for train rides back to New York for quick weekends with Lil and Rema and accounts of his lonely train rides back to Sampson. Any trip away from the barracks seemed to lift his spirits. In January 1944, Irving got a weekend pass and went to Ithaca, where his cousin Johanna was a student at Cornell University. He made several other trips to neighboring towns when he couldn't get a pass to get back to New York City.

Oblas suffered another setback in the summer of 1944. On August 17, he wrote, "Bad news today—I failed the exam for Y1c [Yeoman First Class]. It was the first part that ruined me; on the typing shorthand I was practically perfect—and if they averaged all of the marks, I would pass. But we have to get 2.5 on all parts—and I only made 2.4 on the first part." His failure was compounded by another job opportunity slipping away. "I heard of a request for court reporter from the Bureau of Personnel and investigated it. The location of the job is unknown but most likely is in Washington. I thought it over all morning and was going to ask Van Brunt about it and call you tonight. I was tempted to ask for the change in assignment because it would be a new experience for me and maybe a change for the better. Just when I made up my mind, I found that another yeoman, a former court reporter working in that dept., had decided to take the position because his daily horoscope said he would soon travel. Seeing that he works in that dept., they gave him the first choice for the job. There's nothing I can do about it since I'm not even supposed to know about the opening officially. Oh, well—looks like I'm fated to stay at Sampson. And who knows where I'd be better off?"

He was soon to be better off, when Lilyan and Rema joined him. Oblas's gain was a loss for his Veterans History Project collection; once his family was reunited, the letters stopped, and we have no more documentation of his life in the Navy until August 1945. Then he shipped out to California to prepare for duty in the Pacific Theater. He wrote Lilyan a postcard from every stop that train made, from Buffalo and Niagara Falls through Chicago, Denver, and on to California. All of these vintage postcards are in his collection. Oblas left Sampson on August 6, the day that the U.S. dropped an atomic bomb on Hiroshima. The sailors heard the news during their train ride and speculated about its effect on their future.

Not long after Oblas arrived in San Francisco, he learned that Japan had surrendered. After several months of idleness at Camp Shoemaker, a base outside of San Francisco, he was sent to Bremerton, Washington, to prepare paperwork for decommissioning ships. In January 1946, his tour of duty with the U.S. Navy finally completed, he took a train back East to be reunited with Lilyan and Rema.

"Sub Spotted—
LET 'EM HAVE IT!"

LEND A HAND—Enlist in your Navy today

{ CHAPTER THREE }

Under Fire

Naval recruiting poster, ca 1942.

FREDERICK STILSON 1918

"The trenches before Verdun," reads Frederick Stilson's caption to this photo. Arguably the most horrific battle of World War I, Verdun took place the year before America entered the war. Stilson's engineer corps could only wonder at the evidence of utter devastation.

World War I

"Many of us called it the ride of death, for we were riding to what was to be the biggest battle of the war."

No one was prepared for this war, for the relentless bombardments, for the months spent in trenches knee-deep with water, for the threat of gas attacks, and for casualties on a scale never heard of before. For two-and-a-half years, Americans recoiled from the horror, then plunged into it themselves. Even then, their attitude was typically optimistic. A marine like William Nice, with 12 years behind him putting out brush fires all over Latin America, would rightly look on the Great War as the kind of challenge he had been building up to. For teenager Herbert Kohls, the war was an accelerated life lesson, and for Midwestern postman Vincent Reed, it was simply a matter of survival.

VINCENT REED

Army; Memoir

Reed was stationed in Germany and France with Army's 358th Infantry unit. The following selection from Reed's memoir is from the night of August 17, 1918.

Just as we started out, two German airplanes flew overhead; immediately, every anti-aircraft gun in the vicinity opened on them. We stood there in the shade of the trees, for it was a moonlit night, and trembled with excitement, or was it fear, for this was our first experience.

We could see our way plainly. We had no more than started when the men began ditching overcoats, extra hobnail shoes, and everything that they did not need. Many times a shell or two would drop near these woods and someone would holler, "Gas! Gas!" We would put on our gas masks, but there was no danger.

While in our first position our only water supply was about two miles distant in the town of Mamey. The road leading to it had a screen of branches about six feet high to screen the road from view of the German front lines. A detail of men was sent for water just before daybreak each morning to bring water for the company in the canteens of the men. One canteen of water would have to last all day, for drinking and shaving and washing. We had one bath in Mamey in cold water from a shower which had been rigged up in the half-ruined buildings.

Just across the field from us was a main traveled road, which led to the front-line trenches. As the allied troops were preparing for the St. Mihiel Offensive, this road was crowded at all hours of the night with loads of ammunition and supplies.

We soon realized the need of a dugout, so we went to work on one. It was 25 feet long, 10 feet wide, 7 feet deep. We used it only one night, but it was well worth the effort, for that night the Germans gave us a terrible shelling, so we were thankful for the protection the dugout afforded. The next day we started for the front lines and the St. Mihiel Offensive from which many of our men never returned.

On the night of September 11 we turned in all of our surplus equipment and moved out of our position to join the rest of the regiment for the march to our front-line positions. I shall never forget that night as long as I live. Just about dark, it began to rain, and it rained all night. We ploughed our way across the fields through mud and water. Going up a short hill, we had to step over some wires stretched across the field. As I stepped over, my foot slipped and I fell. I fell with my head down hill, so I had a terrible time turning into a position where I could get on my feet again.

The St. Mihiel Sector covered an extent of thirty miles, and artillery had been moved in until, figuratively speaking, they were placed hub to hub. They opened up at 1 A.M. with a terrific barrage which lasted until 5 A.M. When the guns over a distance of thirty miles opened all at the same time, it seemed as though the end of the world had come.

Reed's company advanced through the fields attracting enemy fire. They scattered.

By this time, we had reached the cover of some brush down in the valley. Above us, about 30 yards away, were the German trenches. They were almost entirely abandoned. As we went toward them, some of the men had captured a bunch of Germans and they set up a howl of joy. The trench was a very deep one and had been lined with concrete walls, making it very strong. Our artillery, however, had torn it all to pieces. We crossed the trench and into the woods. There were a few German snipers in the woods, but we finally drove them out or killed them.

I could not begin to describe the destruction caused in these woods by our artillery. There were holes 15 to 25 feet in depth caused by the big shells our guns had sent over.

We went on and came up in the rear of another machine gun nest about 15 yards from us. We shouted to them and they came out. I was standing in front with my rifle and bayonet toward them as they climbed out shouting, *"Kamerad, Kamerad,"* There were about 12 of them. I felt so jubilant that I did not know how to act. I was so tired and worn out, and under such a nervous strain for the last 15 hours that I felt terribly like shedding a few tears of joy and excitement.

Reed's memoir also describes the night of October 18, 1918.

On Oct. 18, led by Major Allen, we again started for the front lines. We marched all afternoon through some of the most desolate country. It had been terribly torn up by shell fire. Woods had been almost totally leveled. Great holes were all over the fields and sometimes in the road, showing how terrible the fighting was during the opening of the Meuse Argonne battle.

About 4 P.M. a few shells fell near us. I ducked into one of the shelters when, all of a sudden a shell fell just across the hollow from me. My arm had a funny sensation, and upon looking at it, discovered that I had been hit by a small piece of shrapnel. I examined my arm and found it was only a scratch so I put on some iodine and bandaged it.

From this position we moved on the night of Nov. 10th across the open and into a town. There had been rumors that the war was nearly over, but we did not believe any of the reports.

The next morning I walked out into the backyard and found everything covered with a killing frost. As I walked along, I came to a bed of strawberry plants in a hotbed. Then there was a greenhouse, the glass of which was broken and the plants inside killed by the frost. Farther, I found a rose bush with a perfect rosebud on it. It had ice all around the outside of it, but I picked it and pressed it.

THEODORE KOHLS

Army; Diary

Theodore Kohls was born in Watertown, Wisconsin, on June 13, 1902. On April 12, 1917, six days after the U.S. declared war on Germany, he enlisted in the Army. Though not yet 15 years old, Kohls claimed he was 22 and was accepted into the service. Kohls died in 1948; his widow Johanna survived him until September 2001. After her death, their daughter Marlene found an incomplete diary of her father's war experiences. Following are excerpts from that diary.

Our division went into [the Montdidier] front on the first of May. Here is where we experienced real war for the first time. It was continuous shell fire on us all the time. Many times our chow details were shot to pieces and we were held without something to eat. This close fighting kept up till the morning of May 27th, when 150 Germans made a raid on my company. We immediately started killing Germans. We fought them for about 30 minutes when the Germans retreated and left two-thirds of their men dead behind them.

We kept up the fighting for a whole week. One night when my platoon was on a wiring detail, the Germans started a gas bombardment. It was my first time in real gas; we immediately put on our gas masks. Early in the morning we went back to our trenches. We laid around for the day. We couldn't stick our heads above the trenches, some German would take a pot shot at us. Toward evening I thought I was getting a cold, for my voice started getting rougher. We stayed in these trenches for six more days; my cold was getting worse, or what I thought was a cold.

We were relieved by the French on this front. Shortly after we were relieved I got so I could only whisper. I then went on sick report and was told by the doctor that I was gassed. I was sent to a hospital where I stayed for three weeks without my voice improving a bit, so I went downtown and drank all the cognac in sight, came back a drunken fool. But the next morning I could whisper; after that I was getting better every day. I was then sent back to my outfit.

On July 14, 1918, Bastille Day, Kohls was selected to parade in Paris and then enjoyed a 38-hour furlough. His diary begins again on the evening of July 17, 1918.

After supper we at once slung our combat equipment and started on our hike to our place on the lines. Everything went all right for the first part of the evening, but toward midnight we ran into tanks and artillery that was moving into its place in the line. It started raining and was pitch dark. Many times a man fell down in front of us and then you heard some cussing. It wouldn't pay to say the words in this book.

The German shells were landing all around. When we looked to our right and left we couldn't help admiring the sight, although it was a matter of life and death to us.

At 5 o'clock that morning we got in position on the Paris–Soissons Road, and five minutes later we went over the top. The bullets were coming at us like hail. Some of my best friends are sleeping near that road today. We couldn't advance but a few yards; our dead were lying all around. So we withdrew to the other side of the road and waited for a report from headquarters. Our orders were to stay where we were and hold our ground. So we laid there all day. At five o'clock that night, we got orders to go over the top at once, to go till we were all killed if necessary. We crossed the Paris road and carried the heights beyond by storm,

Gas drills were an important part of training during World War I. Frederick Stilson's caption on the photo above reads, "15 minutes a day on gas drill. This was obligatory on every officer and soldier in the command." Stilson demonstrates three positions for wearing a gas mask (below, left to right): Over the shoulders "at all times within 12 mile limit"; in position on the chest "for instant use, 3 mile limit"; fully deployed for gas attack.

but many a Yankee seen his last sun that day; they were lying so thick that we couldn't walk without stepping on them.

We went over and kept going till I was wounded in the left hip, which was the first time I got a taste of cold steel. I laid there until night. Major Roosevelt, the son of the ex-President, lay wounded thirty yards from me. When night came, I was carried off the field to a first aid station and sent back to Field Hospital No. 3.

Kohls was transferred to several different hospitals and finally shipped to Limoges, France, to Base Hospital 28. After spending seven days there, Kohls's division went to the front and saw action; then they were relieved by French troops and returned to the rear lines for some rest.

This place was a town where we was stationed the first time we were in that sector. Here is where I lost many of my buddies. From here we got on trucks, but not till we had witnessed French people returning to their shell-torn homes. We spent hours watching them dig up valuables that they had buried before flight. We rode all night on the trucks passing through the towns where the civilians were sleeping. Many of us called it the ride of death, for we were riding to what was to be the biggest battle of the war. Out of 250 men in our company came songs of home. After riding all night we at last came to our destination. We got off and had to hike 22 miles to our billets, as usual finishing with our big hill. This happened to be the biggest one we had met so far. We had it easy for three days, when came the biggest forced march the First Division ever made. Day after day we marched, hiked like humans into hell.

We could hear the guns and knew that the big battle was on—-

Kohls's diary ends here.

WILLIAM FREDERICK NICE
Marine Corps; Newspaper article
William Nice's collection was found in the early 1980s when a house in Roselle, New Jersey, was being cleaned out and readied for sale. Nice, who was born in Philadelphia in 1882 and died in 1965, had given some mementos to a friend. The material, consisting of military papers, medals, correspondence, a photo album, and a newspaper article, had been in the possession of the friend in Roselle until he died, leaving no immediate heirs. A real estate agent passed on the material to Rosemarie De Nicola of Chester, New Jersey, who in 2002 donated it to the Veterans History Project.

Nice enlisted in the Marines in 1905 and was involved in action in Haiti, Santo Domingo, Mexico, and Nicaragua. When the U.S. entered World War I, Nice was headed for Cuba to protect an American-owned sugar plantation from a rebel upris-

ing. He returned to Philadelphia and on June 14, 1917, sailed for Europe on the DeKalb, *an interned German liner. The article, from the* Asbury Park Sunday Press *edition of September 10, 1933, is titled "Gunner Nice of the Devil-Dogs" and is excerpted below. Nice's unit arrived at St. Nazaire on June 26th and remained in the Bourmont training area until March 14, 1918, when his company entered the war on the Verdun front. They spent two months holding the line in the region of Les Eparges, but the first real baptism of fire was received when the Second Marine Division was sent in as support for the First at Cantigny.*

In 1918 the hell of Chateau-Thierry broke in its awful devastation, threatening Paris as it had not been threatened since the dark days of 1914. Into the thick of the fight went Gunner Nice to bring back Lieutenant Somers, who had been wounded. There were few in that party who returned, but Nice did, despite a wound in the back. The bullet which struck him is still imbedded there. Lieutenant Somers, however, died soon after. Nice was sent to the first aid station and remained there overnight, running away and rejoining his command the next day for fear of being transferred. There he got his first citation, and later there was pinned upon his breast by a French general the Croix de Guerre. "He kissed me on each cheek," commented Nice. "I remember it well for he had been eating garlic." One of the exploits which figured in his decoration was the raid he made in command of 16 men upon a machine gun nest. They captured 26 Germans and two machine guns. "The woods were alive with machine guns," said Nice. "One of the worst nests was in a wooded depression, and death came spurting out of there in a constant stream." Shell fire was poured into it and then the boys went into the mess, and Floyd Gibbons, the newspaper correspondent, was with them. The Germans had pulled off a clever trick. They were operating their guns with lanyards stretching to the top of the depressions. Strings of ammunition containing 1,000 cartridges were operated by weights.

"There was poor Sergeant Jerry Finnegan, one of my pals, who haggled a precious can of salmon open with his bayonet and had been told by a lieutenant to 'damn well fix that bayonet and get on with the war.' Two hours later Jerry lay dead across a Maxim gun, his bayonet thru the body of the gunner. There was Hill 142 there, and the Germans wanted it desperately. They sent wave after wave over and their dead were piled all about it. We ourselves, the 49th, lost 62 percent of our company. We let Red Cross workers among the Germans pick up their dead and wounded until the wind lifted the cover on one stretcher and showed the snout of a machine gun. Then we let them have it. As one German wrote, 'The Americans are savages. They kill everything that moves.'

WILLIAM FREDERICK NICE CA 1917

*Nice enlisted in the Marines in 1905 and saw action in a half dozen
Latin American countries by the time he served in World War I.
Nothing prepared him, however, for the horror of combat in France.*

"But God, how the boys suffered in taking Bouresches. Lieutenant Robertson got there with 20 men out of some hundreds who had started. Whole platoons were shot down. The whole Bois de Belleau was a machine gun nest. But the Americans took it and here the Germans, who had rolled up tired French divisions all the way from the Chemin des Dames, were stopped good and plenty. And later in French general orders, the woods were named 'Bois de la Brigade de Marines,' after us.

"Then we bumped into the Aisne–Marne offensive at Soissons next, in Foch's drive in July 1918, when the whole western front moved. But I forgot to tell you that we paraded in Paris on the Fourth of July after Belleau Wood and you never saw a wilder welcome than the French gave the boys. Well, on July 18, 1918, all the guns in the world opened up for a five-minute barrage and we charged with the Senegalese. And remember, we hadn't had food for two days and had gone three nights without sleep. That's where I lost my orderly, little Tritt. We found him dead under the branches of a fallen tree.

"While there I was sent out on patrol one night to locate the enemy. We found them all right and they found us. We had 56 men. The Germans cut us off from our battalion and there was a lively scrap in which we sustained 37 casualties. The rest of us managed to fight our way back. We were cited in both French and American orders for that scrap and the day's work in general.

"I was hit in the right forearm, but it was only a flesh wound and I stayed with the company. We had advanced over six miles, captured over 3,000 prisoners, 11 batteries of artillery, over 100 machine guns, and the like. Some of those guns were turned on the retreating enemy.

"We were under the command of General Foch. As a matter of fact the Second was his command of shock troops and he sent us wherever hell was popping. That was how we came to get a crack at the fighting in the St. Mihiel offensive in September 1918. There was one machine gun nest that bothered us like the devil, and I and four men were sent out to silence it. It was a hot crawl to get close enough to heave hand grenades, but we did it and killed eight gunners. After that we had a little relief. The French thought enough of the incident to give us citations."

Nice fought in the Champagne offensive and its battle of Blanc Mont ridge, the taking of which Marshal Petain hailed as "the greatest single achievement of the 1918 campaign—the Battle of Liberation." On October 3rd the Marines took the "apparently impregnable" Blanc Mont ridge. The German army retreated to the Aisne, with some units of Marines going beyond the objective and caught in "terrific flanking fire." Nice was wounded, and was threatened with court-martial if he did not go to the rear for treatment of his wound. Nice did, but encountered another officer, a captain, who encouraged him to leave the hospital the next day and return to the front.

Nice's company was in an exposed position "where to remain was impossible." He told his commander, Captain Hamilton, "I've organized the company sector with 20 men, Captain. They're all we got left—you and I make 22. Lord, I'm tired, but what I can't see is why we didn't get ours, too."

That was where Nice was reported killed, and word to that effect was sent back to the States. But later came the correction that he was but slightly wounded. It was hell to have been in the Blanc Mont offensive, and Maj. Gen. John A. Lejeune, commanding the Marine Corps, wrote to the officers and men of the Second Division: "To be able to say, when this war is finished, 'I belonged to the Second Division, I fought with it at the battle of Blanc Mont ridge,' will be the highest honor that can come to any man."

Nice's division joined the First American Army in the Argonne Forest for the great offensive of November 1st. On November 3rd it captured the heights of Vaux. On the night of the 4th it advanced to the Meuse River. And on the night of the 10th, the eve of the Armistice, it forced its way across the river.

"We were ordered to take the heights upon the other side," said Nice, "and we did. But our casualties were 68 percent in doing it. At that, I don't see how any of us got across. I think every man who crossed was given a citation by both the American and French armies."

CHARLES RESTIFO 1944

"Bad, swampy terrain. Japanese were hidden—lots of casual-
ties," Charles Restifo wrote on the back of this photograph.
A combat photographer in the 161st Signal Photographic
Company, Restifo accompanied Gen. Douglas MacArthur
through much of the campaign to retake the Philippines.

World War II

"It's funny, but no one seemed frightened."

Twenty-three years after the Armistice, America plunged into war once again, in much more dramatic fashion than the steady buildup to its entry into World War I. Donald Finn, born in Canada, raised on an Idaho ranch, entered the U.S. Navy in August 1939. Two years later he found himself stationed on Ford Island, in Pearl Harbor, normally a choice duty assignment. But at the far end of the Pacific, the Japanese Empire was expanding, and even if Japan's conquered territory was still thousands of miles away, it wasn't clear what would be the inevitable outer borders of the new empire. The December 7th attack on Pearl Harbor was a shock to be sure but, judging from the reactions of several of Finn's buddies, not all that big a surprise, either.

DONALD FINN
 Navy; Memoir

I was seated on the edge of my bunk vainly trying to make up my mind whether I should shave before going to Mass or wait until afternoon chow and shave just before catching the one o'clock liberty boat when the high-pitched whine of an airplane engine pulling its freight out of a dive forced itself upon my consciousness.

Then there was an explosion as of a charge of dynamite being set off. The two sounds seemed to have some connection. Everyone crowded to the windows opening on the handball court and looked out. There was a cloud of black smoke and flying dirt seen between the edges of the buildings that intervened between the barracks and the hangars and ramps, followed by another explosion and the sight of a low-wing monoplane pulling out of a dive and standing almost on its tail. It was awfully close to the ground.

For the space of a couple of deep breaths, there was silence and then somebody said, "The yellow bastards." Then everybody began talking at once, grabbing clothes and getting into them. "How in the hell did they get in here and where the hell did they come from?" Everybody was asking everybody else.

I said to Van Brocklin, who was cursing the Japs heartily, "Well, it looks like the real thing," and he answered, "Yeah, and I'm glad of it. Now we can give them sons of bitches what they have been asking for." It's funny, but no one seemed frightened, though by now several bombs had fallen and the barracks trembled slightly once. Several guys raced downstairs to look out over the harbor from the main entrance. I stayed inside, myself, my curiosity being just as strong but discretion a little stronger.

An ensign came in and stood on a mess table, motioning for quiet. Everybody immediately began telling everybody else "to pipe down." The resulting hubbub was worse than before. When quiet was restored, orders were given that dispersed the men to different points on the station to turn to and begin resisting. The only resistance being put up so far was by the anti-aircraft on the battlewagons, cruisers, and other ships tied up in the harbor. Their five-inchers whanged away regularly, easily distinguishable from, and mingled with, the bomb explosions.

Coming into the mess hall now were sailors clad in oil-smeared undergarments, dripping wet, many of them burned and dazed. Soon after they arrived, word circulated that the *Oklahoma* had capsized and the *Arizona* was set afire, the *California* listing and the *Nevada* hit. We began to appreciate the enormity of what was going on.

There were many of us taking advantage of the lull in the bombings that came now. We poured out of the exits and entrances, being careful not to bunch up, and began legging it for the hangars, glancing frequently upward in the direction of possible strafers. But there were none. There was no danger to be seen until one got to the paint stripping shop. In front of it was a bomb crater and small plunks of concrete and glass scattered about for an area of 50 yards. There was a crater in the floor of the shop, too, and the roof bulged. That was the first bomb destruction I had ever seen, and it was impressive.

Our hangar was ablaze, its windows mostly in pieces on the ramp.... Some planes had not yet been hit but could not be got out into the air because the crater was between them and the water.

A truck drove by with a load of shovels and picks and everyone snatched one, prepared to fill in the crater. Planes started coming in again. We made for the hangar, getting under benches, behind steel doors, anything to stop flying bullets and falling wreckage. Several muffled thumps came from the direction of the battlewagons in the harbor. The attackers were not aiming for us here on the island.

There was a call for gunners to man guns that were newly mounted on rooftops but had no one to man them. Volunteers answered in a hurry. Every fifty caliber and thirty also was manned by a lot of suddenly serious plane captains and second mechs. Full of fight, too, and unmindful of the leaking gas from punctured gas tanks. It got darker all the time from the smoke of burning oil. There was oil all over the harbor, evidence of the damage inflicted on the battlewagons.

We were not bothered the rest of the day. In all, the raid lasted little over an hour. Three planes from the *Enterprise* came in for a landing at night. They were promptly shot up [by friendly fire]. What a fiasco! Somebody would shoot off a warm-up burst and instantly the sky was alive with fire, and everybody who wasn't manning a gun frantically sought shelter from the bombs he was sure were already on the way down. The order was not long forthcoming from way high up that the next so-and-so to let off a burst without being ordered to do so would find himself in very hot water.

Morning came at last—myself, I hadn't slept a wink and I don't believe anybody else had either. The skipper's big black eyes were bigger, more expressive than ever. All planes that could fly were taking their turns in the air. All flight crews remained at the hangar, and they were all drawing on, or rather raiding, the storeroom for helmets, goggles, and flight jackets. It was almost anarchy.

Soon I got a hop, my first in a PBY 5. Certainly looked sad to see Pearl Harbor from the air. Mr. Moore said into the phone to Ensign Mosley, "It is a terrible thing." The test hop became a tour of inspection for all hands—we all gaped and exclaimed at new views of destruction. Hickam Field looked especially hard hit and we circled that a couple of times, not being able to take it all in on the first bank.

We came down with a very good idea of the damage the raiders had wrought. All that could have been avoided if there had been one hour's warning of the approaching planes. No use thinking about that now. Impregnable Pearl Harbor! We thought! It is to laugh!

A war fought on the land, at sea, and in the air, combat in the Pacific was demanding in ways unknown to U.S. armed forces. American soldiers, sailors, and marines were pushed to the limit of endurance, bravery, and resourcefulness in battling the relentless Japanese one island at a time. Fliers faced enervating stretches over deceptively beautiful ocean waters, wrapped around missions that demanded precision. Sailors were on the lookout for torpedoes from beneath and kamikaze pilots from above. And in the jungles, soldiers and marines battled disease, suffocating humidity, and an enemy that would rather die than surrender.

SIDNEY RICHES

Army; Pacific Theater; Letter to his father, July 27, 1942

Guess we'll be on our way pretty soon. Order came thru today that all of our equipment has to be freighted to San Francisco by the second of August. The enlisted men have to turn in all their heavy clothing like overshoes, overcoats, etc., and are all being issued light clothing. We don't know where we're going or exactly when but it will be soon, no doubt about that. Sure hate to think of leaving and facing the possibility of not coming back but, what the hell, somebody has to do the job and it might as well be part of the Riches family as it was in the last war. *[His uncle Albert served and was killed in World War I.]*

JOSEPH STEINBACHER

Army; Pacific Theater; Memoir

There were thirteen thousand troops packed into the *General John Pope*, including three thousand black troopers in the lowest holds.

We sailed out under the Golden Gate Bridge as we left the harbor and I naturally wondered if I would ever return. I looked up at the huge steel structure as we began to hit the ocean swells, causing the *General John Pope* to heel over back and forth. I felt slightly queasy so lay on my back on the steel deck watching the tall masts move back and forth across a sky covered with large fluffy clouds. I knew I was really on my own now with no one to look after me. I certainly would not look for any of the military personnel for help, especially the officers.

JAMES BAROSS

Army Air Corps; Pacific Theater; Memoir

If we were scheduled to fly, we went to bed early, eight o'clock or so, some men shaving before going to sleep so as not to have to in the morning. We were told that natives, if we were forced down in the jungle, did not respect unshaven troops. So we shaved. Sometime early in the morning, usually about two or three, we would be tapped on the shoulder and the CQ would softly say, "Time to fly, Sergeant," and we would get up quietly, not waking others in the tent.

After dressing and getting our radio kit, .45 automatic with holster and machete, we would go to the mess hall for an early breakfast. Sometimes we would be given a package of sandwiches made up by the cooks, but that was only for the longer missions.

Then to the briefing tent. In front, on a raised bunch of boxes the details of the mission would be given. The weather officer would give us some idea as to what weather we could expect on the way and over the target.

The armament officer would tell us what size and type of bombs had been loaded by the armorers. If we were to do strafing, we were usually loaded with 28-pound parafrags, in clusters that would go out in a long line. A parafrag was a parachuted, fragmentation bomb. The parachute slowed it down so that it did not detonate right under our plane, which was usually just 20 or 30 feet above the ground. They were fused usually with three to five second delay fuses so that the plane could get safely forward of the bomb before it detonated. Fusing was important!

The communication officer would tell the radiomen the codes of the day. We had a "strike" code, which changed during the day, a weather code, and a communication code. These were put on very thin paper, edible, and we were to dispose of them, if captured, as they were important to intelligence. We were given lead-covered code books with which to compute the code we would use to relay to the ground the results of the mission. The purpose of the lead cover was to cause the book to sink into the ocean if we had to land in the water.

Finally, the intelligence officer would tell us what our primary target was, and the secondary and the tertiary.

At one briefing we were told that there would be no friendly planes in the area, we would have no escort, and that we were on our own. As I was looking out the windows, I noticed in the left window, while on the way back from the target, a bright light, then saw it was the reflection of the sun off the side of a plane. Most of our planes at that time were painted olive-green. We had no shiny aluminum planes that I knew of. The plane was creeping up on us from about seven o'clock low. I watched it and watched it and got ready. I was going to take care of that Zero for sure!

Boy oh boy, I was ready! I checked my left waist gun, made sure it was ready to fire, and watched. It was almost in range and I was drawing a bead on it, leading it just right and allowing for drop and all that and ready to press the trigger. Boy!! Just as my thumb was slowly mashing down on the trigger I saw it more clearly, and it was one of ours!! A P-51!

I held fire and the incident was over. That pilot, who knows who he was, never knew how close he was to being a statistic!! At debriefing, they said they did not think he was supposed to be so far north, but????

CHARLES RESTIFO

Army; Pacific Theater; Memoir

November 1943, I was assigned to Bougainville, a long, narrow island about one hundred fifty miles long, five degrees south of the equator, directly east of New Guinea, one hundred percent humidity, one hundred eighty inches of rainfall per year. The airfields were very important here for reaching Japanese air bases farther north. The joint effort of Army, Navy, and Marines initially surprised the Japanese, but it was generally fierce fighting until April 1944. Each day three photographers would cover the fighting. All photographs were top secret and sent to Washington by radio phone.

One day I went to squadron headquarters just to look around. Out on the field was a P-38 plane with the hood up. Looking at the engine were three men—one pilot and two mechanics. I struck up a conversation with the pilot, saying, "You have a pretty good racket flying this little baby." He said, "Speaking of rackets, you have a pretty good one yourself running around shooting pictures." He introduced himself as Captain John Maietta from Pennsylvania.

I started photographing him with his plane. I said, "How about taking me up for a spin?" I thought the photos would be good P.R. He said, "There is not much room in these planes." He opened a lid over the cabin. We both examined the space. There was a metal plate behind the pilot's seat about two feet by five feet. I climbed into the space between pilot's seat belt and the metal plate just deep enough to accommodate my body and simulated fastening the belts. He asked how it felt. I answered, "I would not want to go around the world this way, but it is not too bad." He said, "Let's go up, I want to check the pressure gauges." I had about two feet of clearance above his head for the camera. I strapped on the chest chute he handed me. He explained that in the event of being hit in action the plastic hood above would release and open automatically. During an emergency, getting out of the rear seat would be more difficult than the pilot's seat, the chances probably non-existent.

John got in, and in a few minutes we were ready to take off. Up and off the ground quickly, he leveled off at ten thousand feet. The engines roared and conversation ceased, as we could not hear each other. He had told me to tap his shoulder if I wanted something. I set my camera at two-hundredths of a second. Captain Maietta started sweeping the sky right and left and up and down. We were over water when he spotted a small Japanese vessel shooting at our plane, its gun power too little to do any damage. Captain Maietta took a sight of the

SIDNEY RICHES 1945

Action near Lingayan, March 1945 (top). Sidney Riches' caption notes, "That's my helmet and foxhole pillow left side!" Riches served with the 40th Division in the Philippines, where these photos were taken. Riches lies wounded (above) on January 24, an incident described in the following pages.

ship…. He kept diving until the automatic gun fired. He hit his mark. As he came out of the curve, the Japanese ship was on fire. During this time I was shooting my camera, holding it freehand, not an easy thing to do during a dive. The pilot reassessed the area and headed back to Bougainville base. He said, "That was easy. Ordinarily I would not have bothered with such an easy mark."

Two days later, Captain Maietta called to ask me to go with him again. I went up. This day I would not get any photos, as he was moving from hitting Japanese ships, then planes, and I could not hold the camera sight on the targets. The third day he wanted me to go up again. After looking at the gun camera film, I realized I could not get good pictures under these conditions. I told him I would not go with him this time. I waited at the squadron headquarters while he was on his mission. It was ten at night and he had not returned. Neither he nor his plane were ever found.

I drove my jeep back to the barracks and picked up the pictures I had made of him. He had liked them so much. I placed them in an envelope and sealed them shut. I went to his quarters and was told not to touch anything of his. The following day I mailed his photos to his family in Pennsylvania. Sometime later I received a thank you letter, stating they had received the pictures and asking if I had any information about him. I wrote back and explained about the last few days and that he liked to play pinochle. He was well liked, and all at the camp were saddened by his death.

SIDNEY RICHES
Army; Pacific Theater; Memoir
The drive down the Luzon Plain (Highway 1) toward Manila was underway with only slight rearguard action. On January 24, 1945, I endeavored to set up our command post in a defiladed area while simultaneously one of our rifle units was engaged in a firefight just yards away. A native scavenger entered a small cave nearby but immediately emerged yelling, with a Japanese GI on his tail, but who, on spying me, ducked back into the cave. Startled and having no time to fire my Thompson, I knew it was time to earn my pay and go after this guy, as I was the nearest person to the action. I cautiously inched my way to the entrance, about ten feet away, but he ran out, simulating a grenade. Firing a burst, I backpedaled but missed by a country mile. I hollered for a grenade but, surprisingly, no one near had one. (We all carried grenades subsequently.) Going again for the cave, he emerged, this time with a live grenade. He tossed the grenade as I hit him with the rest of the clip, fell to the ground, hearing his grenade explode

in back of me. Arising, I said to myself, "Hah, he missed me," but as I reached back to get another clip from my pack, I felt blood.

A fragment had entered my crotch area and I was bleeding profusely. The medics stretchered me back to the aid station, where I joined a couple other damaged guys for an ambulance trip back to a field hospital, where I was patched up.

BEN SNYDER
Army Air Corps; Memoir
November 12, 1944, "Somewhere in the Pacific."
There is no question that the Air Corps is considered an elite arm of the military. We are now equipped with gas stoves, rubber mattresses, and the latest equipment in flying gear. Quonset huts should be going up soon and a regular mess hall is on the drawing board. So if we should tumble out of the wild blue yonder somewhere east of Suez, we will do so in relative comfort.

November 20, 1944. You can regard this as my first "battle communiqué." Intelligence has finally lifted at least some of the curtain of secrecy. I am able to tell you that we have flown five combat missions against targets in the Caroline Islands. Under the peculiar system of defining "missions for rotation," only four count toward the forty which we must survive before we can turn "Short Run's" silver nose back towards the mainland. ["Short Run" was the name of his plane.]

Thus far, combat flying isn't as described on the silver screen. Fortunately we fear nothing more than the unknown. Having experienced the regimen, there is a certain sense of comfort thereafter. True, there is a surge of nervous anticipation just before the "run," but nothing which I would describe as fear. Too much concentration is needed, compacted into a few minutes, for emotion to prevail. And when the going becomes particularly dangerous (as it can from time to time), one seeks to tap into the reservoirs of faith.

December 7, 1944. Three years ago today, a number of us were having dinner at the Phi Gam house in Chapel Hill when the first electrifying shocks of the Pearl Harbor attack were flashed over radio. The anniversary was "celebrated" by a successful mission against an Imperial target now some hours behind us. This is being written on the return leg, up forward in the bombardier's compartment. The hours drag by interminably. With no threat of interception, our enemies are the endless sea and the tiny island somewhere up ahead that we seek.

January 8, 1945. The war drags on apace. We fly when the weather permits; long periods of boredom interspersed by moments of tension as the bomb runs begin.

Now that we have more or less settled into a fairly predictable routine, the combat phase is separated from all the rest. Once on the ground, we become absorbed in such ordinary matters as opening gifts, which are finally arriving some weeks after Christmas.

January 21, 1945. Palau Islands. Perhaps by the time you receive this letter, we will be in Sydney, Australia, on our ten-day combat rest leave. The first of our crews go Down Under tomorrow. By departure time, we should be halfway through the required forty missions.

That will equate to about 200 flying hours. Nerves are jangled and dispositions frayed. I now recognize the wild light in Bill Wright's eyes after flying 50 missions over Italy as a gunner. Sometimes the strain is almost unbearable. It's the waiting which is the most difficult. Thinking, planning, briefings, running check and re-checks, often afraid to think too far ahead. The building of suspense has a deathly quality.

JOSEPH STEINBACHER

Army; Pacific Theater; Memoir
Steinbacher was stationed in New Guinea in 1944, where he turned 21 and his company didn't see much combat. In February 1945, they moved on to the Philippines, where Steinbacher realized they were on their way into "real action."

The lieutenant stated that we would stay in these Japanese foxholes for the night. I didn't like the look of the whole setup, certainly not with those Japs up on top of Hill 255 waiting to pour fire down upon us sleeping in the cul-de-sac. I saluted the lieutenant and asked as politely as I could if it would be okay for several of us troopers to move up on the hillside. He replied that he didn't give a damn what I thought and where we dug in as long as we went up the hillside..

I lay down in my shallow trench and stared up at the evening sky. I had chopped through a nest of little red ants and they were really biting me. I mashed hundreds and finally got rid of most of them. I felt just like one of those little ants. If I didn't get killed in this damn war, I would really need a lot of luck and probably some help from the Almighty.

I finally dozed off and had a good sleep. Suddenly, along towards morning as the sky was just beginning to get light, my eyes snapped open and I was instantly awake. Just then I heard a whistling sound, and a number of mortar shells, one after the other, came hurtling down into the cul-de-sac. We jumped up as soon as the explosions stopped, grabbed our equipment, and scrambled down the hill to see if we could help. Other soldiers that had been close by in the area were already there and they were just hauling out the last of the bodies. The

JOSEPH STEINBACHER 1944

An infantryman, Steinbacher titled his memoir of fighting the
Japanese Nine Lives, *reflecting his ability to escape death time*
after time in horrific battles in the Philippines. He was proud of
his resourcefulness, but he also admitted to being lucky.

lieutenant and the sergeant were dead, along with three of the troopers, while
another was badly wounded. I had been right about the spider holes; I didn't get
much satisfaction from that fact.

Along a highway, the company encountered Japanese troops at a roadblock.

There was a wide, deep ditch along each side of the highway and a wide-
open field beyond the ditches on both sides of the highway. Most of us clambered
down into the right-hand ditch, then out the other side to set up our perimeters
in the open field and dig foxholes. Scattered mortar fire was falling on the field
as we rushed to get a hole dug where we could at least have some protection. I
looked over to where a friend, a red-headed private from the intelligence platoon,
was making the dirt fly. Just as I glanced that way he received a direct hit from a
mortar shell and was blown up right in front of my eyes. I just about crapped my
drawers, and then, sure that my friend was dead, hollered at the others nearby
that we might all be safer in the deep ditch next to the highway.

The soldier next to me complained that he was about out of M1 ammo. "I'll try to find some," I answered, and immediately took off to the left along the ditch. I moved along bent over as I still was not sure all the Japs were out of action across the highway. After traveling a short distance I noticed a dead soldier sitting up against the back of the ditch. He had a well-filled ammo belt around his waist, and I immediately rushed over to pull off the belt. I looked him over for a wire or a booby trap, saw no problem, so bent down and, after unfastening the belt, tried to pull it free of the body. I felt something slippery all over my hand, and paying no attention, finally was able to jerk the belt from behind the body. My hand was completely covered in the dead trooper's blood. I shuddered as I wiped my hand off as best I could on the soldier's uniform and hurried back to my place in the line.

The soldier grabbed a clip, shoving it into his M1. "Sorry about the blood," I said. He answered, "No problem, makes the shells slip into the breech real easy."

In the ensuing battle Steinbacher's battalion managed to overwhelm a larger force of Japanese soldiers.

A war correspondent I had seen came strolling up and sat down nearby. "Tough battle," he ventured. "How many Japs did you get?" "I didn't get any as far as I know," I replied. He chain-smoked for a while and finally wandered off. To my horror I learned many years later that the reporter had put in the newspaper of my hometown that I had stated I had probably gotten a couple. Since that incident I have never trusted a newspaperman to tell the truth. Too often they will twist the facts to fit the occasion as they see it. To my great surprise and elation, our battalion had been awarded a Presidential Unit Citation for action at the roadblock. I guess this was why the newspaperman came around; we were now front-page news.

In a small town outside of Manila, Steinbacher found a rare moment of respite.

It is raining lightly as we stop in the town plaza. We each pick out a spot around the edge of a square where we can lie down for the nite wrapped in our poncho. We ate our meager k-rations and got ready to turn in. We noticed a large house near the square is bright with lights. A curtain and a large window are open and a beautiful young Filipino woman sat at a piano and began to play classical music for our entertainment. She played wonderfully well to our music-hungry ears and it was music that we knew. We watched entranced for a long time, standing in the gently falling rain thinking about home. She stood up, closing the window and curtains while we all cheered. I don't know about the other troopers, but I slept all night, waking refreshed the next morning in time for breakfast.

HENRY WILAYTO
Army; Pacific Theater; Interview

For some GIs, the Pacific Theater held a different kind of horror from the intense island by island experience of fighting the Japanese. Henry Wilayto, a young Army sergeant, had drawn what looked like a choice assignment when he was shipped off to the Philippines in 1941. But the Army did not prepare him for what would happen in the wake of Pearl Harbor.

I worked in the commissary as an auditor and saw all the famous people—General MacArthur, General Wainwright—come to John Hay, which was a recreation and rest camp. At the end of the eight months, we heard some airplanes flying overhead. I came out of the commissary and this lieutenant colonel said, "Look at those beautiful B-17s." And they opened their bomb bay doors, and they hit us. They were Japanese planes.

And that was the only time they did any damage to us—killed one American who had just got there the day before to work in the officers' club. We were so green—we had no infantry training, no close order drill. They wouldn't allow us to have any guns; they said we would hurt ourselves, and it was true. We were running around with machetes protecting the camp. We were there until the 23rd of December. There were about 30 of us that marched out. We got out into the jungle, and the officers called us together and said, "Here's 20 pesos apiece, you're on your own." [I thought] What kind of army is this? We called the officers together, and said, "Look, you're in charge of us. We're not going off on our own. We don't know this area." And they said, okay, and we marched through the jungle out to the main highway, Number Five. There were thousands of cases of Type C rations lined all up and down the road, left by the American troops.

Overwhelmed by superior numbers and decimated by starvation, American and Filipino troops surrendered to the Japanese on April 9, 1942, on the peninsula of Bataan. Thus began the infamous Death March to the prison camp near Cabanatuan.

We marched, and I had no food for six days and very little water. You didn't dare drink water from the streams because there would be dead animals in them farther up. After six days, somebody gave me some iodine and said, "Look, when they stop near water, dig a hole a foot away, let it fill in and fill your canteen up, put some iodine in it and stir it up and let it sit for a while, and drink it. There won't be any bacteria in it." So I got a little to drink that way. Finally, I passed out. They always marched you early in the morning, sat you down about 11 o'clock, and stayed in the field until four in the afternoon, in the hot sun, 110, 115 degrees while the guards sat in the shade.

Everybody says what a terrible thing the Death March is. I'm wondering how Americans would have handled it if they had 15 to 20 guards for 5,000 prisoners. You could be out of sight of a guard for maybe two minutes at a time. Any time somebody fell and nobody would pick him up, the Japanese shot him because they had no way of taking care of anybody that fell by the road. So they killed, by bayoneting or shooting, about 650 Americans.

When I passed out, a buddy pulled me into the shade. The Japanese let us go into the river that afternoon—why, I don't know. The moisture going through my pores helped me a lot.

Wilayto got something to eat from a Filipino family and actually got a truck ride to the next stop, about three or four miles up the road. At the end of the march, the Japanese crowded their captives into boxcars of a cargo train.

If you died, you died standing up. If you had to urinate or defecate, you did it standing up. We were on that train from 8 o'clock in the morning until about 5 o'clock in the afternoon.

We had to march 12 miles, those of us who were left. When we arrived the next day, the Japanese commander stood up on a box and said, "You are not prisoners of war. You are captives. You surrendered. You did not fight. If you break our rules, we will kill you or we will do something worse." And they did something worse. We lost 23 men every 24 hours.

The noncoms didn't have to work, but Wilayto volunteered for the job of graves registration officer. He was given 30 men to dig graves. He asked for a chaplain to be sent out once a week to do a service. When one didn't come, the men did the service themselves. Wilayto soon discovered that the Japanese were cutting their rations.

When we found out we weren't getting enough to eat, a hundred of us just automatically came together to march down to the captain's quarters, the man who was in charge of our area. They were all following me. We walked past ten barracks, and I turned around to say something and I got seven guys in back of me, because we were getting closer and closer to Japanese headquarters. So I looked at 'em and I said, "Fellas,"—now I'm not patting myself on the back; I was scared because I know how people got beaten up—"no use seven or eight of us getting beaten up. Why don't you appoint me a committee of one. You stay out of sight and see what happens."

He spoke alone with the captain, who told him he would see what he could do.

And that day we had a fourth meal: pancakes made with rice flour and syrup from cane sugar. And the men were saying, "Wow, can we do this tomorrow?"

Wilayto built up his cemetery detail to 90 men.

When I took over the job, the men were working 50 minutes every hour in the hot sun and getting a ten-minute break. There was a guard tower about 200 yards away, and they were always looking at us. So I figured if we kept looking busy, they wouldn't know what the heck we were up to. I arranged it that they would work for ten minutes and then rest for 50 minutes, but because of the number of men digging graves, I was able to keep the men moving.

He left the camp on his birthday, January 4, 1944, and was put to work in Manila as a stevedore. With regular rations, he gained back 50 pounds.

We had a softball field, a boxing ring. We worked one day, got the next day off, worked one hour, got the next hour off, loading civilian cargo ships. The reason why we were treated so well was that the Swiss Red Cross was looking at how well we were being treated by the Japanese, so we were a show camp. We had a good life there but we tried to destroy what we could.

The men poured water on a shipment of rice going to China. The rice would expand and be spoiled by the time it got to its destination.

Another time we were loading alcohol in 50-gallon drums and we unscrewed the caps and put them upside down. The ship got out in the harbor, there was a spark, and BOOM, the ship blew up.

Ten days after that act of sabotage, Wilayto and a number of other POWs were put on a ship for Japan. Conditions were miserable; Wilayto lost 18 pounds in 10 days. He and the other prisoners were kept in the cargo hold most of the voyage. Buckets were lowered with rice and for sanitation, and most of the men didn't bother to try to keep them separate. "So I didn't eat for 18 days, just traded rice for water." *In Japan, he was put to work in a nickel ore mine.*

It was 13 months; I couldn't have lasted another one. My toes had turned green; they were rotting away. I was down to 135 pounds.

In August 1945, Wilayto and his fellow survivors were liberated by American forces.

June 6, 1944, Normandy Beach, France. "I was thinking,"
recalled Navy officer Tracy Sugarman as he observed the
armada of ships, "there was no way of stopping this."

It didn't start with D-Day—June 6, 1944—but it may as well have. While American
GIs were working their way up the boot of Italy, plans were being made for the
biggest invasion of them all, on the beaches of Normandy in France. From there,
Allied forces would begin the big push to liberate France and Belgium and Holland
and break the German Army's resistance. Before crossing the English Channel, how-
ever, there was an ocean to sail, as Alvin Dickinson and John Earle note.

ALVIN DICKSON
    Army; European Theater; Diary
June 1943: I awoke feeling the vibration of the ship's engines. We had started.
From the accent of the steward I guessed that we were guests of the Royal Navy.
Later I found out that we were riding on the *Queen Elizabeth*, the largest ship in
the world. I was more amazed to find out also that we were totally alone. The
Queen Elizabeth, as I understand, made solo trips back and forth across the
ocean without any escort because the ship was a little too fast for any destroyers

to follow. And we wonder why they were never hit by any torpedoes. The *Queen Elizabeth* changed course every five minutes. They had it figured out that a German U-boat torpedo would take seven minutes to hit the ship. They couldn't get any closer; the British had just discovered sonar and so they could detect any U boat [that got closer]. I was a little leery, but it made 27 crossings of the Atlantic and was never hit, so evidently their theory was correct.

The entire trip was much like a pleasure cruise to me because everything was so different and I was excited about everything I saw. But hidden underneath this was a feeling of tense waiting—waiting and wondering if the terrific explosion of a torpedo would strike near you in the next minute. When the ocean trip began, all electrical devices were called into a central room, the reason being that they send out waves that German submarines may pick up. I turned in my electrical shaver.

For entertainment aboard ship we had Glenn Miller's orchestra with the movie actor Brod Crawford as a front. The band played on deck a couple of afternoons and played for an all soldiers' show in the lounge. In addition there were movies on the covered deck every night and there was enough talent on board to form many small bands that played all over the ship....

At night blackout rules were rigid, and rightly so, too, because one light could sink a ship. Two men were placed in the brig for opening a porthole during a blackout.

JOHN EARLE
Army; European Theater; Memoir
As entertainment officer for 5,000 Infantry men, I thought it would relieve tensions on our troop ship voyage to Europe during WWII if I passed out harmonicas. Could not find any before leaving but did buy 250 Kazoos. We passed them out as they boarded ship. You could imagine what a din that 250 Kazoos made on a crowded troop ship. Needless to say by morning not a one was left on board.

TRACY SUGARMAN
Navy; European Theater; Letter to his wife, June 1, 1944
Sugarman was a Naval officer who in the spring of 1944 was in England, training for the Normandy invasion. He was to command a group of four LCVPs (Landing Craft Vehicle Personnel), 30-foot support craft that were carried over the English Channel on the larger LSTs (Landing Ship Tanks), the 280-foot flat-bottomed vessels developed to land troops and cargo on open beaches.

My darling Junie—

Hope this gets out to you—it will be the last word from me for a <u>long</u> time. DON'T WORRY, angel—I'll get in touch with you <u>first</u> chance I get. Believe me, darling, I'm feeling wonderfully well and absolutely squared away for anything that may come my way. For this wonderful peace of mind I have you to thank, Junie.

Interview

We were finally secured one night and sealed to the ship; we were saying D-Day is going to be tomorrow, and they called the officers up to the wardroom. They gave us our orders, and they gave us a book showing Utah Beach, which was as thick as a Manhattan telephone book. And in that book were the names of the men, the officers commanding, what kind of troops in what sectors on what beach. This was this kind of stuff we had gotten from our intelligence and the underground: what kind of gun emplacements were there, what kind of backup gun emplacements were behind the beach. Sounded like a piece of cake. Well, it didn't turn out that way. The night we were sealed, we turned on the radio, and we heard [Nazi radio propagandist] Axis Sally. We had just looked at these maps that we were about to use to hit the beach, and there was an arbitrary line drawn about five miles off the beach, which we called the Mason Dixon Line, and that was where our small boats were to assemble. And Axis Sally is talking to the Americans and she's saying, "We know you're coming and we'll be waiting for you at the Mason Dixon Line." And I thought, Oh my God, if they know that, what else do they know?

We were supposed to leave the next day, and it was postponed one whole day because of the weather. And as a small boat officer, my job was to go out through the fog and find all the ships that were in my group and pass on the new orders: "We're not going." I'll never forget what a weird safari that was, finding our own ships in the harbor because it was so soupy. Then when we finally did go, the fog had cleared, the storm had somewhat abated, it was sunny and a very rough channel. We just pulled out of our harbor—we were in Salcombe at that point. All these LSTs would pull out of Salcombe and get in this procession. And out of Portsmouth, and out of Dartmouth. You can't imagine all these ships coming out. And meanwhile you have thousands of airplanes overhead. So you have this procession, and instead of going toward Europe, they're going along the English coast. We joined it late morning, maybe early morning on D-Day. And then when we got to a certain point we would head off to our port direction. Looking back and looking ahead, there were ships as far as you could see. I was thinking that there is no way of stopping this. You could see the planes overhead diving toward the beaches and you could hear the explosions. And then there were these cruisers with the big guns that were firing over us. It sounded like someone throwing trolley cars past you. Meanwhile you're maneuvering to stay in step with all your boats.

We left the LST about one o'clock in the afternoon. We didn't hit the beach until about four o'clock. Then as we were finally headed for Utah Beach, off to my left, I could see—I had glasses—this cliff that was Omaha Beach, and on this long shallow beach, there was what appeared to be cordwood. It was 2,500 dead Americans. I didn't know it then; I found out in the next days. And in the next days I went over to Omaha Beach, to climb Omaha Beach because I had to go back to England to pick up some gear and we had a landing strip on top of Omaha Beach. I had to climb that cliff that the Rangers took under total fire on all sides. I was twenty-two, I was in good shape, I was carrying nothing, and nobody was shooting at me, and I think it took me over 25 minutes to get up that cliff to the airstrip up on top. To this day I will never understand how we took that beach.

Minesweepers did what they could to clear the Channel, but mines would still pop up.

The worst thing I saw in the war was in a storm I think ten days after D-Day, when an LST was coming through a storm, trying to land, with all the men on the deck queued for chow at lunch time, and you could hardly see them, it was so windy and wet and stormy—it was the worst storm they'd had in a hundred years there, almost wiped out the beaches for weeks. And I saw this ship blow up, and all of a sudden those men were in the water, and we went rushing out in our LCVPs trying to rescue them. I made a drawing of that about four days later, because it was such a nightmarish experience of trying to rescue men that were drowning, and you'd reach for them and you could not reach them and they'd get swept away. I was able to sort of forget about it, making that drawing. And 60 years later, someone who saw that drawing recognized himself going down the line from the bow with his buddy and he called me and he said, "That was me!"

Letter to his wife, June 12, 1944
My darling Junie,

I hope that long before you get this note you will have received the cable I gave to one of the officers who was returning to England.... I'm swell, darling—honest to Pete—but like usual I'm working—rather than being worked too damn hard! I find that this invasion stuff is nothing more nor less than a hell of a lot of work. After a bit the unusual and dangerous elements fall into place—and you

ALVIN DICKSON 1945

Dickson, an officer with the Eleventh Armored Division, shipped out to Europe in June 1943 on a voyage he compared to a pleasure cruise. When this picture was taken, he had survived nearly a year of combat, including the fearsome Battle of the Bulge.

become pretty indifferent to them. I've seen a good deal. The news we get seems very encouraging, but it's fragmentary and mostly scraps picked up from different men coming back out from the lines. You probably know a great deal more than we. I'm going through the process now of shaking down all the sensations and sights I've felt and seen and trying to figure out my relation to the whole set-up. I don't think I was scared. If I was—it wasn't at all the kind of fright I had imagined. At the time you are just too busy and excited to figure out whether you're frightened. There is no cause for worry or despair when you don't hear from me. Know that every chance I get I'll try to write.

WILLIAM ARNETT

Army; Interview

William Arnett enlisted in the Army in January 1941, eleven months before the attack on Pearl Harbor brought America into the war. He shipped out to Europe in the fall of 1943, landing in Belfast, Ireland. In April 1944, his unit moved to England and they landed in France on Utah Beach one month after the Normandy Invasion. Arnett was in a tank destroyer unit. By the time Arnett's unit landed on Utah Beach, the fighting had moved inland about five or six miles.

We could see at night what looked like heat lightning, but what it was was the artillery. And it was continuous and it was all night long. Didn't worry me any because I would never get hurt.

The next day, they moved up and into a field.

And there were some cows there. And the man who owned them came in and got his two cows out. I said, "We're not going to steal your milk or anything." He knew what he was doing I found out a little while later when they started shelling us. It was a nice, warm sunny day; it was fairly quiet in our area. I was sitting under a tree, didn't have duty then, and I heard this shell coming in, and, although I'd never heard one before, I knew what it was. And I rolled over on my side, and it exploded, and I jumped up to run for a foxhole. I didn't know the Germans shot more than one shell at a time, and there's another one right behind it that was covered up by the sound of the first one going off. When that one exploded, it jarred me real, real bad, and I was completely numb all over. I jumped into the foxhole and I looked down and the back of my hand was all covered with blood. And since I couldn't feel anything, I had to feel my hand to see where I'd been hit. I couldn't feel any place that was broken. And then I brushed my hand against my leg and I felt that leg and it was all right. Then I saw that the blood was running off my nose. That really scared me because I didn't know how much of my face was gone. But I got out of it pretty good—very, very lucky.

The first soldier killed in our outfit was killed by a guy who was on sentry duty. He was trying to relieve the sentry. Everybody's scared to death, they don't know what they're doing. And if you're moving around at night, it's very, very dangerous. It almost happened to me later on.

We lined up to get our meals, and because we were penned in close we had our kitchen trucks with us. We got all in a line to get our mess kits filled and the shells started coming in. And of course that was the end of the meal. And the next day we did it again, and the same thing happened. So then we decided we would fool the Germans. We were eating at 12 o'clock; we would eat at 11. But then we got in line and here the shells come in again. And we didn't realize it, but they were watching us!

You did feel stress—not all the time. After a while you realized that your chances were getting dimmer all the time for the simple reason, as Bill Mauldin wrote, "You felt like a fugitive from the law of averages," because you do know that you can be missed only so many times.

WILLIAM WHITING

Army; European Theater; Memoir
Whiting entered the Army in June 1942, as a 20-year-old. He was in the Army's
802nd Field Artillery Battalion, which was among the wave of troops that poured
into France after the Normandy invasion. The men of the 802nd saw their first
action in August, and by early December they were three or four miles southwest of
Sarreguemines, France, near the German border.

On the 7th we all moved into other quarters. We had somewhat grown accustomed to seeing dead German soldiers, and by this time did not give them more than casual glances. I had not seen any that were badly disfigured or dismembered. Even though they were the enemy, once they were dead you could no longer hate them. You could not help but remember they were or had been someone's son, husband, father, brother. Usually their wallets had been removed from their clothing, rifled, and discarded on the ground, with family pictures scattered. Often their ring fingers had been cut off for the ring. Any pistols they had were gone. It was sad but not upsetting. But I never did get accustomed to seeing dead American soldiers.

A wounded German was turned over to Captain Murphy, CO of A Battery, by a civilian. The German thought it was safer than surrendering by himself. We had not heard of prisoners being shot by U.S. soldiers, but I am sure it happened. Or perhaps the Germans were saying so to discourage their soldiers from surrendering too readily. A great many German prisoners had passed through our area in the preceding month, being marched to the rear under infantry guard. Most of them did not seem unhappy. They were happy to have survived the war. Some had been on the Russian front and fighting for several years. To be captured by the Americans (or *Amis*, as they called us), in contrast to capture by the British, French, or especially the Russians, was known to the common German soldier as the "golden capture." One prisoner marching through our area was reported to have said to one of our guys that he was luckier than the American, since he was going to America and our guy was going to Germany and more combat.

By Christmas Eve, Whiting's company was embroiled in the Battle of the Bulge,
fighting in the Ardennes Offensive.

On the 24th we fired 33 missions totaling 690 rounds. It was very cold and clear, and our Air Force was out in strength, a tremendous help. The Air Force had difficulty telling friend from foe, as there was no fixed front. We had brightly colored luminescent panels, about three feet by six feet, that rolled up when not in use, that we put on top of our vehicles to identify ourselves to the fighter pilots. The panels did not always prevent American planes from attacking American positions. The American fighter-bombers almost always flew in groups of four, and the Germans were always single planes. We on the ground had no trouble telling friend from foe. There was no German air force (Luftwaffe) of any consequence. Probably more American positions were attacked by American planes than by German. We had a standard joke that if there was a single plane above us we did not have to worry, as it was German. If there were four planes above us we did have to worry, as they were sure to be American. One day we saw four American planes diving on and strafing and bombing an American position we knew was a nearby American artillery unit. That was back in Lorraine. It was rare that that happened. The American fighter-bombers were of tremendous help to the infantry and tankers, no question about it, even though there were occasional mix-ups.

DONALD SPENCER

Army Air Corps; European Theater; Letter to his family, December 14, 1944
Spencer had hoped to become a pilot in the Army Air Force, but he washed out of that program and settled for being a gunner. His company arrived in France in October 1944, and he flew his first mission on November 19th. He kept notes on each mission in a small notebook, which he brought home after the war.

You asked me in your letters if I had been over Germany yet. Well I guess I have been over Germany a few times, and also Belgium and Holland. It seemed rather strange to me the first time I was over Germany that there were people just like all others, and yet they were the very people who had caused all this. I did not realize what our enemy was until they started shooting at us. Then it made me feel good when I heard our bombardier say "bombs away," for I knew it was our way of getting back at them, many hundreds of times. Also I knew that our work for the day was over and then we were headed back home.

There isn't any place that looks as good to me as our home field after a cold, hard mission. After the mission is over and after interrogating and we are back in our barrack, we sit around and talk about what we saw, how thick the flak was, how light it was, etc. Then the excitement of the mission wears off, and we get cleaned up to go eat or to go out and throw a big one, if it was really rough.

NATHANIEL RALEY

Army Air Corps; Memoir, Interview

Raley was a P-38 fighter pilot, fulfilling a boyhood dream to fly combat aircraft. His first missions were out of Tunisia, escorting B-17 and B-24 bombers to Italy. For a time he flew out of Libya over Crete, trying to help British troops evacuate from Greece. His first combat mission was in August 1943, when he bombed an electric plant in Italy. Flying close to Mount Vesuvius was the first time he was fired upon. As he noted, "You come to expect it but never take it lightly."

On February 10, 1944, I was leading the squadron on a dive-bombing and strafing mission in support of American ground forces at the Anzio, Italy, beachhead, south of Rome. This was my 48th combat mission; I was now twenty-one years old and still the youngest pilot in the squadron. I began firing at a truck and saw my bullets shatter the windshield. While I was firing my guns, someone yelled on the radio that I was being hit in my left engine. I was forced to shut down that engine and feather the propeller. Soon, I was over another flak battery and they finished shooting me down. I finally reached the reality that I would either crash and burn to death or bail out at below the minimum altitude. I chose the latter and reached an altitude of about 300 feet. I was going to count to ten (as instructed back in pilot-training school) but I probably counted to "one" and quickly realized that I could never get to "ten" before my body hit the ground. The parachute opened properly, and I swung back and forth two or three times and hit the ground on a backwards swing; I somersaulted backwards, got out of my parachute harness in a couple of seconds, and stood up with my back to several dozen German soldiers only about 50 yards away. I hated to face the reality that I was about to undergo a drastic change in my "life style."

They stood me before a masonry wall, pulled back from me, and began to form a line about ten yards in front of me. It began to appear that they were going to make an execution out of it. About this time, a German noncommissioned officer appeared, waved his hand at my apparent firing squad, and they quickly disappeared. The NCO asked (in English), "Are you badly wounded?" I told him I thought I had only flesh wounds. He took me to an Italian farmhouse.

Three guards drove me to a doctor. They brought out a large plate of meat and potatoes for me. I was not really hungry, but I ate it all. It was the beginning of my never refusing food. Whenever food is offered, eat it. You never know when the next meal is coming. When I had finished, they brought out a bottle of Italian wine and said (in French), "*C'est la guerre.*" I thought that they might be trying to get me intoxicated for the interrogation. I drank one glass and thanked

NATHANIEL RALEY 1943

In the cockpit of his P-38, Raley flew escort missions out of Tunisia. Later, while strafing at Anzio, Italy, he was shot down and taken prisoner. His identification photo from his last stop, a POW camp in Germany, is pictured below.

them for it. Had I known what soon lay in store for me, I would have consumed the entire bottle.

Raley was transferred to several holding facilities of varying quality. At one, he arrived just after the one bowl of soup a day was served. This was my first full day of absolutely no food.

I had a very cold night ride to my next POW camp, which was near the Italian town of Laterina, southeast of Florence. Conditions there were the worst I would encounter during my POW experience. I don't use curse words, but it was a hellhole. We received one-half cup of thin, watery soup twice a day on weekdays and only one half-cup on Sunday. We got a small amount of black bread. We got water only once a day. There were lice and fleas on the straw on which we slept. I lost a lot of weight.

My next experience was being locked in a boxcar for three days without food or water. We eventually arrived at Moosburg, Germany (Stalag VIIA), and were taken to a building to get a shower. We were ordered to strip naked in the snow about a foot deep, and put all of our clothes in a bag to be put under steam pressure to kill the lice and fleas.

I was called before a German officer in a small one-room building in which only the two of us were present. He explained that even though he wore the uniform of a German officer he had been designated to assist the Red Cross as part of Germany's cooperation with the International Red Cross. I had serious reservations about the validity of this.

Raley refused to fill out the form he was given, beyond the standard name, rank, and serial number. The German officer would say, "Oh we know you've been shot down for some time now, so this information isn't really important," *to which Raley would reply,* "Oh, if it's really not important, then let's forget it."

After several hours of this, he began his threats. He said that I was most uncooperative and left him no choice but to turn me over to the Gestapo for torture. He said that I would be fortunate if I could even walk when they got through with me. In complete exasperation, he threw me into solitary confinement.

Raley was then moved to Stalag Luft I, a POW camp near Barth, Germany, a city on the Baltic Sea.

I was shot at twice there. The fences were actually two fences, each about eight feet high, about ten feet apart, with coiled barbed wire between them. Additionally, there was a single strand of barbed wire, on posts about two feet high, and about ten feet from the main fences. This marked a "death zone," where guards in the towers were authorized to "shoot to kill" without warning if a prisoner even touched that wire or a post. I did not know that, as my previous prisons did not have such a wire. While walking, one of my shoelaces became untied; I put my foot on one of those short posts to tie the shoelace. The guard in the nearest tower shot, and the bullet hit the dirt a few inches away. He could have killed me on the spot, but out of "kindness" had only given me a warning shot. Initially, we could go outside during air raids; this was a great morale booster. Eventually, we were ordered to stay inside the barracks whenever the air raid siren sounded. On one occasion, I had my head out the window of my room while watching an air raid. A guard, on the ground, shot at me but the bullet hit above the window, three feet above my head. I then saw the guard who had shot at me; he was only about 50 yards away and could easily have killed me.

At night, some English-speaking guards would crawl under our barracks to listen to our conversations; some guards were quieter than others, and we could not hear them. We began to hear a clumsy guard and were able to spot his approximate location (it should be noted that the floors had numerous cracks). Then someone quickly poured boiling water over that spot. We ran out of the room. The guard fired several shots at the source of the water but no one in the room was left to hit.

We received Red Cross parcels sporadically, but when we did get the parcels, the Germans would cut back on the rations they gave us, which consisted mostly of black bread (with sawdust as one of the ingredients) and potatoes, which we ate without peeling them; we threw nothing away.

By the end of March 1945 things were beginning to change for the better. It was suddenly "discovered" that there were 50,000 Red Cross parcels to be sent to Barth. One German major visited our barracks and in tears told us that he was forty years old, had been a professor of English in a university, that this wife and children were already safe behind American lines, and he was supposed to await the arrival of the Russian army. We urged him to desert and try to get to the Allied lines and surrender to the Americans.

May 1 was a weird day; there were no Germans and no Russians. During the day, several guards returned, without guns, but with their wives and children, asking to be let back into the prison. It was sad, but they were refused admission.

That night, the first Russian patrol entered the prison. The POWs were invited to come into town, and those who did witnessed frightful brutalities by the Russian soldiers. The POWs were instructed in a radio address by General Eisenhower to stay within the prison compound, and shortly afterward, a fleet of B-17s with skeleton crews arrived and picked them up, 30 at a time. The POWs marched through the town and got on the planes, which never cut off their engines. As Raley recalled, "I don't think I looked back."

By Land, Sea, and Air

Few photographs in the Veterans History Project collections show actual combat. A soldier is not likely to snap pictures when the twin instincts for self-preservation and helping comrades override all other thoughts. Nevertheless, as the pictures on the following pages suggest, there was time for reflecting on war's awful price on the landscape and on the human psyche. The advances in weaponry, particularly in the air, where dirigibles gave way to speedy planes and then to high-flying jets, made destruction and killing arguably more efficient. But on the ground, from World War I's trenches to the Persian Gulf's desert, technology couldn't diminish the messiness of war.

Scenes from World War I-era France. A portion of a road through a shelled area (left), and a Navy dirigible over St. Nazarie (below).

Rod Hinsch (opposite), served in the elite Special Forces unit in Vietnam and saw plenty of combat action.

Belly gunner Bill McGlynn served
on a B-17 in the Army Air Corps
in the European Theater. A photograph from his collection
(opposite, above) shows a B-17
dropping bombs over Europe. The
handwritten caption on
Raymond Dierkes' photograph
(opposite, below) reads:
"Gooseberry June 1944 Under
Fire." Dierkes served in the Navy
and was involved with the
Normandy invasion. James Walsh
(this page, above right) was an
ammunition bearer in Korea. He's
pictured here (center) with Staff
Sgt Dean Warren and another private, Hartland Clouse. His caption
reads in part, "Shooting is a training problem." Joanne Palella poses
in the Kuwaiti desert with a
Bradley tank that had been hit by
an M1 tank during the Persian
Gulf War (this page, at right).

JAMES WALSH CA 1951

"This is a real war picture," reads the note on this photo. "What I mean is all the guys in it really felt the effects of war. The next day we moved out on hill 440 and one was killed, two badly wounded and one cracked up. Two of us made it off. Me & the one sitting up."

Korean War

"It was…madness to fight for the next hilltop, for there was no end."

The first flashpoint of the Cold War, in Korea might have seemed like a mismatch: the mighty United States, which had helped win two World Wars, against the tiny nation of North Korea. But the Koreans—and their Chinese allies—had terrain and weather on their side. Plus, a willingness to take casualties in great numbers that astonished even GIs who remembered the Japanese ethic of World War II, to die rather than be captured. In two bloody years, through numbing winters and over a seemingly endless progression of desolate hills, the battle waxed and waned—and eventually came to a standoff that remains unresolved a half century later.

PAUL STEPPE
   Marine Corps; Memoir, Interview
The best part of my equipment, aside from my weapons, were the new boots issued in late fall. Everyone had seen movies about the seriousness of taking care of their feet. The gravity of that was due to the many foot soldiers of the various countries fighting under the United Nations Colors getting frozen feet during the winter of 1950. Many toes, feet, and legs were amputated due to frostbite that was either not treated immediately due to the war situation or ignored by the afflicted. These newly issued boots that I now have were a gift from Heaven. Requiring only one pair of socks, the boots are waterproof and insulated and have at least an inch and a half sole and larger heel. They are a little heavy but absolutely great! They keep my feet warm and comfortable.

   The United Nations forces had established a front line of defense, called an "MLR," or Main Line of Resistance.

The night watch starts just before darkness sets in at the end of another long day. Everyone has finished their evening meal, the canned heat is out, the weapons have been checked, loaded, and ready for use, extra ammunition is accounted for and placed in logical locations, and the wristwatch is checked for accuracy. It is entirely up to the two persons assigned to their bunker how long each watch will last, but generally it is two hours in cold weather and two to four hours in the warmer months.

The same activity is occurring in each two-man bunker across the entire MLR. The sentry expects something to occur when it is least expected; therefore he must discipline himself to always expect it. The sentry feels totally alone in the darkness. No talking, no whispers unless there is a need, no humming, and doing nothing but watching and listening. These cycles of anxious and tense moments wear on the sentry. Soon he is ready for sleep, just to get away from the presence of war.

Steppe's battalion saw its first action in June.

With every mortar shell that came in screaming, I thought it had my name on it. My eyes caught something moving to my left about thirty yards away. I turned and saw an NKPA soldier moving southward on another smaller ridge line consisting of soft dirt or sand, which made running away difficult. I sighted him with my rifle and pulled the trigger. I know that I hit him, but so did about four other marines. The guy was picked up off the ground from the impact of the bullets and moved sideways about a yard and fell dead. I didn't feel any remorse for that soldier, perhaps because I was not the only one that shot him. I had heard that the first kill was the most difficult, and many marines were killed because they hesitated in squeezing the trigger before the enemy did. The soldier was running away from battle. He could have been shot by his own colleagues.

That was the way it was, waiting, attacking, digging holes, attacking, waiting, and more hills to climb up and down. That was Korea and its famous mountain ranges. Engagements were sometimes swift with little defensive reaction, but often they became fierce, and men were killed or injured and most were never seen again.

I think your worst war memories are your buddies being killed. It's a buddy system. You have a bond and brotherhood when you're overseas. Watch the man on the left, you watch the man on the right, and they do the same for you. They do best by replacing that man as soon as possible, to keep you talking, to keep you occupied. I lost six buddies over there. And they were senseless. That's when I started considering war senseless, when I started losing my buddies.

On watch, December 24, 1951: My buddy was awakened at 6 P.M. and he prepared to stand the first watch. After being relieved I went to sleep and slept soundly. Two hours later, at about 8:00 P.M., I went outside to relieve my buddy from his watch.

While scanning areas toward my left, I heard a "pop" over my head to the right flank. I knew it was a grenade because I saw the fuse from the Russian grenade flicker several times. I yelled out, "Fire in the hole," and bent forward and heard another "pop." By then I was bent over on my knees and partially around a corner of the trench. Both grenades landed to my rear and exploded. The first one merely threw dirt all over the place, but the second one found me. It blew my right boot completely off with its shrapnel and injured my right foot and buttocks.

Steppe was removed from the battlefield. The story of his long journey home continues in Chapter Six.

James Walsh

Army; Memoir

In the fall of 1951, Walsh got his introduction to life as a private in the Army infantry.

I was the best ammo bearer. Each ammo bearer carried two cans of ammunition into action plus backpack, equipment, and carbine. Challenged by the section's ammo bearers to run an uphill race with as much ammo in hand as possible, I lugged six cans, each weighing 20 pounds and holding 250 rounds, up a never-ending climb to win the honor of "first idiot ammo bearer."

In charge of the 3rd section of machine guns was 1st Sgt. George Shoemaker. "Shoe" pushed his squads to clean weapons and spare parts, check ammo, draw fresh water and combat rations while ranting, "No combat infantryman cared if he ever fired his weapon in a second firefight, having survived the first. Yet, if war he must, an infantryman cared about the fire support he got after he crossed the line of departure, the "LD." He wants every weapon the Army and Air Force could fire will precede him, cover him, then follow up along with the men climbing the hill. An infantryman doesn't want limitation. He wants a choreography of shells, napalm, and bullets dancing with him as his partner. It gives strength to legs heading into the enemy's trenches!"

My first glimpse of dead GIs caused more surprise than sorrow. I knew GIs were as likely to die in battle as was the enemy, but I hadn't ever seen a dead GI. Here were a half dozen laid side by side. They could have been in a

JAMES WALSH CA 1951

There were battles fought in Korea to be sure, but much of the war was spent waiting, watching for enemy movements, your rifle ready to pick off an enemy soldier.

funeral parlor, so neatly arranged were they. None had limbs missing. Their bodies were still in full field dress. Bodies that once were full of vigor were waxen, pale of face and hands, blood spots staining their fatigues. A lone rifleman guarded them. He could have been at prayer the way he knelt over them. I let loose a prayer of my own for the repose of their souls with God this moment.

Why did the sight of dead GIs stir so? Because the vague fear I had of the terrible consequences of war had become manifest. There followed the recognition that life lived in combat could be very brief. I felt mortal, not helpless, never hopeless, just fragile. It was an enervating sensation. I controlled it.

As if they were sharp knives thrown from the brow of overhead clouds above my head, F-84s sliced through the smoke of the firefight, blazing cannons flashing. Suddenly, plunging pieces of metal bit hunks out of my sand bags and in the earth around the fighting hole. I thought I was being hit from behind by the enemy. I grappled with Clouse to swing the machine gun around. He resisted, his eyes questioning my sanity. Then, as if all the Eighth Army's 155 howitzers had at that moment fired simultaneous bursts more resonant than deep thunder, my auditory senses swelled to near eruption. In confusion, I grappled Clouse to one side and took possession of the gun hole's deepest level. His knuckles bonked my helmet a few times while letting me know ear-shocking sound waves always followed the planes' dives to targets. Aware at last, my heart throbbed a bit more slowly and slid out of my throat. The F-84s had turned the battlefield into a charnel house. Pleased with themselves for leaving a crimson glow on the far hill, they shook wings and flew away. My first glimpse of airborne's fiery oblivion hurled at Chinese infantrymen shocked me. I said a prayer for them, another of thanksgiving this infantryman wasn't over there.

My hands moved dirt while my mind worked over Smith's phraseology, "killer from a distance." It was less than a year ago when the fingers of my hands were folded in seminary chapel prayer. Now they pulled a trigger and turned knobs to traverse and search for communists to kill. Had I ever metamorphosed! Transformation from seminarian to soldier was done by natural agencies, changing me from the goodly to the deadly. I was convinced a former follower of Confucianism was as likely as a former follower of Christianity or Judaism or Islam to rediscover his beliefs in a foxhole under fire. Combat was war between believers. Disbelievers were safely back stateside in the chairs of universities.

In those gun pits all wild with wrath, soldiers who'd never met before or would meet again except on the battlefield, fired artillery, mortars, machine guns, and rifles to wound and kill for a hilltop between lines. It was madness when there was talk of a DMZ! Madness to fight for the next hilltop, for there was no end.

MAX CLELAND CA 1966

*Max Cleland (seated, facing the camera) insisted on serving in
Vietnam. "I felt that I needed to take my place on the line," he
recalled. He paid dearly for that feeling when, in April 1968,
he was severely wounded by a grenade.*

Vietnam War

"You could never let your guard down."

Vietnam echoed Korea in eerie ways: the difficulty of telling friend from foe, extreme weather and difficult terrain, and an enemy seemingly unafraid of death. This time, America had even more firepower, not to mention a distinct advantage in technological capabilities. But for the soldier, it still came down to the same uncertainties: the booby traps in the jungle, the mines buried in the roads, the surprise attack on a patrol. And the fabric of military discipline began to fray: soldiers fought among themselves or, worse, refused to fight, well aware of their short-term status "in country."

RHONA KNOX PRESCOTT
   Army Nurse Corps; Interview
Vietnam from the air is gorgeous. It is all green like Ireland, all shades of green. You can see the divisions of the rice paddies separated by handmade dikes. It is very hilly and fertile and of course it has the sea all around it. It was gorgeous coming down.

When I came down, it radically changed. We were not allowed to disembark right away from the airplane. We were told to put on our helmets and to run single file to a site on the tarmac—to go as quickly as possible and not to look back. When the doors opened, the heat just kind of hit us in the face. It was close to 130°. We were being fired at; there were snipers there along the runway, somewhere in the bushes, that they hadn't been able to remove. We were told just to run, so that we did. Nobody got shot. It was a real eye-opener!

CHUCK HAGEL

Army; Interview

It's hot, it's unfamiliar, it's oppressive. There is great angst, uncertainty. It was 6 o'clock in the morning, and even at 6 o'clock in the morning the heat was oppressive. We were walking toward the processing area, and a bunch of the grizzled old veterans who were coming to get on the bird that we were on to go back home were shouting things at us, "Hey baby, Charlie's gonna love you. They're gonna cut your ears off," saying every outrageous thing that you could imagine. We were all staid, stolid, marching along, not going to let any of this affect us. Of course, it did. You never forget that entry point; you always remember what it looked like, what you did, and what you heard. The whole thing closing in on you in a way like you'd never experienced anything.

MAX CLELAND

Army; Interview

Cleland has previously written about arriving in Saigon and the staring of the people who are waiting to get on that airplane to get out.

Replacement troops have what Patton used to refer to as "the valor of ignorance." And the hardened, experienced troops have that hollowed-out look in their eyes, what became known as "the ten-thousand-foot stare in the ten-foot room." They're the ones: been there, done that, got a few holes in their t-shirt.

As the movie *Platoon* shows it, the tension started immediately. The moment the door opens and the heat comes in the tension begins, and you never shake that tension as long as you're in country.

CHUCK HAGEL

Army; Interview

Hagel's battalion base camp was the farthest of any into the Mekong Delta.

I walked a lot of point, and my brother Tom and I together walked a lot of point, which was all right. You know what happens to a lot of point men. But I always felt a little better when I was up front than somebody else. You have the front position; you also have the responsibility of not walking your company into an ambush or a trap. Booby traps were a way of life; you dealt with that all the time. At night we would sweep roads, and we needed to do that because at night VC would get on these roads and plant bombs, various imaginative booby traps. Or they would do something to continue to keep us off balance. Our APCs [Armored Personnel Carriers] would run those roads at night. We were sitting ducks riding in the APCs because it was so dark you couldn't see in front of you and you couldn't use lights. You didn't find it particularly healthy to be in those Armored Personnel Carriers.

When the Tet offensive began, they were headed into Long Binh and an ammunition dump blew up right in front of them, vaporizing the two Armored Personnel Carriers in front of his APC, or "track." Although Hagel's unit had lost a number of its officers and senior enlisted men, it went on to engage the Vietcong in the Battle of Widow's Village, an area that had been set up by the South Vietnamese for the widows of their soldiers. The Vietcong had killed the children and the widows living there and were using it as a staging area for an attack.

We drove the VC out of that village—fought all day, took a lot of casualties. Then they assigned us to house-to-house fighting in Saigon. As you know, the enemy got into the embassy and they were everywhere. We had a hard time getting rid of some of them, fighting house-to-house in Saigon after Tet hit.

It was during this time that his brother Tom joined his unit.

And my mother was a little concerned about that. But my mother is a very strong woman, and I think she thought overall if we were both going to be there, it was good to have us together.

On March 28, 1968, both Hagels were wounded.

We were on an ambush patrol. We knew that the VC had been in this area. We were walking through a very dense jungle, and we were crossing a stream. One of the point guys hit a trip wire in the stream. There were large Claymore mines that had been placed in the trees, so when the trip wire was hit, the Claymores exploded. Took down the guys in front of us, hit me with shrapnel in the chest, and Tom got shrapnel in the arms and I think the chest.

After a brief firefight, they were able to evacuate the dead.

It was hard to get in with choppers because it was so dense, and then of course you got problems with security of bringing those choppers down so low.

The captain asked if the Hagel brothers could make it, and they said yes, and then he asked if they would walk point and lead them out.

I was as afraid that night, I think, as I'd ever been because it was dark, and when it gets dark, it's <u>dark</u>. We almost hit another booby trap—Tom saved us. It was a live grenade hanging with a thin wire. It would have gotten me, but he grabbed it and defused it.

Hagel spent three days in a field hospital; the doctors left some shrapnel in him because the pieces were too close to his heart. In another month he was back in the hospital with a new wound. Hagel's unit had gotten a call late at night to investigate a village that had reportedly been infiltrated by Vietcong. Hagel's truck was the lead track going in. They found nothing in the village and departed. Hagel's truck was the last track going out. The Vietcong hit an APC with a 500-pound mine detonated by VC hiding nearby in trees.

The fire came up and burned me up and down on my left side, my arm. My brother Tom was unconscious because of the concussion. We were also experiencing some machine gun fire from the jungle. By the time our other tracks could turn around and get back, I got everybody off our track because I was afraid it was going to blow with all the ammunition we had in those tracks. My brother Tom had blood coming out of his ears and his nose; I didn't know whether he was dead, but I threw him off and fell on top of him. By this time the machine gun fire had gotten even fiercer and heavier. But our tracks were coming back to get us. Tom had a concussion and had been hit with shrapnel. Both of my eardrums had been blown out. And until they could secure the area, they couldn't bring any choppers in to get the wounded out. I remember sitting on that track waiting for the dust-off [chopper] to come and thinking to myself, *If I ever get out of all this, I'm going to do everything I can to assure that war is the last resort that we, a nation, a people, calls upon to settle a dispute.* The horror of it, the pain of it, the suffering of it, people just don't understand unless they've been through it. There's no glory, only suffering in war.

THOMAS HODGE

Marine Corps; Interview
Hodge, a native of Springfield, Massachusetts, was 19 years old in 1968 when he was drafted by the Army, but he chose to enlist in the Marines, "because I knew I was going to Vietnam and the Marines did the best of training." Hodge was trained to be a truck driver.

Every person in the Marine Corps is qualified as a grunt, or a ground pounder as they call them: infantry. No matter what your MOS, whether you're a Remington Raider—that's what we used to call typists—or a nurse or doctor or cook, if they needed you out in the bush, that's where you went. At least you know how to fire all the weapons. I was stationed up near the demilitarized zone. In the Marine Corps you try to secure the high ground; better to look down on the enemy than look up. When they said in boot camp that the life expectancy of a truck driver was three days, it was very true. You go to an amusement park and you have a line of ducks and you're shooting at them; that's about the size of a truck driver in Vietnam. We run in convoys; convoys

CHUCK HAGEL 1968

Hagel (right, with his brother Tom), atop an armored personnel carrier, volunteered for duty in Vietnam just before he was to be shipped off to a posting in Europe. He was wounded twice, the second time when his APC ran over a 500-pound land mine.

have a machine gunner every fifth truck. We run a 30-truck convoy, maybe three tanks at the head of the convoy, two tanks in the middle, two at the end. Above our heads we have these helicopters, the Cobras, Huey gunships. We call it the suicide convoy, because a lot of times on these convoys if a round hits one [truck carrying artillery rounds and ammunition], the whole convoy goes up in a row.

This was an everyday thing, 365 days a year. There was no Sunday or Monday or Tuesday. You never kept track of the days; it was just survival.

Coping with that is not something that you learn in school. You have to go into a cold mind. We run 18-hour days. Sometimes I would go two or three days without sleep. If you've got a little man named Charlie chasing you, you don't worry about sleep.

Sometimes we'd go out on patrol at night time, no lights, no cigarettes; the man in front of you was about two feet in front of you, so you really don't know what's out there. Here you are, ten, twelve thousand miles from home walking

RONALD WINTER 1968

Ronald Winter, pictured in his quarters in Quang Tri, Vietnam,
left college to enlist in the Marines. In Vietnam he flew more
than 300 missions as a machine gunner aboard helicopters.

around in someone else's backyard that you don't know. It's very scary.

We had minesweepers that ran the road before us. Minesweepers usually go about 20 minutes before the convoy pulls out. Usually we don't find mines. Uusally when we come back, we find mines. Because while we're gone, the enemy would put mines in the road. They have what they call pressure detonated mines. Let's say one of our B-52s drops a bomb and the bomb didn't go off. They would take this bomb and bury it in the ground. Maybe a jeep might roll over this mine and it doesn't go off, but a truck carrying ammunition is heavy enough to set this mine off. I used to try to ride what they call the lead truck. The lead truck in the convoy was sandbagged, so if it hit a mine it would blow up; you'd just get a little shaken up.

This sort of stuff goes through your mind every day you go out in a convoy and come back, you always say, Is it going to be my day to come back? I just happened to be in the wrong place at the right time. Your friends, your buddies get shot, the best thing you can say is, Better him than me. You just have to think that way.

RONALD WINTER
Marine Corps; Interview
Winter, a helicopter gunner, arrived in Vietnam in May 1968.

I flew 300 missions as a machine gunner. A mission meant that you had to go into a hot zone where fighting was taking place. More often than not, some of the firing would be coming at you. There were missions we were on where you would go in and there was a lot of firing but none of it directed at you. But it was still a mission because you were where there was fighting going on. Sometimes you'd take the mail, which was always a big deal. Then when things were getting really hot, you had to go in on a medical mission. That was dangerous because you were taking people, and they were trying to keep you from taking people out. When you were bringing replacements back in, same thing, you got a lot of shooting there. There were troop lifts where they had identified a concentration of the North Vietnamese troops and they wanted to attack. You would spend an entire morning taking flight after flight of infantrymen in and setting up zones and blocking forces. Those were usually very dangerous. And the most dangerous of all were reconnaissance missions. The recon teams were anywhere from five or six up to 14 or 15 guys who would go out in the field and look for concentrations of enemy and troop movements. They would radio all this information back in: Sometimes they would call for air strikes, sometimes they would call in artillery strikes, and sometimes they would get caught. Sometimes you would take them out and they would immediately get surrounded and you had to turn right around and go back and get them.

Sometimes when you would go into the zones, there would be a lot of firepower come your way. You could just see them start at the beginning of the helicopter and literally in your peripheral vision see the bullet holes as they worked their way down the side. My job there was to get an idea of where they were coming from and stop them from doing it. I had a .50 caliber machine gun, which was the largest weapon an individual can use in the entire U.S. arsenal, and it spoke with tremendous authority. The bullets in it were armor-piercing, tracer, but we also had explosive rounds. One in every five would explode, and what that meant was that if it hit you, it blew up. And if you hit someone in the hand, their arm was gone. It was a devastating piece of weaponry.

There was one time where one of the guys I shot was brought on board, and that was a little difficult because he was much younger than I thought. And of course, when your people are trying to prepare you to fight and go kill someone else, they're trying to give you as mean and horrible an image of that person as they can, and that's the only way you're mentally prepared to do what you have to do. This guy had a pack, and there were personal effects in it, and there were pictures of his home and his girlfriend and him, and I said, "Boy, that was a human being." That was different. And then you get an idea, like, What on earth? I mean, here I was at twenty, and what's this kid doing here. You don't think of it till later, he's no more of a kid than you. We were all pretty young. More in the years afterwards I thought about that.

MAX CLELAND

Army; Interview

For about eight months the war was manageable, but then the North Vietnamese decided to counterattack and put it on the line. That became the Tet Offensive, which began 1 February 1968. Apparently, General Westmoreland used the Cav as a blocking force to secure the Marines at not only Danang but at Hue. And we were astride Highway One when three North Vietnamese divisions came down. That's where the First Air Cavalry Division and the Marines and other units got shredded, and we lost a lot of people. You can't take away from the enemy their ability to die, and that's what the North Vietnamese had, and their willingness to die. So that's what they did, by the tens and twenties of thousands. But it gave such an emotional shock to this country. We lost 15,000 men in 1968, more than four times the number that the French lost at Dien Bien Phu.

Cleland volunteered for a big relief mission in March.

I've done crazier things, but I can't remember what was more crazy than that. I don't know, there's something about combat, the moth to the flame thing: Let's get this sucker over with, let's do it, because Vietnam for American troops had a big frustration level. You'd go somewhere and you'd fall back. And then you'd go somewhere else and you'd fall back. You never had a sense of winning. We ended with this war of attrition against experts in wars of attrition.

He was promoted to captain on the day of the Tet Offensive, though his commander couldn't get to him for 26 days to pin the two bars on me. I thought by volunteering, getting there, being part of this, and winning this sucker, we could win the war and be done with this. This nutso stuff—the lost lives, the craziness, the lack of goal-setting to accomplish the strategic objectives—all that would be over. And so that's what I saw in the battle for Khe Sanh, and I hung it all out, and the country hung it all out. And then we broke the siege, and I got wounded the day the siege was actually broken, April 8, 1968. And of course after the Khe Sanh base was taken they plowed it under and evacuated it. Now how does that make you feel?

Cleland was wounded in a way that a soldier doesn't like to get wounded: By accident, a circumstance that he admits made recovery more difficult.

I came home feeling very guilty, very embarrassed. Yeah, if I'm such a great, wonderful military leader, why did I get wounded? Why did I get wounded this way? I call it a freak accident of war, but that's war. I could have gotten killed the night of the 4th of April when we had 20 or 30 Russian rockets coming in. Just another click on the sight of a North Vietnamese gunner and I could be number five—there were four killed on the hill that night.

I recall a bit of my evacuation because I was awake to it. I fought going out of consciousness because I thought I would never wake up. But that was just a personal fight. Really, it was the people around me who saved my life. They tended my wounds, cut off my clothes, tried to make a tourniquet. My right arm and leg were blown off immediately, left leg was amputated within the hour. They got me on a medevac with IVs, and one of the things I remember is, I looked up to the medic and asked, "Am I gonna make it?" and he said, "You just might."

Persian Gulf War

"They didn't do a head count in this war."

The Veterans History Project is just beginning to document the Persian Gulf War of 1990-91. Its combat stories have, for the most part, not been told, in part because the duration of actual fighting was so brief. This was also a war with a big differ-ence, the first in which women officially came to fight, to do the heavy lifting that had previously been reserved for men. As Joanne Palella, a ten-year Army veteran when the U.S. came to the aid of Kuwait, tells it, going into the desert gave her and her sister soldiers a chance to participate more fully in the experience of war.

JOANNE PALELLA
Army; Interview

We left for Saudi Arabia on January 6, arrived on January 7. We didn't know if we were going to be bombed going over. I'd say the worst pressure and stress were the first two weeks in the aluminum buildings, because starting about three days after we got there we were bombed every night from about nine o'clock to five o'clock in the morning. We really didn't sleep much, and we did-n't know if there was going to be gas. They didn't hand out bullets for the M-16s. Not that you could fight that with bullets, but it was a little bit paranoid for everyone there, not having any defense for things that were coming out of the sky.

We lived in aluminum warehouses by the piers for several weeks before we were sent out into the desert. I was in country for nine months. I was an ammu-nition specialist and a truck driver, so one of my jobs was to haul explosives. I also hauled the M1 tanks and Bradley tanks and worked with explosives for my

JOANNE PALELLA 1991

Joanne Palella took this picture in a place U.S. soldiers called Death Valley, an area of immense destruction and carnage in the Kuwaiti desert.

company. There were no casualties in my unit; there were a few injuries.

One of the horrible experiences that I remember—and I'm glad that the smell has finally left me—was when we went into this place called Death Valley in Kuwait. Our military had bombed it for three days straight; there were thousands of military and civilian vehicles—the Iraqis confiscated whatever civilian vehicles they wanted to use. They ran one big convoy; it was like they were colored with a red Magic Marker: Hit Me, Hit Me. And the planes did for three days. Afterward we had to go through there and pick up the tanks that partly survived and had to clean up and pick up explosives. If there was dead inside the tanks, scrape them out, leave them for the engineers. The engineers made quite a few huge holes—they didn't do a head count in this war—they just piled them in with equipment and covered them up. And it just stank horribly.

A good memory was when we were in our vehicles in convoy. There was plenty of Kurdish children that were starving, and we got to feed quite a few of them some MREs. I enjoyed doing that.

When asked to compare her experience to veterans of other wars like Vietnam, Palella had this to say:

We had electronic equipment to know where everything was when we got there. However, when we were going to blow up bunkers, we would be driving and not even know we were on them, the terrain was so monotonous. We could see for twenty miles, and they could see for, what, three feet inside the jungle? I'm glad I didn't have to go to the jungle.

{ ONE MAN'S STORY }

Corbin Willis

*"It struck me so funny that I didn't have the energy
to pound ten nails into place."*

Ted Williams was the most famous American to do it. He served in both World War II and the Korean War, as a fighter pilot in both conflicts. But 1.5 million other Americans with less famous credentials than the Splendid Splinter also served their country in the two major American wars closest in chronology to one another. Among them was Corbin B. Willis, Jr. This native of Fort Morgan, Colorado, was born in 1922 and began his military career in January 1941 as a private in the Army Air Corps. Willis was trained as a P-38 fighter pilot, but there was a greater need during the war for B-17 pilots. As he notes in a memoir of his World War II experience, "Our class was switched to multi-engined bombers and we had a choice of B-17's or the Army Tank Corps—a take it or leave it ultimatum."

Willis became a B-17 co-pilot. On November 6, 1944, he and his crew were on their 22nd bomb mission, three short of the 25 required to go home on rotation, bombing a ball bearing factory and military complex area in Magdeberg, Germany. They were hit by antiaircraft shells and dropped to an altitude that made them "quite a 'sitting duck' target for ground fire." Willis bailed out and hit the ground on his back. A German Tank Corps soldier fended off an angry crowd of civilians that had gathered around Willis, who wound up with two black eyes and a swollen jaw.

Of the nine crew members who bailed out, four were killed on the ground by civilians, including the radio operator, who was wounded in the plane and killed on a stretcher on the way to a hospital. "They were mostly incensed," wrote Willis, "by the British RAF 'pattern bombing' of Cologne for the last six nights. You wouldn't really expect them to greet you with roses, so I understood their feeling. I'm sure my own family would be out there swinging and hitting in like circumstances."

CORBIN WILLIS 1944

*Heavy ground fire forced Corbin Willis (front row, right) to
bail out of his B-17 in November 1944. He survived internment
in a POW camp and went on to fly combat missions in Korea.*

The five survivors were put on a train to Weisse, Germany, an interrogation center
for POWs. "I must tell you about the training we received at our air base in Britain,"
Willis wrote. "The RAF had allowed some of their intelligence officers to be captured by the Germans and after they were interrogated by the Germans they were
liberated and flown back to England to tell all of us about what to expect when we
became POWs. We were told that the German intelligence service was thorough.
Any information we gave would be verified by the other crewmembers in a clever
use of words and intimidations. There would be no physical force used on us but
they could use fear and reprisal in their questioning. We were told that they would
seek confirmation of each question and answers from our facial expression and
responses. If we lied they would detect it from our expressions. So they taught us
to practice non-expressive eyes and facial responses; even though the replies were
either right or wrong they would not reveal the truth."

Soon Willis and his crew were loaded onto a troop train. "Our guard slept most
of the time. I took out his pistol and examined it out of curiosity but knew it would
be useless to keep it or attempt an escape from a military troop train." The
Germans furnished them with bread made of sawdust and potatoes. They had tea
from a Red Cross food parcel. Four of them shared an 11-pound box of Red Cross
goodies that was supposed to be allotted to one person.

At their camp, organized escape committees hoarded food and supplied cloth-ing and money acquired in barter with guards and civilian personnel. "The grate of our stove was lifted out at night and a crew entered the tunnel being dug under the barracks. Bed slats had to be used to shore up the sandy soil to prevent its collapse. When it came my turn to give up my bed slats, it required using one of the horse hair blankets as a hammock nailed to the sides to support my weight. I remember that I was losing weight rapidly and had little real strength, so when I was given the ten nails necessary to hold the blankets into place, I was able to only pound in seven and that was the end of my strength. I sat on the floor and actually laughed, it struck me so funny that I didn't have the energy to pound ten nails into place."

Willis recalled, "Many letters were shared because many of us never received any letters while in prison camp. In fact, I received all my letters after the war was over, when the sacks of mail piled in the prison camps were found later. For morale reasons, they were not given out to many POWs by the Germans." Willis had been listed as Missing in Action. A telegram sent to his parents and his wife listed the four crew members killed by the civilians and said the fate of the other crew members was unknown, "as the bomber blew up."

As the Russian Armies were advancing toward Berlin, Willis and his fellow pris-oners were put out on the road toward a camp many miles away, at Moosburg. It was winter, the temperature below zero, and whenever the column stopped, "some POWs fell down face first in the snow and we had to revive them and get them on their feet to keep them from freezing." When they arrived at Moosburg, they were shocked at the conditions in the camp. In March, when the weather warmed up, many chose to live in tents outside "to escape the cramping and stench."

Hidden radios brought encouraging news of the Allied advances. According to Willis, Gen. George S. Patton "learned of our plight and spearheaded a column toward our camp." On April 28, 1945, Willis and his prisoners were freed. The son of Patton's Chief of Staff was in the camp, "and the first tank through our gates was his and he carried his son in his arms out to his tank." Then Patton arrived, "riding in the back seat of his jeep. What a target, with his chromed helmet and his pearl handled pistols. He looked us over and saw our physical condition, so he told his sup-ply officers that each man would have a square meal that night out of the 7th Army's rations." Patton was taken aside and told that the prisoners' stomachs would not take heavy food, so he ordered soup kitchens set up. "We had such a potent soup that for three days I could barely hold water on my stomach," Willis remembered. "It was too rich; it killed some POWs." The Red Cross came in with doughnuts and coffee, and "it killed a few more POWs." Finally, the men were airlifted to a location where their diet could be controlled. Rice did the trick, because "rice was the easiest of all foods to digest. It expanded in our stomachs and caused us to be full."

Willis's return home after the war is told in Chapter Six. He stayed on active duty in the Air Force, and in 1951, he was stationed in Nagoya, Japan, as a deputy finance officer, when, as he says in his memoir, *My Korean War Experience,* "it became apparent that they needed spotter planes to help in the air and ground conflicts. They screened all pilots and all those pilots stationed in Japan that had ten hours or more of trainer planes (the AT-6)." Willis had over 800 hours in that aircraft as an instructor pilot at Randolph Air Force Base, near San Antonio, Texas, so he was a logical recruit for what would be known as the Mosquito Squadron.

"Our combat missions," he wrote, "started at the crack of dawn. They were all over enemy territory and we would spot troop movement, vehicle movement, or gun emplacements, then call in air strikes, ground artillery fire, or troops to enter the area where the activities were spotted.... We would circle the area to be hit, until the planes or artillery were ready—then we fired a smoke rocket into the area, so the planes could have a visual reference to start their bomb run, or the artillery would know the area and could pattern-shell it with their heavy guns.... I sat in the back seat as an observer and called in the air strikes."

Weather was "a real factor" in deciding where and when to fly. One day, when the ceiling was below 100 feet, Willis's group commander, who was in the company's forward base, ordered the planes up. When Willis told him that conditions were not favorable for flying, the commander insisted. The commander eventually let Willis off the hook, having checked the conditions and verified how low the ceiling was, "but he never forgot the incident." Willis finished 50 missions, and then the commander assigned him to a two-month tour as "Forward Air Controller," attached to the Army's I Corp. "We were in a security boundary, patrolled by South Koreans, and of course you could not tell a North Korean from a South Korean, so we were always on the alert for penetration."

One day, Willis did get to witness some brutal ground combat. "Waves of North Korean and Chinese troops were screaming at the top of their lungs and running forward, in waves, into our guns. The ones without guns had clubs and whistles and they would stop and retrieve a gun that another soldier had used before he was hit. The casualties were enormous, but if they wanted a position, they would expend all their troops to overrun it."

Willis survived that day and lived to write about his harrowing adventures in two wars. He retired from the Air Force in 1961, not yet 40 years old but experienced well beyond his age.

{ CHAPTER FOUR }

They Also Serve

*John Enman examines the aerial photographs he helped create
for pilots in the China-Burma-India Theater during World War II.*

*Mas and Sergeant Hiramatsu, two Japanese-American col-
leagues of Warren Tsuneishi, at Camp Savage in Minnesota. They
were training with the Army's Military Intelligence Language
Service School to translate captured Japanese documents.*

The Specialists

*"It goes without saying that knowing enemy intentions
is half the battle."*

At the entry point of service, every GI is assumed roughly equal, but some are quickly separated from the pack, by dint of their unique skills or background, to perform in specialized units. Fluency in a foreign language would lead to intelligence work; college students with degrees in the sciences got to apply their knowledge to fight deadly diseases; lawyers were called on to make sure that POWs were being treated humanely. These GIs sometimes got so wrapped up in their work that they would forget the dangers that lurked, but they never lost sight of their mission, to help win the war.

WARREN TSUNEISHI
> *World War II; Army; Memoir, Interview*
Warren Tsuneishi described in Chapter One how his Japanese-American family was interned at the outset of World War II, but he was able to finish his college education at Syracuse University. At the urging of his older brother Hughes, who was already in the Army's Military Intelligence Service Language School at the time of the Pearl Harbor attack, Warren signed up for the same program. He was sent to Camp Savage, Minnesota, to learn to read and translate Japanese military documents. In June 1944 his group was named the 306th Headquarters Intelligence Detachment of the XXIV Corps.

We received jungle training in Oahu, and then some time in late summer we boarded a troop ship for a leisurely ocean voyage. The XXIV Corps was part of the Army that "returned" to the Philippines with General MacArthur, landing on Leyte Island on October 20, 1944. My MOS was 267, "Translator," and most of my "intelligence" activities consisted of translating captured documents. I recall staying up all night following a Japanese airborne attack, translating a captured top-secret operational order found on the body of a member of the attacking forces, spelling out in detail the mission, objectives, personnel, and equipment carried by the airborne force. The mission was to knock out airstrips being built by the Seabees, and then link up with Japanese ground forces on Leyte. Needless to say, their mission failed. Another document I translated comprised secret information on the force defending the Camotes Island, situated between Leyte and Sajmar.

Initially when we were sent out, we were assigned bodyguards to protect us from our own troops. We were not trusted to be loyal citizen soldiers working on behalf of the U.S. government.

The XXIV Corps was part of the 10th Army in the Battle of Okinawa, landing on April 1, 1945. Classic Japanese strategy called for bitter defense at the water's edge in repelling any enemy landing force. XXIV Corps headquarters staff was on the beach on D-Day, and we soon learned why there was virtually no resistance on the beachhead. I was involved in translating a top-secret operational order laying out the strategy for the defense of the island: Let the enemy land with their full forces and supplies with minimum resistance; take up dug-in defense lines on an escarpment bisecting the island; let the Imperial Navy kamikaze attack and destroy U.S. naval and supply ships; and then destroy the invading forces, cut off from the supplies, at leisure. It goes without saying that knowing enemy intentions is half the battle.

There were tons of top-secret documents strewn around. They were not conscious of document security. We were told, for example, that we could not carry any diaries into the battlefields. I left all my personal diaries with a friend's family in Hawaii before I left. The Japanese didn't have any restrictions; they carried their diaries into the field. Mining the diaries was very important for what the Army calls Order of Battlefield Information. The Japanese military apparently thought that it didn't matter whether the documents fell into our hands because no Americans could read Japanese in any case—or very few.

RAFAEL HIRTZ

World War II; Army; Interview

Hirtz was recruited from the Army Signal Corps to join the fledgling Office of Strategic Services (OSS), largely because he was fluent in French and was familiar with Europe, having spent part of his youth there with his family.

We were always very careful. We always tried to let the French know if we were going to do something, about blowing something up, so that the civilians would get out of the territory. The old OSS was a pretty decent group, even though admittedly there's not anything you're not willing to do if you wanted to get in. You're always a volunteer. Only once in my life did I say no to an OSS "suggestion." That was a weird one; they wanted to assassinate Hitler. There wasn't any chance of success. We looked at the plans, and they admitted it was a suicide mission. I said, "Well, a suicide mission is different from a mission where you know there's probably no way it can succeed and at the same time you know that it is a suicide mission." I said, "That doesn't make much sense."

The SOs were special operators who went in alone; there were also teams of three: one Englishman, one Frenchman, and one American, all fluent in French and German. These operators were always dressed in civilian clothes.

My group had a choice, depending on the mission. Some missions we went in as civilians, some missions we went in in full uniform, so that theoretically if you were captured you might not be immediately killed. But of course, the German high command knew who we were, and they had orders that there was to be no mercy shown, that if we were to be captured, we were to be examined, and all the information gotten that they could get was to be gotten out of us, and then we would be shot.

We were in constant touch with headquarters, and if we didn't have a radio or it was lost, we could listen to the BBC, which was sending coded messages all the time. There were thirty of us on the first mission to go in, and we left from Carrington Field, a secret field in England. The planes were painted black. The first mission we had was to work in conjunction with D-Day, as Patton's troops were going through Brittany to take Brest, where all of the German long-distance submarines were being built. Our job, rather than destroy, was to save bridges that we could, so that Patton's armored group could cross the bridges without anybody stopping them. Our job was to train the French underground and arm them. We had the weapons parachuted in. We trained the people how to hold a bridge, and then we went and took the bridge.

I had two missions in Europe and one in China. We were sent originally with the idea of going through French Indo-China, which of course became Vietnam, because everybody spoke French and they were very anti-Japanese. We were supposed to contact Ho Chi Minh, who was very anti-Japanese and at that time was pro-American. The French command in the area refused us permission to parachute into French Indo-China, because, they said, "This is our colony, and you're not going to fool around in it." So they sent us into China itself. We trained the first paratroopers in the history of China. We organized 20 commando units. I trained the second commando unit and parachuted in with them and 11 Americans. That was into south-central China, behind the Japanese lines. It was literally hell. There was no food available; you had to live off the land, and there was nothing to live off. We survived actually on about a bowl of rice. We were supposed to be supplied by the air, but there were more important things going on in Asia than our small groups.

I barely made it out of China. You were living off the land; there was no way you could keep yourself clean. It was a difficult situation. I had just about every disease known to man—yellow fever, jaundice, amoebic dysentery. I came back on a hospital ship, and I think I was 128 pounds.

JOHN ENMAN

World War II; Army; Memoir
During World War II, Photo Procurement Detachments were established to secure and process aerial photography for two purposes—strategic planning of air strikes, naval bombardment, or troop landings, and producing maps that were both current and accurate. John Enman's job was to record on 1:1,000,000 maps, at scale, all aerial photographic coverage flown in the CBI (China-Burma-India) Theater.

We were reduced to being the India-Burma Theater, as the China area was separated and put under the command of a Chiang Kai-Shek favorite, Maj. Gen. Claire Chennault, former head of the mercenary Flying Tigers (by 1944 legitimized as the 14th Air Force), and married to a Chinese. Stilwell wound up commanding on Okinawa and died two years later. Chiang Kai-Shek also disliked the British, presumably for sound Chinese historical reasons, so we had to keep two sets of maps, those that showed all sorties, including those over China, and those where the sorties ended, rather abruptly, at the Chinese border. The latter were for use by British Intelligence; the former by our own, the O.S.S.

On days off during all of our tour in New Delhi, a small group of us took in all we could from local hikes and day-long Sunday excursions in a company vehicle through the countryside to a few weeks' leave at one of the several cool hill stations. Truck tours, as to the Taj Mahal, occurred occasionally (usually through the Red Cross), but the Delhi area, center of Mughal India, was a trove of Muslim architecture plus some of Hindu, Sikh, and British origin, which in the months we were there were amply photographed in black-and-white with the unit's 4x5 and 8x10 cameras.

RAFAEL AND MARY HIRTZ 1945

Rafael and Mary Johnson Hirtz after their wedding in New York. The couple met on the job; he was an operative with the Office of Strategic Services; she was an OSS translator.

There were those who preferred spending their free time drinking beer at the enlisted men's or the NCO (non-commissioned officer) bars and who came home knowing little more of India than when they first arrived. Some of the British were the same, and for their beer drinkers we were a godsend as their beer ration was two pints a month, ours a case (eighteen pints) a month. Some of us swapped a case of U.S. beer (like Iron City, Falstaff, and Griesedieck) for a fifth of such as Johnnie Walker, Black or Red label. Cold beer was had only at the aforementioned bars, so our unrefrigerated cases satisfied the British, who preferred their brew tepid.

Downtown New Delhi was then relatively new, as the entire planned town had been built in the 1930s by the British (likely at Indian expense) and it contained numerous book and native craft stores, movie houses, and a variety of good restaurants. Nearby was the Town Hall where each Sunday evening a classical music concert was put on by the All-India Gramophone Society with professionally printed programs and notes concerning the performances, presented on 78 RPMS. One week some British service men and women staged an enchanting floodlit evening presentation of *A Midsummer Night's Dream* among some old ruins in Lodi Gardens, with Mendelssohn's "Incidental Music" wafting from speakers hidden in trees. Since then, each time I hear that music their entrancing production flashes through my mind.

DENTON CROCKER CA 1944

Denton Crocker's unit studied and proposed methods of exterminating malaria-bearing mosquitoes in the Pacific Theater. A colleague stands outside the unit's tent in Gusica Meadows, New Guinea (top). Denton Crocker in his tent (bottom).

DENTON CROCKER

World War II; Army; Memoir

When ground troops began to fight in the South Pacific, the power of malaria to disable the men became apparent almost immediately. On Guadalcanal, for example, casualty figures due to malaria rose to over 100% (repeat admissions to hospital giving the odd statistic of more admissions than there were men). The response was to form special units with the responsibility of bringing these numbers down through control of the carrier species of mosquitoes and through educating the troops in preventive measures.

Two kinds of units were formed. Survey units had the function of mapping the area assigned for study, identifying those species of mosquito present that were carriers of malaria or any other disease (such as dengue fever), and then making recommendations for control. Control units had the job of actually carrying out the control and were supplied with the equipment to do it.

Crocker was assigned to a survey unit. Their first duty station was New Guinea.

Of all the vast South Pacific, New Guinea seemed then and continues to seem the most wild, dark, and "primitive." So there I was, on February 25, 1944, at the age of twenty-five, with an undergraduate degree in biology to help me understand what I saw.

As we stepped off the ramp, Bill Brown was just ahead of me. Bill, a friend from Pickett and New Orleans days, was a Harvard student of entomology, especially ants. His first act ashore was to reach into a shirt pocket, pull out forceps and a vial of alcohol, and begin collecting ants.

Crocker and his unit were to stay in an area called Gusica Meadows, near Finschhafen, New Guinea, from April 28 to September 10, 1944.

The land war in this area had been won; for ships it was different. One day, standing in the noontime mess line, I looked toward the harbor to see a plane low to the water heading for the outermost vessel, the place where ammunition ships anchor away from the others. Unopposed, the plane continued straight for its target and struck. Both disappeared in a great cloud of smoke. I cried out, "Did you see that? Did you see that?" No one else had, and as I was explaining what had happened, a great blast struck us; the large mess tent shook violently and we all ducked. A kamikaze pilot had achieved his glory, and only a disappearing cloud in the sky remained as evidence of what had happened.

Work fell into a pattern, mapping the area for which we were responsible, collecting and identifying mosquitoes, developing recommendations for control, and writing reports. It was, of course, a hot tropical climate, but in this open grassland the humidity must have been low because to me it was not as oppressive as New Orleans. On many an afternoon, back in the forest hills, I could hear a murmur, which, growing louder, became a rushing sound and finally, a drumbeat as rain hit. After 15 minutes or so the sky cleared, the hot sun emerged, and soon all was dry again.

Here at Gusica and later on Mindoro in the Philippines I felt that I was a real contributor to the war effort, and for the most part I was enjoying it.

Crocker also wrote frequently to his fiancée Jean-Marie.
Letter to Jean-Marie, June 12, 1944

Yesterday (Sunday) was a very wonderful day. Cassel, Dziepak, Miles, and I took off just after dinner for a place about 25 miles from our camp to see the men in another MSU [Malaria Survey Unit] with whom we trained in New Orleans, and also to see a Lt. Col. Chaplain, a biologist and dean of St. Albans College in Green Bay, Wisconsin, before entering the Army. I should mention first that I actually, on a Sunday morning, arose for breakfast and did a good pile of washing. After boiling my clothes, I went down to the river with Roecker and rinsed them out and took a swim in a good-sized pool Roecker had discovered. The water was cold, and after 15 min.. we were quite blue and goose pimply enough to call it quits.

Crocker was next stationed in the Philippines, arriving there in November 1945. He tried to continue the survey work, and again fortune was with him when it came to encounters with the Japanese.

One day Bob Diener and I were returning from a hike into the hills when we encountered an infantry patrol heading for where we had been. The officer in charge said, "Where the hell have you guys been?" We told him roughly where, and he said, "Well, you're plenty lucky, because Filipino scouts have reported Japs back there and we're on the way to clean them out. They probably didn't shoot you two because they didn't want to give away their position until they could ambush a larger party."

PATRICIA SEAWALT

Persian Gulf War; Air Force; Letter
Seawalt had completed 13 years in the Air Force and received an honorable discharge when Desert Storm broke out.

The Army Oil Analysis Program was a big part of maintenance for both ground equipment and aircraft. The only problem was the Army did not have an MOS for Oil Analysis and it had always been contracted out. Until my discharge,

I was the only one qualified to do oil analysis, as I was a lab chief and project manager and physical science technician III as a contractor. Although the Army had two mobile labs, they did not have the personnel to run them. I contacted FORCECOM and then I reenlisted to run and train ten selected soldiers to man one of the labs for deployment.

We dealt with millions of flies and our mess tables were so covered with them the tables looked black. Showers were allowed only at the end of the day and for ten minutes in length. On several occasions the water delivered for our showers was in the same trucks that had hauled petroleum products earlier. The toilets were impossible to keep clean, due to the large number of units using them. Disposal of the waste was by burning, due to the fact the people contracted to empty them did not show up very often.

Weather conditions. By 0430 it was usually around 105°F. Rainy season: usually flooding and constantly wet. Winter: extremely cold at night. We had scorpions, snakes, bugs, and fleas to deal with as well as more flies. A lot of bugs, fleas, and flies were feeding on dead bodies and carcasses of herds of goats & camels found dead in the desert for no apparent reason.

As I said, there were also good memories, meeting new people. One of my duties was to work with and teach selected Arabs about oil analysis. At first they refused to have anything to do with me because I was a woman. Earning their respect was one of my greatest accomplishments. They began calling me "Madam," and when I left country they gave me perfume called "Madam." They also allowed me to eat in the same dining room. Women are usually made to eat in a separate room. Mornings during breakfast three male Arab teenagers would show up at my table and ask me to check over their English homework. Then in the evening they would report their grades.

I was required to travel between sites to meet with various leaders to report, repair equipment, and to pick up reports. Most of the travel was in the desert as well as across the borders. On one occasion a major had asked me and my driver if we could deliver a four-wheel drive to a location we were going to. Without a thought I said sure. I got in one vehicle and my driver the other. We had to go through a checkpoint at the border. While waiting in line it dawned on me it was illegal for me to be driving. New female military personnel were allowed to drive only military vehicles and must be in military uniform. I did not have a military four-wheel drive, but a civilian four-wheel drive, surrounded by Saudi military. My driver was waved thru the checkpoint. It was my turn. At the same time, two cars filled with civilians were in line next to me. All the Arab soldiers except one went to search the car. The one left took one look at me, looked to see what his comrades were doing, and very quietly motioned me on. Between the time I realized what I had done and the time he waved me on, I had pictured myself in a Saudi prison. In the Saudi prison system your family is responsible for bringing you food, water, clothing, blankets, etc. If you have no outside support, you die.

STEVE BUYER

Persian Gulf War; Army; Interview
After graduating from the Citadel, Steve Buyer declined a Regular Army commission. He went to law school and got his degree, and then served on active duty for a short time with the Army, practicing as a lawyer in the JAG Corps. He decided to go into private practice in his home state of Indiana but stayed in the reserves. Then in November 1990, he got the phone call: His reserve unit was being activated to go to the Middle East. He had to wrap up loose ends on his practice in a few days; he got the call late Wednesday night and was in uniform on Saturday.

I got assigned to Dhahran. Five of us were going to be airdropped into southern Iraq to set up some advance logistical bases. My nickname was "Combat JAG," to give you an idea of my personality. I wasn't your typical JAG officer. Normally you don't take a lawyer with you to do a behind-the-scenes mission. I was more than just a lawyer; I was a good soldier. We prepared for that mission, and at the last minute it was canceled.

Believe me, there is so much lawyer stuff to do. The thing about bringing military reservist lawyers to a theater of war is you're not caring about a military career. Lawyers are tough; they do their job and give you hardcore advice, and if the commander doesn't like it, you say, "Well, tough, I don't care what you like or dislike. We're going to do this the right way." You're not worried about a career.

Buyer was assigned where the prisoner of war camps were being established.

There was so much to be worked out. Not everyone in the Coalition Forces wanted to matriculate prisoners. Our forces as they swept through southern Iraq were like a vacuum cleaner. They swept up everyone. I was setting up my own process for tribunals. And no one else had done that. There wasn't anybody I could turn to and ask, "How do you do this?" In law school we had to read a book on the Geneva Conventions, and I don't know why, but I remembered it like I had a photographic memory.

I remember inspecting the camp for the first time. I told the colonel [in charge], "You have over 500 latrines built facing Mecca and Medina, and we cannot have thousands of Iraqis urinating in the same direction in which the

PATRICIA SEAWALT 1990

Patricia Seawalt outside her company headquarters in Garden City, Saudi Arabia. Seawalt was a retired Army reservist who reenlisted to apply her special knowledge of the oil industry during the Persian Gulf War.

Saudis pray. You're going to have to turn them." That's the first time he realized that this lawyer is going to be a royal pain.

When you go down the Geneva Conventions, it mentions cigarettes. You've got 44,000 under wire, and we're trying to do the best we can. And they smoke. Give them their cigarettes. First [the American officers] were like, "Don't give 'em matches." What are they gonna burn? What I wanted to do was to bring them to calm. Matter of fact, to bring calm at the Iraqi prisoner of war camp, I made sure they got what they wanted: Madonna. They just wanted to listen to Madonna. So we rigged up and piped in Madonna music. Many of the different tribes of Iraq listen to Western music. So if I can get 'em their cigarettes and let 'em listen to Madonna, and they don't cause any problems, amen.

Every day was different. Here's a classic example of a lawyer moving fast. The lawyers for the International Red Cross show up. They want to investigate a complaint upon the United States. So I met with them, and they said, "The complaint is you're feeding the Iraqis pork. And you're to feed them food they're accustomed to in a prisoner of war camp." And I said, "You know, you're correct. But look around here: This is all concertina wire. We've got thousands of Iraqis under wire. We've got them in tents; we've got shelter for them. We've got sleeping bags, water, latrines. You see, this is not a fixed facility; this is a transient camp. And under a transient camp, that's all you have to do, provide for the basic necessities and treat them with human dignity. No pictures, we keep everybody out, there's no torture." And he said, "You're right," and they left. You know what? I made it up. There's no such thing as a transient camp. But it made sense.

Three stories of officers in support of the men at the front lines offer a small sample of the hundreds of such positions filled in every war by men and women eager to do their part. John Wister, a Harvard-educated landscape architect, entered the service in 1917 at the age of 30 with the idea of training to become a storekeeper, and was assigned to keep track of ammunition. Edward Schrock was a Naval officer who volunteered for duty in Vietnam and found himself assigned to the delicate job of escorting reporters in country. Jacob Younginer was a munitions expert who was pressed into service in Vietnam when an unexploded bomb needed to be defused.

JOHN WISTER
   World War I; Army; Memoir
Wister's memoir consists of letters he sent home during his 18 months in Europe. He opens with a long introduction, excerpted below. Wister served in France as an enlisted man in the Ordnance Department in what was at various times called the L. of C. (Line of Communications), the S.O.R. (Service of the Rear), and the S.O.S. (Service of Supplies).

I was never at the front, never heard gunfire, never saw an enemy soldier. That was true of about one million of the two million soldiers of the American Expeditionary Force, but they usually did not admit it!

I did not like the Army. I never met any soldier who did. The men I was with enlisted voluntarily. They were not drafted. Most of them, like me, were nearly beyond draft age. Most of them, like me, never had their draft numbers called.

Wister had volunteered for a special program in procurement, for which the Army stressed the need for experienced businesspeople. He sailed for France on November 26, 1917, and arrived in St. Nazaire on December 10. His group was split up, and the 25 men saw service in nearly every important depot and ammunition dump from the base ports to the front lines.

Instead of following theoretical instructions, they had to use their common sense and to improvise. Their job was to receive ammunition, store it, and deliver it quickly and efficiently when called upon. As far as I know all but two of these men made good in the positions to which they were assigned. Yet the promised promotions were never forthcoming.

On arrival in France I was assigned to the most important Ordnance Depot in the AEF. It was not the largest, but it was nearest the front. It was by far the best from the point of view of climate, topography, and accommodations.

The apparent complaints in my letters do not reflect any bad temper about my own lot, but rather my general resentment against the whole Army system of pretense and lies. I believed and still believe that the high command, from general down to lieutenant, was incompetent, and that it used the censorship to keep this truth from the folks at home rather than to keep military information from the Germans.

Letter to Morris L. Cooke, "noted Philadelphia and Washington Engineer and Efficiency Expert," April 9, 1918

I am glad you found a man that liked the Storekeeping Course. He ought to be preserved in alcohol and exhibited with Barnum and Bailey's Circus!! But seriously speaking, of course the courses vary.

The chance to visit factories, etc. was of undoubted value but was poorly arranged. Some of the lectures by outsiders were splendid. The best was by a young storekeeper from Midvale. He spoke from KNOWLEDGE. A poor one was by an Atlantic Refining Co. man who took a whole hour to tell us that in storing, barrels should not be stood on end. That was absolutely all that he told us, except that gasoline vapor was explosive. The latter remark we found interesting, and wondered if he would mention the fact that the earth was round. He didn't.

But enough of this subject. Spring has come. France is exquisitely beautiful. We are very busy, time flies. Shipments come and go and the depot grows in size and in interest, and as you predicted, things go smoother. Our friend red tape, however, is stronger and healthier every day.

The gardening of France is so far ahead of ours in orderliness and taste that I shall miss it when I return. It is so wonderful to be in a country where all around are world famous Horticulturists, some of whom I have corresponded with for years, and most of whose names I know as well as my own, because they are attached to plants I have known and grown.

Letter, June 7, 1918

It is not strange that I make no allusions to the war. I am not in the war, tho' of course I might be at any minute. Last week during the bad time we got no papers. When the papers do come, they contain very little reference to the war, and what they do say is often so vague that you can't make a thing out. A month later I usually receive a Philadelphia paper telling all about it. It's a great system of getting news by way of America.

EDWARD SCHROCK

Vietnam War; Navy; Interview
Schrock's first assignment, in 1964, was on an aircraft carrier in the Pacific. He and several officers volunteered to go to Vietnam. After taking survival training back in the States, he was posted to Danang, arriving in October 1966.

I actually had orders to go into the Riverine Patrol in the I Corps area. I thought, This is going to be great stuff. Now I look back and think—foolish. Because it was very, very dangerous. But when I got [to headquarters], they said, "We notice you had collateral duty functions on the carrier in public affairs. We are just being inundated with news media right now, and we need people to help move them throughout the country. Would you be willing to do that for a while?" I said, "I don't mind." Of course, I did that the rest of the time.

I was able to travel a lot with the media and see a lot of the action that went on. Had I not been in that role, I wouldn't have seen any of that. It was fascinating. Got caught August 30, 1967, ten days before I was supposed to leave to get married, took Marvin Kalb and a CBS film crew with him up to DMZ, and we got into a firefight and ended up staying in a bunker for a couple of days. We couldn't get out, and those news guys were panicked, wanting to get out of there. And I thought, Here I am, days from getting out of here and going home and getting married.

Danang almost reminded me of a European town. Lots of buildings and houses crowded together like any busy city; beautiful waterfront—the Danang River was just spectacular. We lived in a real nice building. Lots of motorcycles, lots of bikes, lots of these little jitneys you would see in the Philippines. I had access to a truck, and I'd get several guys after hours and go out in the country, which was probably not the smartest thing to do. Every single day I was there we heard rockets go off; every single night you could go out and see the mountains and hills ablaze. It became a way of life; you just had to hope it didn't hit you. It never hit the center city.

One of the most difficult aspects of being there was going with the news media to the Navy hospital, because I had never seen anyone who was missing limbs. That was my first experience with that. And there were some kids there—and they were kids just like myself—some of whom had no arms. One fella I remember had no arms or legs, and part of his face had been blown away. It was the first time I got physically ill. I can see him to this day. Every Friday I would take the news media out to the Danang Airport as they loaded the body bags on. Watching those body bags go on that plane, I thought, There's somebody in there whom somebody loves at home. And they're waiting for them to come home, and their hearts are broken. Death was all around you; it was just an everyday occurrence. I think those two images were the most difficult to retain, and I have retained those.

JACOB YOUNGINER
Vietnam War; Air Force; Interview
In April 1967, Younginer began a year's tour of duty in Vietnam.

I was the youngest advisor to the Vietnamese. That started my EOD [Explosives Ordinance Disposal] career. When the U.S. Air Force put a bomb out in the field one day, the commander came in and said, "You guys are gonna have to go out and get that napalm out of the way so the farmer can come in and harvest his rice." So we went out and took care of it and didn't realize the danger in it. God takes care of fools and poor people, and he took care of us that time. After I returned from Vietnam, they sent me to EOD School, where I learned how much danger I had been putting myself into. Scared me a lot, but from then on I knew what to do, instead of just going out and doing what I thought was right based on my munitions experience. I had a nice five-year career in EOD.

EOD is what the civilians call the bomb squad. Anytime there's a problem with a munitions item, an explosive, the EOD team is responsible for going out and taking care of it. In civilian life it's now a lot easier in most cases, because when we did it most of what we did was a manual operation. Now, when you see it on TV, there's a lot of these remote devices, robots and all that, going in and taking care of the actual bomb. When I went out to take care of it, my hands were my robot. I can't talk about it, but a few times in my career we were involved with nuclear/biological weapons. You had to be trained for every possibility. To survive all that, you had to be pretty good at what you did. We lost a few people along the way that I knew personally, and that was always a very traumatic experience because it was such a small, close-knit group of people. Most of the time everybody knew somebody.

The Entertainers

Far from concert halls and theaters, GIs serving their country in a foreign land crave a living, breathing reminder of home. Armed Forces radio carries the hits of the day, a sheet is strung up, and an old movie projector runs a scratchy print of a recent film, but there is nothing like seeing and hearing a singer, a comedian, a dancer, or an actor familiar from the movies or television. Bob Hope, Marlene Dietrich, Marilyn Monroe, and countless other entertainers sensed this. Their tireless efforts to connect, however briefly, with soldiers, sailors, and marines imprinted dazzling memories for men and women longing for a break from the grim realities of war. These performers, accustomed to lives of comfort and ease, sometimes braved enemy fire and often put up with spartan quarters and performing venues to offer their own special brand of support to men and women in uniform. Some of the veterans in the Veterans History Project collections were themselves entertainers, and their stories express the joy of performing for a captive but wildly appreciative audience.

Janice Bickerstaff Yeoman (far left) performs with the Theresa Landry Dancers as part of a USO show for servicemen stationed in Rhode Island, 1967. She worked with the USO as a singer and dancer for five years.

Robert Krishef (above, left) a sergeant serving in Korea
with the 2nd Infantry Division, earned major brag-
ging rights when an unknown photographer snapped
this picture of him, a buddy, and Marilyn Monroe,
who was visiting the troops. Martha Raye (left) was a
frequent attraction during the Vietnam War, earning
the nickname Colonel Maggie from her friends in the
Army's Special Forces unit. She autographed this
photo to Rod Hinsch, who served as her bodyguard.

Bob Hope logged more miles than a space shuttle entertaining the troops, beginning with World War II and continuing through Korea and Vietnam. Hope attempts to keep up with the tap dancing Nicholas Brothers (above) aboard the USS Ticonderoga, China Sea, 1965. The Nicholas Brothers, Fayard and Harold, also performed for the troops during World War II. "A sore tooth," reads the caption on USO dancer Patty Thomas's photo with Hope (opposite). Her collection includes photos of performing in the Pacific Theater during World War II (bottom, left and right).

ISABELLE CEDAR COOK 1942

*Isabelle Cedar Cook (left) enlisted in the Army not long after
America entered World War II. Here she's seen with some of
her nurse pals during their Atlantic crossing to North Africa.
She would serve in Africa, Italy, and France.*

The Nurses and the Red Cross

*"The patients were really scared, and you had to try
to pass some kind of confidence on to them."*

*They are the first to see the awful effects of combat, and it's their composure and
professionalism that are the key to any GI's recovery. No matter where the hospital
is, in the North African desert or in the jungles of Vietnam, the nurses are there, full
of good humor, devoted to every patient as if he were her own brother. Their stories
are among the most heartbreaking of all.*

ISABELLE CEDAR COOK
   World War II; Army Nurse Corps; Interview
We went on a troop ship that was the *Louis Pasteur*. Originally, it was a French
luxury liner, and it was converted to a troop ship, manned by a British crew. We
didn't know our final destination. We ended up in Casablanca. We spent about
three months in Casablanca, because the Germans were still fighting in Tunisia
and [our] general hospital was supposed to be set up in Mateur, just outside of
Tunis. When the Germans were defeated in North Africa, then we got our orders
to proceed to Tunisia. I was one of the ten nurses chosen for the advance set-up
party. We traveled 1,500 miles across North Africa in an open 10-ton truck. And
the heat in May [1943] was unbearable, but we managed. We slept in pup tents
and ate K rations. One night we got to spend with the French Foreign Legion,
and we got a real hot meal and a bed to sleep in.
   *When they arrived at Mateur, it had been bombed out and people were living in
caves. Cook was put in charge of housekeeping for the new hospital.*
   Here I am, twenty-two years old, never took care of a house in my life. [The
head nurse said], "You can probably get the townspeople to do the laundry."

Well, there was no town; it had all been bombed out. We took over this French army barracks that had been used by the Germans. There were still some Germans who were so badly wounded they couldn't be moved, and there was one German doctor. The rest of our unit arrived; they had had a terrible experience going across country in cattle cars. One of our nurses had died, the heat was so terrible. We set up our entire hospital in about eight days—800 tons of equipment.

The nurses and enlisted personnel had tents. There were five of us in each tent. Outside latrines and outside wash stations. We were getting the sirocco winds from the Sahara, and it was pretty bad. Within about five days after we set up the hospital, we began receiving patients by air. We were taking care of casualties from Sicily; the Sicilian campaign had started. We were acting as an evacuation hospital rather than a general hospital, which takes care of the more severely wounded and those who need to stay much longer. We received about 2,000 patients, and as a result we had to open another thousand-bed hospital in tents. We all did double shifts. The heat was so unbearable for the patients; we did have Italian prisoners of war, and they set up extra tarp over the tops of the tents and they would run cold water over it to cool it.

We stayed in North Africa for about one year; we took care of about 5,000 patients during that time. Bob Hope came to entertain. And of course our social life was just wonderful, with 100 nurses and about 100,000 servicemen in the area. We had about six nurses that married doctors from the outfit; they set up individual tents for each couple, and that was called Honeymoon Lane.

We followed General Mark Clark's army [into Italy]. We were supposed to be sent to Rome, but the fighting was still going on in Anzio, and Rome had not been captured, so we were set up in an orange grove outside of Naples, near the king's palace. Originally, we took care of French colonial troops and Arabs and Senegalese, and we had no interpreters. Following that, we got American soldiers wounded from Anzio and Cassino. We stayed in Italy about nine months. We were able to get leave now and then. We went to the Isle of Capri; that was quite an experience.

We were transported to France after the invasion of France. We went through Marseilles, then on to Aix en Provence. All this time, we had been living in tents; when we arrived in Aix en Provence, to our great delight, they took over a resort hotel, and we lived in this hotel. They even kept all the staff on, so that we had a French chef. It was amazing what they could do with dry powdered eggs and Army food.

We took part in the VE Day parade there on May 7, 1945. They invited all the

ISABELLE CEDAR COOK CA 1942

Cook (left) and a friend wash that sand right out of their hair in Mateur, Tunisia. Enduring primitive conditions was part of the job—a small inconvenience compared to their patients' wounds.

foreign troops to march in this parade. We're marching down the street and all of a sudden I looked up at one of the lamp posts, and hanging from the lamp post was a man with a big sign across his chest that said COLLABORATEUR. They had hung the collaborators. It was a horrifying sight to see them swinging from the lamp posts. They had all the women who had consorted with the Germans heads shaved and made them march at the end of the parade, the people watching the parade throwing rocks and stones at them.

I had worked in the orthopedic section, but in Italy they were so short of nurse anesthetists that they decided to train two nurses to become anesthetists. We had a major who was an anesthesiologist, and he took over the job of teaching myself and one other friend of mine. So we were doing that the last year and a half I was in service. *After VE Day, it was decided that one nurse anesthetist from each unit would be sent to Paris for a training course.* It was such a hardship for me to go to Paris and spend six weeks there that I reluctantly agreed.

JEANNE URBIN MARKLE

Vietnam War; Army Nurse Corps; Interview

Markle spent 30 days in Long Binh waiting for her hospital to open. She was assigned to post-operation duties with the soldiers who had had surgery.

We waited and waited; we were ready to go and there were no patients. We were there at war and there was no war. I can remember the first sound of the helicopters, the loudspeaker going, "We're getting an arrival, we're getting an arrival."

Their first patient was a 42-year-old sergeant who had had a heart attack. Within a week, the First Division, the Big Red One, landed 50,000 troops, and the hospital immediately started getting 25 or 30 casualties a day.

There were times when our surgeons were operating 72 hours on their feet. The surgery suite was one big Quonset building, and it had four surgery tables on each side. They were operating on eight patients at a time with eight teams. There were no walls. Today we would go, "Oh my, infection control." But then it didn't matter.

My ward had 33 beds. In those days we didn't have anything but penicillin, and we had to draw it up and shake it and add it to the IV bottles. I remember one night having to do that to 30 IV bottles, and I was the only nurse. We worked 12 hour shifts, 7-7, and we rotated. At night it was just me.

The patients were on cots, high up off the floor. We had no running water. Every morning at 4 o'clock, the corpsman would go out and set a fire under a big barrel of water and let it heat until 6 o'clock. Then we got a pitcher and dipped it into basins and put some cold water in it and started bathing the boys. If there was someone in the next bed that had one arm he could use, he got up and started bathing the boy next to him. And if one had no legs and was in a wheelchair but had arms, he would help. These were seventeen, eighteen, nineteen, twenty-year-old boys, and they were just as scared as I was. It was wonderful how they took care of each other. If it hadn't have been for them, we couldn't have got the job done.

I think one of the things that struck me the most was when we ran out of bandages and we had to use the *Stars and Stripes* newspaper until we got more dressings sent from the United States or the depot. No wounds were closed in Vietnam until seven days after the surgery. It's called delayed primary closure. Every patient coming out from surgery had packing in his wounds, no matter what they were. All wounds were dirty, so you wanted to leave them open so they wouldn't get abscesses underneath. We had to change dressings every two hours. At the end of seven days, if they didn't show any signs of infection, which they didn't because we took such good care of them, then they sent them back to surgery and the delayed primary closure. We kept them for 24 hours and if they were okay, we shipped them to Japan.

I think one of my saddest nights is [when] they brought a captain in. His helicopter had gone down. Because the Vietcong were in there, they couldn't get to him for 48 hours. We finally got down there and picked him up. In Vietnam there was a fungus—the longer you were on the ground, it would get into your lungs and cause an infection, and it causes death. They brought him in that night, and he had lost a leg. We thought he'd be all right, not knowing about this other thing. The day he got shot down, he was due to leave for Hawaii to meet his fiancée to get married. We kept him for a couple of days. [His last night] was a sad night; we coded him five times—we kept trying and trying and trying and trying—and we lost him. It was a sad moment; we had many of those sad moments.

SALLY HITCHCOCK PULLMAN
World War II; Army Nurse Corps; Memoir
Sally Hitchcock's memoir alternates correspondence to her parents back in New Hampshire (the dated material) and her own memories.
November 18, 1944
Yesterday for the first time some of us were put on temporary service at the 54th General where we were ensconced when we first came. I was put on Officers' Surgery. Most of the men were casualties from Leyte.

It has been ages since I worked and I was nervous. The nurses in charge didn't give me an assignment, so I went around to see what there was to do. One man asked me to change his dressing. I did and I relaxed. Then I took all the temps, passed out water, rubbed backs, straightened sheets, the old "P.M. Care" routine. (P.M. Care was a procedure taught early in nurses' training—a late afternoon routine to make the patients more comfortable.)

One of my memories not in a letter was of an event on that Officers' Ward where I was doing detached service. I was handing out basins for back and hand washes, and back rubs. Since this was my only assignment, I went down the left 15 beds to the end, washing, rubbing backs, and straightening sheets.

Across from the last patient on the left was a black officer. I crossed to him to do his care when his left-hand neighbor (an officer) said, "Don't touch me after you've done him!" Such terrible racial prejudice!! I was shocked. The ward was suddenly silent. I turned to him and said, "I won't!" I did special care to the black officer and skipped the offending person. I was angry. I could have made a speech but didn't. I went right up the right-hand row of beds and finished. How terribly unfair and unkind and SMALL!!

Next afternoon I had the same assignment. There were no comments from anyone and I did everyone with no comments.

December 22, 1944

Nighttime is hard for these men who are patients. They can't sleep. One-by-one they come up and talk to me if I'm not busy. They worry about their homes, the wives they have and don't know, kids they have never seen, parents who are elderly, pals they've lost. They verbalize about the horrors of the war they have been in and how scared they were and how little they want to go back.

December 25, 1944

This is quite a tale, being on duty Christmas Eve. This night I will NEVER forget. Among the officers of the 51st, there was a party going on. All the medical, nursing and day staff, many of whom had served for weeks rotating to the front in 48-hour shifts, were celebrating. I reported for my duty at 7 P.M., December 24. I went on, checked my four wards. All was quiet.

But at 7:30 P.M. came the fatal phone call:

"ALL BEDS WILL BE FILLED. HOSPITAL SHIP UNLOADING AND AMBULANCES EN ROUTE!"

I had 80 empty beds! You cannot believe how we hustled getting all units ready to receive the litter-borne men.

I rushed to list the sickest ones so the doctor would see them first. But when he finally came, he had been celebrating too long and too hard. I called my supervisor. Everyone was swamped. She could send me no more help.

"Do the best you can," she said. So I made rounds with the doctor. He was not at his best and a problem for me and for the men who were hurt, but at least I did get a blanket order for dressing changes and IVs and narcotics. Thank Yale for its training. I was able to function.

Before morning report, the ward officer doctor of the night before arrived to see his patients. He had to rewrite some of the orders he'd written the night before. He was so contrite. Nothing awful had happened to his patients, but he and they and I were very glad for a new beginning. The chief nurse congratulated me on a job well done!

Hitchcock and some of her nurse pals were transferred to the Philippines on December 26.

This was my first night on Leyte. We sloshed to chow, a memorable breakfast

*Life at Fort Harding in Baton Rouge, Louisiana, in 1942
is depicted in these photos from Rosalind Westfall Sellmer
(sixth nurse from the right in the top photo). She later
cared for men to be sent home from the European Theater.*

for me! I sat opposite a 1st lieutenant, a patient whose hand was encompassed in a huge bandage.

"Hi, where did you come from?" he asked, eyes twinkling. "We arrived last night from New Guinea," I answered. "Like bridge?" he asked. "Sure do," I said. "Name's Dan," he said. I told him mine.

January 10, 1945

During my off hours, I've been squired around by Dan, the young officer I met that first breakfast. In the evening the group plays bridge, or we sketch or write letters. Our leisure facilities are pretty limited. We have a "Rec" tent, but we sit on boxes or logs and play bridge on a box. There is a lightbulb overhead, the company is fun, and we enjoy the diversion.

January 21, 1945

To get to know all my patients and their problems, I planned to do what we had been taught to do at Yale, go to work early, and make rounds before the doctors came. So having a quick breakfast, I went off to #16 with my notebook in hand. I went up and down the wards, speaking to each patient and listening to his complaints. By the time the doctor came, I had quite a list.

At first the doctor went with me as together we made rounds. But then a few days later, when he came he began to ask for my notes, from which he wrote patient orders. This was very upsetting to me. The patients wanted to discuss their problems with the doctor.

I know I'm griping, but—we are not hitting it off at all!!

February 3, 1945

Now my ward officer and I are not doing well at all. I feel badly for the patients and for me. It's a brand-new feeling to want to fight this man—and he outranks me!!

After a lot of thought I screwed up my courage and went to my chief nurse to ask her to change my assignment.

The next day on the ward when I met the doctor, he asked me who had reported him.

"I did," I replied.

"Why?" he asked. I don't know how I dared to say what I did, but I answered.

"Sir, can you honestly say to yourself that you are giving these men the best care they deserve?"

To my surprise, I was not moved. He was.

To climax all this "to do," Captain McKay told me I was to be the head nurse on the Women's Ward.

March 9, 1945

Last Tuesday, Dan and his friends came for one last fling before they were shipped out. We all went down to one of the pillboxes by the beach (at Tacloban Harbor) and sang and talked. We were popping corn over a fire.

Suddenly they threw sand on the fire and yelled, "GET INTO THE PILLBOX!" We did in a hurry; then we heard it. A lone Jap plane came in low, dropped bombs on the big fuel dump by the harbor. Then the pilot sprayed the beach with his guns. The bullets ripped through where we had been.

Our picnic was dampened but I had a chance to walk along the beach with Dan. But this was good-bye to all of them, Dan, ER, Dunk, Daniel Boone, and Jess, guys we had met when we first hit Leyte and who became our special friends. I'd love for you to meet all of them, so fearless, humble, and yet so full of life.

Hellos and good-byes are so common here. You try to get used to them, but it is hard. These guys really adopted all five of us and their leaving hit us hard. We pray for their safety!!

In April, Pullman came down with amoebic dysentery and was hospitalized for a month.

May 20, 1945

Two days ago I went back to work. At last after too long. I was not put back on #25, my Women's Ward, but on a Men's Surgical. These guys are so young! They've only been over three or four months as replacements and are mostly eighteen and nineteen years old with some wicked wounds. One nineteen year old has an awful chest wound. We both work up a lather when I do his dressing. He calls me "Mom," I call him "Son." But he never lets out a whimper. They are so brave! I've developed a ward nickname—"Happy" or "Skip." It's good to be on surgery again.

We've become, here in the 126th, like a big family. We are all congenial, the nurses, the doctors, the special service people, all the enlisted men. We have all worked and do work so hard! This facility is actually so well cared for and well run, we're like a village.

RHONA KNOX PRESCOTT
Vietnam War; Army Nurse Corps; Interview

Those were really long days. When surgery started (it was usually brain surgery), they had no idea what they would find, and the surgical techniques weren't perfected at that time. It was kind of: Go in carefully and slowly, see what you could find, and test the areas of the brain to be sure that you could cut there without doing more damage. It was a very slow process; once we got into a skull we stayed until the work was done to the best of our ability. We had a lot of cases. We worked really long days, and scary days.

Since there were head injuries it stands to reason that there were also facial injuries. These young fellows on these litters were like Halloween masks; they just didn't even look human. It was really challenging.

One incident I remember because I was the assistant supervisor, so I was pretty much operationally in charge. The hall was filled with litters with fellows on them with decimated faces and skulls and other body parts. It was so filled that you had to kind of shimmy around to get down the hallway. One of the corpsmen just lost it. He just started screaming and crying and slid to the floor. I remember just yelling, yelling, yelling at him that he had to get himself together and go ahead and function. What I remember him saying back to me (between gasps) was that a specific litter contained a person he knew and had gone through basic training with and was in fact his buddy. It was a real moment of truth when he verbalized what he did.

I had to come to grips with the fact that what we were dealing with was absolutely impossible. The patients were really scared, and you had to deal with them and try to pass some kind of confidence on to them. In a way it was so very dishonest, but it was the thing to do to give them the best chance of recovery.

Prescott received orders to be acting chief nurse in a field hospital in the remote Central Highlands.

The hospital was a series of tents, big green tents held up by poles with stakes in the ground. The floor was a tent liner, which was just a kind of plastic and canvas material that sat on the ground that was lumpy. There was of course no air-conditioning; the tent flaps were left open. It was hot. There were a lot of helicopters flying over; their rotors pulled up a lot more of the dusty clay. There was dirt flying all the time, and it was hotter than Hades during the day and it got really cold at night.

The operating room was just one little area with these two little metal tables

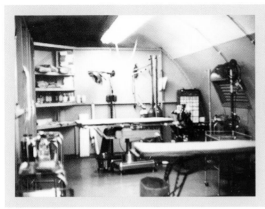

Rhona Knox Prescott's stripped-down field hospital operating room in An Khe (left). Jeanne Urbin Markle watched patients arrive at this helipad (right) at Long Binh.

and an autoclave that was akin to a pressure cooker that we might use at home for cooking. It wasn't really safe. The stuff was old. Since I was acting chief nurse, I decided that the casualties would all just go into the receiving tent where there was more room and more tables and where the doctors posted themselves. That tent became our surgery. It was beyond primitive; it was beyond the MASH movie and TV show. It was dirty; it was a non-sterile environment. We didn't have enough instruments. We didn't have enough hands. Needless to say, we shared things during surgical procedures that were absolutely needed to save lives, but they weren't sterile. We didn't have suction, we didn't have penicillin to irrigate wounds, and we didn't have enough blood to transfuse.

We did have so many casualties right out of the field. They just brought them all in there. The First Cav put their people in that staging unit, hoping that we could fix them and send them back into the war. So, we were way over our heads. We had kids right out of medical school; it was not a posh assignment. It was where nobody else wanted to go, but it was where the greatest need was. Everybody was fresh. Everybody was open to anything in terms of staff. We did improvise, and it was amazing what we were able to do with mayonnaise jars from the mess hall, rubber tubing from wherever, and plastic from here, there, and the next place that we got recycled and built into things like suction machines. We just divided up what intravenous fluids we had and what blood we had and spread it around as best we could.

When we were busy (which was most of the time) we had to somehow block out the smells and the sounds. The smells were of dirty, putrefied flesh and blood. There were insects and there was dust and other organic material that didn't smell good in the area. The sounds were of people crying and screaming and praying, and then there were people on our own staff who were also pretty flustered and muttering back and forth. The sounds were chaotic. The only way to function was to somehow block those things from sensory perception or you couldn't go on. So that is what we did, and I don't know how we did it. I guess there is some innate gift in all of us. I really think it was the hand of God there.

Home was up the hill. We had wooden buildings that you could live in that were a little better than tents. We had cots to sleep on that were at least off the floor, which is more than I can say for the patients, because many of them wound up on the tent floor; there weren't enough cots for them. I don't remember much about being off duty. I think the shower stands out in my mind more than anything, because we were covered with blood and human waste and perspiration from ourselves. There was one shower; it was outside and there was a little tent around it and it was open to the air above. It was a big old water bag. They filled it with water every day. It was heated up by the heat of the sun, so that was good; it was warm water. You just had to run down to the latrine with your towel around you and get your shower quick. You were not to waste water; there were others coming. Some of the fly-boys thought it was comical to fly overhead while we were showering. They got a big giggle, and sometimes we were worried about what might be open to view. The water was so welcome it didn't really matter. That was the highlight of "home," as you say.

Eleanor [Eleanor Grace Alexander] was there when I got there. She was also a captain and so we were more or less on the same level and we became friends. We also took turns covering the operating room, because the person who was really in charge (a major) for one reason or another just didn't seem to be there very much. Whenever the "pushes" came in (which means the mass casualties that would come in by the carload and by the planeload, literally), it was either Eleanor or I who ran it because the major just couldn't be found. We co-supervised that operating room. There was a battle gearing up, one of the battles that turned out to be the beginning of that infamous Tet Offensive of 1968. I was the nurse on that team; there was an anesthetist and two corpsmen. Eleanor wanted to be the nurse on the team, but they chose me because I had the experience.

We had been through a day of heavy casualties in our operating room. Eleanor was off; I was on. I was doing triage and a lot of other things. The day had ended; the casualties were treated. I had gone over to the officers' club to get a beer. I was beat. In that five or ten minutes, the call came. I wasn't in my quarters. Eleanor was close by; my roommate went and got her, and [Eleanor] took my gear (which included my jacket with my name on it), and since time was of the essence she got on the helicopter with the chosen anesthetist and the correct corpsmen, and she went to the duty station at another hospital in my place.

About four weeks later the casualties were under control. She and the team were coming back, and the plane didn't make it. It did indeed crash into a mountain in heavy rain. There is a question as to whether it was shot down (because there were bullet holes found in the fuselage). They were all killed. We don't know if it was immediate, because nobody could get to them for three days, but Eleanor (probably wearing my jacket) died that day, and I lived.

I got the news very soon after the plane was declared missing. Ironically, I had been visiting (unauthorized) a boyfriend of mine back in An Khe, which wasn't too far from where this team was sent, to Pleiku. I was in a plane, without my name on the manifest, coming back to Qui Nhon at about the same time that the team was coming back from Pleiku, unbeknownst to me. I was in the very same model plane, within minutes of hers, in the same flight pattern as she was. My plane landed, her plane (right ahead of us) went down. When we landed, there was talk that a plane was missing. I didn't know at that time it was hers, but when I kind of snuck back in, it was learned that the whole team was missing and the plane was down. So I put two and two together and it didn't take too long to figure it out.

MARGARET (PEGGY) HENRY FLEMING
World War II; Red Cross; Memoir
Fleming's two brothers were serving in the Armed Forces in infantry divisions. "Going overseas as a recreation worker with the American Red Cross seemed like a logical way for me to participate in the war effort." *She worked at the Red Cross club in Reading, Berkshire, England, but transferred to the clubmobile group as D-Day approached. This transfer landed her on the Continent.*

Clubmobile Group F, to which I was assigned, landed on Utah Beach on July 28. We were attached to VIII Corps Rear Headquarters but assigned to a particular division. Thus, we worked our way across Normandy and were in Brittany until the fall of Brest. Another Red Cross girl and I had a day off about this time, so we decided to go to Brest. When the MPs tried to wave us down, we just waved merrily back and kept on going. We were aghast at the condition of Brest, for you couldn't even figure out where streets existed. We were even more interested in observing the truckloads of captured German officers wearing their best uniforms, even after time spent in the bunkers during the siege. We were really indignant that they waved to us!

Eventually, we moved to Bastogne, Belgium. In addition to Group F Clubmobiles, we had a number of supply trucks, one of which I drove for a short while.

My clubmobile was assigned to the 8th Division in Wiltz, Luxembourg, and three of us in the Red Cross visited the different units within this division with our coffee, doughnuts, and American chatter. At this point we were certainly among the most popular women in Europe. The 8th Division had recently captured a huge supply of cognac—much more than it could possibly move. Distribution was according to rank. Somehow we girls were each issued a colonel's ration—12 bottles—and as soon as the newly arrived 28th Division officers got wind of this, most of them dropped by to "get acquainted!"

Coming as it did from the costly action in the Hurtgen Forest, the 28th Division, with over 6,000 casualties, was ready for the quiet of the Ardennes. A large divisional rest center was established in the charming Old World town of Clervaux, Luxembourg.

I lived in the hotel whose name in my scrapbook is recorded as Hotel Bertemis. The same picture shows several buildings just down the street from the hotel, one of which was converted into a Red Cross Club. It had formerly been a bar, or possibly a small restaurant. I had two local girls as helpers and we tried to create a pleasant place for the GIs to hang around and eat a reasonable facsimile of American snack food. We also provided what entertainment we could under the circumstances. My most vivid recollection of this club was that I always returned to the hotel when I wanted to use the restroom because, in quaint European fashion, I would have had to pass through the men's section of the club's restroom before I reached the women's area.

Clervaux was less than five miles from the enemy lines and strategically located between Prum, Germany, and Bastogne, Belgium. VIII Corps was responsible for the weakest sector on the Western Front at this time and consisted of divisions that were either recuperating or untried. Twenty-four miles of this front were thinly under the control of the 28th Division. It was mountainous, wooded, and by now—in mid-December—snowy terrain. It hardly seemed like a good prospect for a major German offensive.

On December 16 around 5:30 A.M. we were all awakened by the sounds of

Doughnuts were a staple of World War II-era Red Cross aid. A soldier in Naples, Italy, grabs a bite in 1944 (top), while the caption on the photo above reads, "Not German issue, but good old Red Cross ones!"

shellfire. After a few hours the shelling stopped and I guess we hoped that somehow the attack had "blown over." At least, that's what I hoped. I reopened the Red Cross Club, although many of the men were being quickly assigned other duties than "resting." I placed a big, brave sign in the window to the effect, "Of course we're open!" The men who came in kidded me about earning a combat infantry badge the hard way. But that afternoon the shelling began again and became progressively worse.

Although we had no idea that we were in on the start of a major battle of World War II, the Battle of the Bulge, we did realize what a serious situation we found ourselves in the midst of. We got word that reinforcements were on the way, but would probably not reach us in time. We could hear small arms fire and knew that German tanks were on the outskirts of town. We went to the basement to try to hold out as long as we could. Soldiers were stationed at the bottom of the stairway, prepared to shoot if and when German soldiers appeared.

I was told to remove the 28th Division patch I was wearing, leaving only my Red Cross insignia, so that my civilian status might conceivably be in my favor if I were captured. As I'm sure many soldiers have done, I gave my parents' address to the two local girls and asked them to write to my folks if I didn't make it.

How did I feel through all this? Scared to death, naturally—but equally determined not to let the men know how frightened I really was. Since then I've suspected that much bravery is enhanced by the knowledge that others are watching to see how you <u>do</u> react!

It was decided to try to get me out of Clervaux, even at this stage. Eight of us (including the two local girls who were felt to be in jeopardy for having worked with the Americans) started out of the hotel with the idea of trying to reach the abbey high on the hill. The main street had to be crossed under fire. Lt. Col. Trapani went first to see if it was even possible to get across, although none of us really expected him to make it. He went fast, firing as he ran. I was next, then the rest of our little group—one by one—between bursts of tank fire from down the street. Miraculously, we all made it across. Lights were flashed on us, and we would all freeze, trying to fade into the stone walls we were passing. I was also worried because the two officers were trying to shield me, thereby endangering their own lives even more.

Once a shot came whizzing by very close and I instinctively hit the ground, whereupon the men thought I'd been hit and started to carry me. I was able to convince them in whispers that I was all right.

After roughly half an hour, we reached the abbey. Hurriedly whispering thanks to our escorts, the two girls and I climbed into one of the artillery trucks and rode with this battery back toward Bastogne. The roads were constantly under attack. Whenever things would get too hot, we'd all climb out and hit the ditch. By the morning of the 17th of December, we'd reached the outskirts of Bastogne. That night I slept in my clothes on a table in the mess hall, and we left early in the morning to drive toward Charleville, France. We spent ten miserable days there in a freezing cold barracks; then we were near Reims in a chateau for two weeks. Christmas dinner that year was cold C-ration hash, bread, and coffee.

I was sent back to Paris to be re-outfitted, as I'd lost everything except the clothes I was wearing. While in Paris, I was interviewed by one of the top newsmen in Europe, Joseph Kingsbury Smith of INS. Incidentally, after my interview was completed, he took me out for dinner.

The Columbus *Dispatch* [her hometown newspaper] carried this story on the front page around the first of January 1945, during a terrible central Ohio blizzard that had stopped mail and newspaper delivery in the county. My parents were quite puzzled when they started getting calls from friends and neighbors saying, "Don't worry about Margaret. She's all right!"

{ ONE FAMILY'S STORY }

The Stilsons

"Keep Warren out of the military as long as possible."

The more members a family sends off to war, the more likely that one will not return. Frederick Stilson and his two sons, Malcolm and Warren, served their country proudly in two wars. Frederick and Malcolm were the lucky ones; though they were shipped overseas, they never fired a weapon and were rarely in harm's

way. Warren, Malcolm's younger brother, served in the infantry and was killed in action leading up to the Battle of the Bulge.

When the U.S. entered World War I in April 1917, Frederick Stilson was living in Illinois, working for the Interstate Commerce Commission. He enlisted in the Army and got an officer's commission in the Engineer Corps. On August 15, while still in training, he was given leave to marry his sweetheart, Essie. Frederick and 4,000 men set sail for France on January 21, 1918.

"On the trip over," he wrote in his memoir, *That Other War*, "I had to serve as officer of the day a couple of times. I found a bunch of the men and some of the sailors in a crap game down in the hold near the stern of the ship. I asked them what they were doing and they said, 'Oh, we got a little game going.' It was against orders, but I turned my back on them and just said, 'Well, have fun.'"

That incident set the tone for Frederick's service in France. He was a tough officer when the situation demanded it, but he also cut his men slack when he thought it made sense. In France, Frederick Stilson and his crews found themselves not just repairing but actually rebuilding some of the rail lines. It was

MALCOLM AND FREDERICK STILSON

WARREN STILSON

demanding work but, as Frederick often reminded himself, not nearly as hazardous as duty in the trenches.

One afternoon he made a reconnaissance trip, using a map that didn't accurately chart the current German position. Only later did he realize that he had come within 600 yards of the lines. "It was late afternoon, bright sunlight, and I guess all were asleep on the other side or a sniper bullet would have winged me easily." Brushes with danger hardly dominate Frederick's memoir. He describes a "musical extravaganza" that he and his men staged in Brevannes, titled "Lost in the Trenches." In the program printed up for the occasion, Lt. F.C. Stilson is credited as General Manager, his nickname "Everyone's Friend."

As the war continued, morale began to disintegrate. One night, after "Taps," two soldiers returned to the barracks "lit to the gills," and a fight broke out. "The next morning I held court in the office. The liquor had worn off, and one of the drunks said he wanted out of this so and so company. I told him he was in it for the rest of the war, whether he liked it or not." Frederick confined the two to quarters for a week. "When we parted in June of 1919 in Camp Devens, Massachusetts," he wrote, "They thanked me for my consideration, as I could have had them court-martialed and set to prison for disobedience of orders in time of war."

After World War I, Frederick and Essie moved to southern California, where their first son, Malcolm, was born in Los Angeles in 1923. Mac was a freshman at UCLA when the Japanese attacked Pearl Harbor and, as detailed in Chapter One, wound up volunteering for the draft in December 1942.

Assigned to become an Army radio operator, Mac wrote in his memoir, "I constantly wished that I had had good eyes, so that I could be in a combat unit instead of in radio." He continued, "I also thought I would never get overseas, which I greatly wanted to do." For two years, Mac was denied his wish. Meanwhile, his brother Warren, two years younger, graduated from high school in June 1943. Mac was full of advice for Warren, at first telling him of the "wonderful possibilities for you in the Air Corps," then writing, "I thought he should go into the army while his schooling was still fresh in his mind," and finally writing in a letter to Frederick and Essie, "keep Warren out of the military as long as possible."

Mac's first memoir reflects his own frustrations, as he is reclassified to be a clerk and then a motor pool dispatcher. A fairly skilled piano player, he finds an outlet for his energies by jamming with fellow GI musicians. Disheartened at his inability to make any kind of progress within the army, he admits, "The bitter truth lay in the fact that the only thing I had learned since I entered the army was to 'goldbrick,'" the popular GI term for shirking work through creative means.

In the fall of 1943, Warren entered the Army Specialized Training Program at Montana State College in Bozeman. The following spring found him in at Fort Benning, Georgia, undergoing combat training. On his way there from Montana, his train passed Kelly Field in San Antonio, Texas, where Mac was posted. On April 28, 1944, Mac wrote his brother a letter about their future:

"Brother mine, when we get back together again, I think we will be a lot closer than we ever have before. When I was younger, I made a mistake in not teaming up with you more often. When we get out of the army I suggest that we go to school together. Rocket engineering will be our goal. What the Wright Brothers did to the airplane, so shall the Stilson Brothers do to the rocketship. After all, why not?"

Six weeks later, Frederick wrote to his younger son:

"I have read your letter of your experiences with a great deal of interest. We certainly didn't get much training in our war. They gave us a lick and a promise and sent us overseas into battle, and I will never forget my first night at the front. The firing was heavy, and we had to stand all night….Try hard but don't take foolish chances. Above all, don't ride a horse out in plain sight of the enemy on a bright moonlit night, as I did once and got the scare of my life."

Warren shipped out to Europe in September 1944. A month later, Malcolm got the word he had been waiting for: "Tonight we were notified that we had been alerted as a group for overseas shipment. The Captain announced that the date will be January 1, 1945, so the next furlough will be the last for at least two years or more."

Warren wrote several letters to his parents from France. On December 8, 1944, he told them about his girlfriend back home: "I would kind of like you folks to let Laura in on this letter of my intentions if she or you call up or go visiting. She is definitely in my future too. I hope you are finding her the kind of girl that you want me to associate with, because I love that gal." His last letter was dated December 9. Frederick wrote him on December 14th, but that letter was returned, along with Warren's personal effects. December 14th was the day Warren Stilson was reported missing in action.

Warren's best buddy, Rodger Gardner of St. Paul, Minnesota, was wounded in the same fight and wrote his parents in December 1944: "Only one thing makes me feel bad and that is that my best buddy I ever had (I can't mention his name) is gone." The *Los Angeles Times* reported in a story in January that Warren was missing in action, and the War Department continued to issue official correspondence to the family to that effect. But in March 1945, Rodger, writing to Frederick and Essie Stilson from England, confirmed Warren's death. Frederick kept after the War Department to back up Rodger's story, but it wasn't until September 26, in a telegram, that the government would do so.

At that point, Malcolm had been overseas for nine months, but he was hardly in harm's way. In his second memoir, *Thik Hai, Sahib*, he describes his 12 months in India (from March 1945 to March 1946), about half of it spent with a Special Services unit of entertainers, all GIs, who traveled from camp to camp, offering songs, snappy patter, and relief from the rigors of war and the boredom of the post-war months. Among his fellow troupers were Andrew Duggan, who later carved out a career as a character actor, largely on television, and Peter Gennaro, who became a respected Hollywood choreographer. Mac Stilson was the troupe's pianist.

There is a tender moment after Mac and his colleagues have visited the Taj Mahal in the spring of 1945. "It is after the show on the next night that I cry for the first time in my army career over the fate of my brother, Warren. He was listed as missing in action just before the Battle of the Bulge near Bitche, France. He had just celebrated his 19th birthday in November in the cold and snow of the battlefield. I didn't know that he was dead, but during the play I went behind stage and squeezed out as many tears as I could. I was all choked with sympathy for myself."

The war ended in August, but the players played on for another month before disbanding. "That night," wrote Mac, "after the show, with an intimation that our tour was coming to an early end due to the fact that several of our group had enough service points to go back to the U.S. soon, we gather together in our tent and over a bottle of whiskey discuss our futures." As the bottle is passed around, Mac announces, "I know one thing I won't be in ten years." To the unanimous chorus of "What?" he replies, "The world's greatest pianist."

{ CHAPTER FIVE }

World War II Home Front

Clare Marie Morrison and Herbert Johns on their wedding day, May 29, 1943, in Cleveland, Ohio. Clare worked at one of Cleveland's USO clubs while Herbert served in Europe.

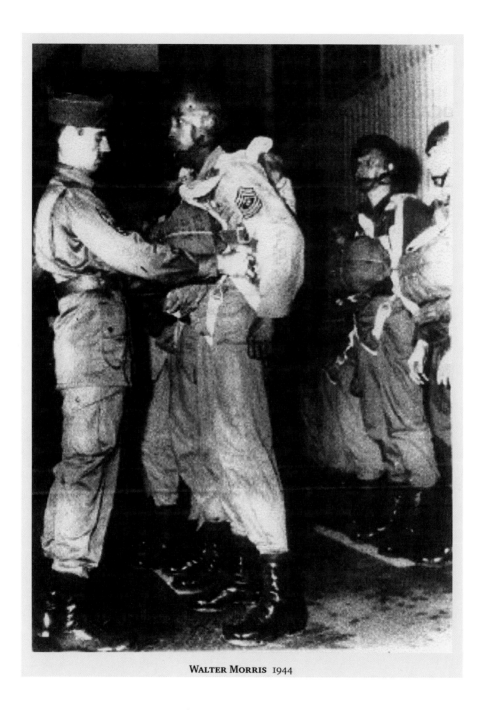

WALTER MORRIS 1944

Morris was stationed at Ft. Benning, Georgia, when he became sergeant of the 555, the Triple Nickels, the first all-black paratroop unit. This photo was taken after his first jump. The unit never saw combat but nonetheless served in a unique capacity.

The Soldiers

*"We were let down—we really thought
we were going to fight the enemy."*

*What could be more frustrating to a soldier, trained and primed to confront the
enemy, than to be left waiting for the call that never comes? Walter Morris, a paratrooper who played an important role in integrating the Army, and Irving Oblas, a
sailor stuck for two years at a training station in western New York, eloquently
describe these feelings. Marie Voltzke had a different experience. Confined for long
hours to a wartime office in Washington, D.C., this young WAVE from a small town
in West Virginia got a liberal education in big city life during her leave hours.*

WALTER MORRIS
World War II; Army; Interview
*Unable to find work as an apprentice bricklayer in his native Georgia, Morris enlist-
ed in the Army in January 1941. He was assigned to be a clerk to interview inductees
and held that position for two years; then he applied for Officer Candidate School.
Twelve weeks into the 13-week course, he was told that he wasn't going to make it,
but that he could reapply in three months. He was given his choice of assignments at
Fort Benning. On the list was an all-black service company at the base's parachute
school.*

Our sole function as a service company was to do guard duty for the parachute school and its properties. Every day at 4 o'clock in the afternoon, when the
white students would go back to their barracks, we would assume our duties and
do guard duty until 8 o'clock in the morning.

Having just left Officer Candidate School, I thought I had the know-how
to run a company, and I saw so many things that were lacking in the

supervisory position of this company, mainly because it was a post for white officers who had washed out of the parachute school. They were assigned as company commander until they could be reassigned. The company commander spent more time in the officers' club than he did at the headquarters of the service company.

The company had the wrong people at the wrong positions. So one day I made out a table of organization, and I had myself as the first sergeant. I presented it to the company commander and he said, "If this is what you want, I'll go along with it." And so the following morning I was first sergeant and I had all my men rearranged.

We were billeted next to the calisthenics field, and every day the white students would go through their training and every day we watched them. It occurred to me that if I could get my men to go through that same routine, it might inspire them. So one day at 4 o'clock the white students left the field, and I gathered all of my men with the help of the NCOs. They worked on exercises, including the fluid roll, a way of hitting the ground and dispersing the shock to your body. An amazing thing happened; after about a week or two of that regimen, I could notice a distinct improvement in their appearance; when you talked to them, they looked you straight in the eye. They started acting like soldiers instead of servants.

One day during our exercises, the general in charge of the parachute school drove by. He saw about fifty colored soldiers running up and down, shouting. He told his chauffeur to stop and he observed us for a while. We had no idea he was there. He went back to his office and told his aide, "Get a hold of that black officer and have him in my office tomorrow morning at nine o'clock."

The next morning, the general listened as I explained what was going on in the field and then said, "Now let me tell you a secret, Morris. In a few weeks, the Army is going to direct me to activate a 555 parachute company, all colored, officers and enlisted men. Would you like to be the first sergeant of that company?" When I left his office and went back to my office, I have to this day no idea how I got back. My head was in the clouds—I might have flown back, I might have taken wings.

In December of 1943 orders came from the adjutant general in Washington, D.C., activating the 555 Parachute Company and Walter Morris as First Sergeant of that company.

I must say that the reason for this was not that I agitated the adjutant general to activate the 555; it was the lobbying of Brig. Gen. Benjamin Davis. He was the only colored general in the Army. He had lobbied President Roosevelt to activate a colored parachute outfit. There were three other men lobbying, too, for more colored participation in the war effort. A. Philip Randolph, Bayard Rustin, and the president of the NAACP, Roy Wilkins, went to President Roosevelt in 1941 and promised that if the colored people didn't have some relief, there would be a march on Washington. That was one thing President Roosevelt didn't need; this was prior to Pearl Harbor, and the defense plants were gearing up and making matériel for the British people who were actually in war. Now, this march on Washington actually came true 22 years later, by the same three men.

The Army then selected 17 soldiers from the 92nd Infantry Division stationed in Arizona, plus Morris and two of his men from the service company.

The instructor was a volunteer, because most of the soldiers did not want to be associated with us. We as colored soldiers in 1941 and 1942 in Fort Benning, Georgia, could not go into the main post exchange or theater. But when we passed the main post exchange and we could look in, we could see the German and Italian prisoners of war sitting down at the same table with the white soldiers, drinking Cokes and smoking. So it's understandable how colored soldiers would have an inferiority complex: "There must be something wrong with us. We're in uniform, but we're not good enough to sit at the table with the prisoners of war!"

We had so many colored people volunteering, this company was expanding so fast that General Gaither called me to his office—he was serving as my godfather—and said, "Morris, I want you to go back to OCS, because this is going to be a battalion—it's too big for a company—and they're gonna need more officers."

Morris went back to OCS and graduated. Meanwhile, the 555th Battalion moved from Benning to Fort McCall in North Carolina. Morris was sent to Fort Sam Houston in San Antonio for further training. The Army pulled some men out of the 555th and trained them to participate in combat, but the war in Europe ended before they could be shipped out, so the assumption was that they would go to the Pacific Theater.

Sure enough, one day orders came ordering us to Pendleton, Oregon. And we said, "Well, this is it. We're on our way to the Pacific." Little did we know that the Forest Service arm of the Agriculture Department was having difficulty fighting forest fires. Some were started by campers not putting out their fires, some were caused by lightning, and some were caused by Japanese incendiary balloons that floated over from Japan across the Pacific and landed in the Pacific Northwest. That was a well-kept secret because the Army did not want the public or the Japanese to know how effective those balloons were. We were sent to Pendleton as part of Operation Firefly; that was the code name for smoke jumper. We had no idea what smoke jumping was; we'd never heard of it. We were let down—we really thought we were going to fight the enemy. Here we were going to learn to jump out of a plane and land in trees, which we were taught not to do, and fight a forest fire with picks and shovels.

No one had told Morris or his commander about the assignment, even after they left by train for Oregon.

When we got up in the mountains, on our way down to Pendleton, we stopped for refueling. I asked the battalion commander if I could go across the railroad track because I saw a general store. When I walked into this general store there were the white loggers sitting around an old pot-bellied stove. Some were whittling, and when they looked up and saw us, they said, "Well, you got here at last!" And I said, "You were expecting us?" And they said, "Oh yeah, you colored soldiers, you paratroopers, are gonna fight forest fires. You're gonna be smoke jumpers." And I said, "How did you know?" And they said, "Well, we read it in the *New York Times*." My battalion commander had never heard of it, so when I got back to the train he scoffed at it.

We used a special chute designed for smoke jumpers that allowed the jumper to maneuver more easily. They had LDRs, Let Down Ropes, to get from the top of the trees to the ground. By the way, that was how we lost the only casualty in the ranks. He was coming down one of those tall pines, about 100 feet tall, and he slipped and fell. We had over 33 fires that we jumped on, and we had over 1,200 individual jumps.

One of the fires I went on was up at Mount Baker, Washington. I had one officer under me and 24 men. This was a big, big fire. We jumped on the fire and we landed. Our equipment was maybe 50 yards beyond where we landed, but the underbrush was so thick we couldn't even get to it. Because the equipment chutes are either yellow or red, we could see our rations and gear and we couldn't get to it. It turned out the good Lord had it rain. It rained all that day, all that night, and we had no tents, so we sat around in a circle, and I had one of our men who was very good at telling jokes entertain us. That's how we got through the night.

The next morning the Forest Service people came up with their mule packs and brought food. The Forest Service being a part of the Department of Agriculture, they had hams and good food, so once they got up we were well fed. The leader of the group asked me if I wanted to retrieve the chutes, and I said yes. He knew of a route to get the chutes, so I went with him and went up and

Marie Brand Voltzke 1945

Marie Brand came to Washington, D.C., from West Virginia to serve in the WAVES. She performed clerical duties and during her off-hours explored the capital.

around and passed a cabin. He said, "I'll bet this is where your chutes are. So we knocked, and a logger came to the door and said, "Come on in, fellas." And we walked in and his cabin was lined with our chutes. The Forest Service guy said, "Morris, do you want to get those chutes?" I thought, for two or three chutes, is it worth antagonizing these people? We might be up here again and need them. I said, "Let him keep the chutes."

For the first five jumps the student is to pack his own chute. That gives him confidence in the jump. It's a wonderful feeling when you jump out of a plane—once the chute opens. Looking down, the whole planet is yours. We had a fine group of men, and they were all focused on the same thing: proving to the world that colored troops were no different than white troops. If you had it, you had it, whether you were black, white, blue, or green.

MARIE BRAND VOLTZKE
World War II; WAVES; Interview
Voltzke enlisted in the WAVES in the early days of World War II and was posted in Washington, D.C., doing clerical work at the Naval Communications Annex.

Checking in for duty, we were given a battery of tests. We sat in pews, no desks or student chairs, in the small chapel located on the Naval Base at the Annex. According to our aptitude, we were assigned to our work section. We were sworn to secrecy, given ID badges to wear at all times on duty, and advised we would be shot if we disclosed our section or the nature of our work. Marine guards checked us in and out. In the meantime, I heard from home that a naval officer had been to my hometown, checking with neighbors, friends, teachers, and employers regarding my character.

My first work assignment was to a room where we sat around a large table and added numbers. We were told what to do but not why or the ultimate results. Our work was logged in on a time clock by a carrier. It was taken out the same way. All scrap paper went into "burn bags." A detailed record was kept of the bags. A misplaced or mismarked bag was a serious infraction.

The job was far from exciting. Another room in our building was dubbed "the little chit house." Intermittently, a WAVE was sent to this room. If her performance was not satisfactory, she returned. I dreaded the day I was sent. Fortunately, I was allowed to remain. In the beginning there was only one other WAVE and our officer, Lt. Theriault. The section grew to an additional officer, more WAVEs, two sailors, and two civilian workers, a man and wife. The number on all shifts was the same, but the combinations varied. The work procedure was the same, but I assumed more difficult. Work that met a certain pattern went in one basket, otherwise into another basket.

In all my time in the service, Lt. Theriault was my favorite officer. On a midnight shift, I took work to him that did not follow the usual pattern. He became excited, and the commanding officer, who was off duty, was called in.

In a few days I was called to go to the Naval Department to receive a commendation. At that time I was a second class petty officer. My reward was that the time between second class and first class petty officer was waived. However, I was required to take the regular first class exam. On February 19, 1944, I received a memo from Lt. (j.g.) Pond, an officer from administration at the barracks, congratulating me on my promotion to Sp. Q first class, stating I was first in the entire Annex. Our classification in the meantime had been changed to a new rating of Specialist Q. Consequently, I became the first Chief Sp. Q on the station. My friends bought my chief's hat, emblem, and patches. All awaited to take my picture the next morning as I exited the barracks.

Arriving at work a few days later, both civilian workers were gone. We were never told the reason. I often wondered if they were spies.

To this day, I've never been enlightened as to what I accomplished or the results of our work in the Pacific Theater. I've never been notified of a reunion or if our work had been declassified.

News from Home

Like millions of other wives during World War II, Marion Gurfein kept in frequent touch with her husband Joe, who served in Africa and Europe. But unlike her fellow correspondents, Marion Gurfein was the publisher of a newspaper. It was called "The Goofein Journal," a monthly with a modest circulation of one copy. In April 1943, Joe shipped out to Europe, leaving behind a wife who would soon learn she was pregnant with their first child. Marion moved in to an apartment in the Bronx with her mother and two sisters. To cheer up Joe and herself, she began to write and design a mini-newspaper on two sides of a small piece of artist's board. She handwrote all the stories—tales of family events and wide-eyed accounts of Joe's exploits—and a photograph or two to remind Joe of how quickly their daughter Marjorie was growing up. Marion also made cards for special occasions—or just any occasion when the mood suited her. Joe kept every "Goofein Journal" and every card, bringing them home to an astonished Marion and their two-year-old Marjorie in 1945.

Marion Gurfein and her daughter Marjorie, circa 1944 (top). Marion used family photos as news pictures for "The Goofein Journal." Some of the cards that Marion created to keep up her husband's morale are pictured on this page and opposite.

"The Goofein Journal" typically contained one story about Joe's exploits and one about the progress Marjorie was making. A "personal ad" placed in one issue read: Mrs. Marion Gurfein requests the Captain to please end the war and come home where he belongs!

The Goofein Journal was about to cease publication when the May 1945 issue (above) came out. But in August 1950, with Joe headed off to Korea, America's smallest circulation newspaper was back in business. The November 1951 issue (below) did prove to be the final one.

Clare Marie Johns
SIGNATURE OF BEARER

PHOTOGRAPH   RIGHT THUMB PRINT
Wife of 2nd Lt. H.G.   61st Bomb Sq

AGE 22 SEX F HEIGHT 5-4 WEIGHT 110

COLOR HAIR Brown COLOR EYES Brown

DRIVER'S LICENSE (STATE) None

SOCIAL SECURITY NO. None

CLARE MORRISON CRANE 1943

When her husband Herbert Johns was stationed at Davis Monthan Air Base in Tucson, Arizona, Clare Johns carried this identification card. Before she received the card, she tried to get on the base and was taken into custody by vigilant military police.

The Wives

"There were a lot of girls who were engaged and getting married.
The time was right for them."

Romance that blossoms in wartime can yield a lifetime of memories or the deepest sor-
row. For any couple separated by the obligation to serve, communication is often the
sole nurturing element. Clare and Herbert Johns were married five months before the
war took him to England, while Marion and Joe Gurfein had less than two years
together before Joe left his pregnant wife for North Africa. The women's memories of
the home front—in Gurfein's words, "an all-woman society"—are complemented by
their devotion to the men whose return they prayed for constantly.

CLARE MARIE MORRISON CRANE
   World War II; USO; Interview, Letters
At the time that we are talking about, my name was Clare Marie Johns. My
maiden name was Clare Marie Morrison. I had it for 21 years. I was born in
Cleveland and raised on the West Side.

   I went to Notre Dame College for Women. I have a bachelor of arts degree
in fine arts and economics. I was in my junior year of college, and our dean of
women asked me to participate in the USO program. It was early '42.

   I had two brothers that were going into the service and my fiancé was in the
service and I had a lot of friends who were going into the service. As a matter of
fact, in our recreation room, I had a huge map of the United States, also the
Pacific area and the European area, and I would put little pin points wherever I
knew a serviceman.

   Our dean of women asked me to go to the USO and look out for our girls
who were going to serve as hostesses. They picked me because I was engaged.

They did not want any of the girls falling for men in uniform. It was called "khaki wacky."

We served food, mostly doughnuts, coffee, sandwiches, and whatever pies and cakes people would bring in. We had an area where you could sing around the piano, or dance, or play records. There was an area where the servicemen could go to rest, and wash up, and in the meantime we would press their blouses or middies.

We had a job because of the Port of Cleveland. Whenever Navy personnel came in, they would have the name of their ship on their headband, and it was thought that this was not a good idea that everyone would know what ships were in port. So we would rip the headband off and just throw it into the waste-basket and put on a headband ribbon that merely said, "U.S. Navy." I wish now I had kept some of the ribbons. What a memento that would be.

Our USO was the main one, located about three blocks from Public Square. We did have a USO in the Terminal Tower Building, but that was mostly for the servicemen who were waiting after hours for their trains to go out.

We would go in around 7:30 in the evening and stay until 11:30. There was to be no dating of service people. Sometimes we would come out, and they would be waiting for us. We would walk them to the square and show them where they could get shelter in the Terminal USO, and then my girlfriend's father would pick us up and take us home.

There was a time when my younger brother was a patient at Crile Hospital in Parma, Ohio. For 16 weeks, I went out and visited with him and with the other people who were being treated. And sometimes I would even talk with the prisoners of war. When they had some free time, they could use the gym or use the swimming pool. I would talk in German to these prisoners of war. They were nice young people, so far from home and lonely.

The home front was very active. We had victory gardens, which supplied us some nice things because there was a rationing of food and gasoline and other things like leathers and metals. A lot of the older men in the neighborhood became air raid wardens and we would have practices. My grandfather was a German immigrant who served through two wars. He was seventy-five years old and was called into his shop. He was a machinist by trade, and he knew the machine tool industry. So as the different shops converted to do Army work, he was called back in for his expertise to set up new machines.

All the service members, when they came back to Cleveland, would want to visit "Old Dutch." My grandfather came from a place in Germany that was on the Holland border, and they had many cultural ways of the Dutch people. As a matter of fact, in my grandparents' garden they wore their wooden shoes like rubbers. They had a regular open house on Sunday night for any service people.

I graduated on May 23, 1943, and the following Saturday, May 29, I was married to Herbert G. Johns. He was a graduate of Case School of Applied Sciences and Western Reserve University. He went into the Army as a communications officer, doing mostly radio work.

The wedding was completely unplanned. There were a lot of girls who were engaged and getting married. The time was right for them. Since my mother had a dress shop, it was not a problem to get a wedding dress. Not the one I probably would have picked, but there it was and I could use it. I just called up my girlfriends and told them, "Just wear one of your petty semi-formal dresses." They had different colors. We had one girl in yellow, one in aqua, and one in peach, and I was in white, or course. It was a beautiful wedding and in a brand-new church. Our parish had built a new church, and the first wedding was supposed to be in June. But I sort of sneaked in and had my wedding at the end of May. So I was the first bride in the new church.

We left from Cleveland Terminal and went to Chicago. It was beastly hot that Decoration Day Weekend. We started to travel west on an old steam train called *The Challenger*. It took us four days to travel west, and we finally ended up at Salt Lake City, Utah.

During our travels to Salt Lake City and then Tucson, I was the person who had to go out and find the quarters for us to live in. My husband, all he had to do was go to base and check into the bachelors' quarters, so he had shelter and food, but I had to make the arrangements to find a room.

When I was in Salt Lake City, most of the townspeople were Mormons, and they'd ask me, "Are you a Mormon?" and I'd say, "No." Then they dismissed me right away. I caught on to it, and when they'd ask me if I was a saint, I would say, "No, I'm not a saint, but my husband is."

When we traveled down to Tucson, Arizona, we were to be stationed at Davis Monthan Air Base. There was a big influx of people into Tucson. There was a big Navy contingent at the University of Arizona and loads of airmen at the Davis Monthan Airfield. They had only three constables in the town, so the whole police force was just Military Police—the town was under martial law. I know I probably pulled a big boner, but trying to get near the air base, I got on this bus. I was going towards the air base and I imagined that I would see a sign, "Welcome to Tucson, we have a room for you," but this did not happen. We were pulling onto the base, and the MPs were coming on the bus to check passes. But I

Victory garden of Anton Herman Walters, a family friend of Clare Morrison, was typical of home front gardeners who offset grocery store shortages of fresh vegetables with their own produce.

didn't have a pass! So the provost marshall came in a jeep and hauled me away to some type of military establishment. I told him that my husband was there on the base and that he was going to bring me over to introduce me in a couple of days. So I told him my name. A few minutes later, a lieutenant came in and said, "I never saw this woman before in my life!" and here it was a Lieutenant Johnson instead of Lieutenant Johns. But I did get photographed and fingerprinted and did get my pass.

I had a little job. During my high school and college years, I worked in a dress shop, so I found employment in a dress shop where I lived. I could even walk to the dress shop, which was at Broadway and Country Club Road. It was interesting because we had a lot of starlets from Hollywood. They would make motion pictures right behind the little shopping area near the dress shop where I worked. The movies, which were Westerns, would be filmed out in the desert.

And they would come in to buy their handbags and lingerie and jewelry. And, of course, when the servicemen were paid, they'd come in to buy gifts for their mothers and friends.

We came back to Cleveland in October of '43, because my husband was being shipped from the Pacific area to the Atlantic area. We knew then that he would be going to England.

I tried to write to him about every other day. I can remember how we would watch the mailman go down the block and then turn around and come down our side of the block, and we would just sit by the window and wait to see if his shoes would turn up our walk. And if they did, we would get so excited.

V-mail was something to expedite your letters—to get them over to the service people quicker. They had two post offices—one was in New York and the other was, I believe, in San Francisco. You would purchase this sheet of paper and you would write your letter on one side, fold it up and write the address on the other side. The postal service would photograph it, reduce it about half of the size, and then send it off overseas.

My husband censored his own letters. He was very careful not to mention anything he shouldn't mention. Some young people tried to have a code to say where they were, but I don't think it really worked.

Letter from Herbert Johns
March 18, 1944
Last night we had a party at the club. I had a pretty good time. I didn't drink much. I still have no hankering for hangovers. Needless to say, I missed you very much.

I moped around most of the evening and went home around 10:30. Seeing all the other fellows dancing and having a good time with their girls made me so darn lonesome & homesick for you that I just up and left.

Letter From Herbert Johns
May 9, 1945
Honey, the big day has arrived at last. One half of our job is now finished. Let us pray that Japan will soon follow Germany on the road to complete surrender. I sure hope that I can get home for a spell. These are the alternatives. Either we go direct to the S.P. [South Pacific] or to the S.P. via the States or we stay here to occupy Germany. However, your guess is as good as mine as to the final outcome. In the Army one looks for the worst & hopes for the best. The best of course would be to see my Honey again.

On May 19, after censorship restrictions on mail were lifted, Herbert wrote Clare a long letter describing all of his duty stations during the war. At that time, he was stationed in Châteaudun, France, a town about 70 miles southwest of Paris.

Letter From Herbert Johns
May 20, 1945

Today was a pip for yours truly. This morning we had a physical exam. It might interest you to know I'm disgustingly healthy. No chance of getting out of the Army that way. However, at this particular moment I am very much under the weather. I can hardly move my arms. You see, in addition to getting an exam, they brought our shots up to date. I accumulated the amazing score of four shots & one vaccination. That is enough to knock down a horse. It is my own fault, though, as I had been putting it off for some time.

The other major event was the totaling of my points. I have 71. One needs 85 to be considered for release. I guess I stay in the Army. I wouldn't mind that so much though if they would only send me home.

God Honey I sure do miss you. Even more & more. It hardly seems possible that soon we will have been married two years. Lord, I hope that I see you soon. I'd give a lot to see you again. This business is definitely N.G. [no good]. Well, if we are lucky perhaps it won't be long. Honey, I must sign off now as my arm is killing me.

Interview

When servicemen went off to war, their parents or their spouses could purchase a little flag emblem that you would put in the window and it would have however many stars. First we had one star, then two stars, and then we had three stars, because my husband and two brothers were in. And then, if one of the soldiers perished, they had an embroidered gold star that could affix over it.

My husband served all of '42, '43, '44, and half of '45. The war in England had ended May 8th and they were processing them to go to Japan. There hadn't been any talk of any furloughs for them to come back home before going. I guess nobody knew of plans for the atomic bomb. It was all secret stuff. But it was during this process when they were giving shots to go to Japan that they discovered my husband had leukemia. It was a rapid illness—he died within ten days of the discovery. [Herbert Johns died on July 14, 1945, en route to the U.S. for medical treatment.] That was a very sad time for us. I had to tell his older parents, who were in their late 60s. He was the youngest of the family. It was a sad time for them.

I must comment on the Red Cross. When we got the telegram that he had died

CLARE MORRISON CRANE 1945

The In Service flag that hung in the window of the Morrison family.
Each star represented a relative in the military. The black stars
are for Clare's brothers, the gold star for her deceased husband.

at Gander Field in Newfoundland, the Red Cross let me have a phone call all the way to St. John's, Newfoundland, to talk to the base there. And they assured me that it was a military funeral with all honors. From his dog tags, his religion was noted, so he was able to have the last rites of his faith. He was in repose there until '47 or '48, when they finally abandoned that cemetery and brought him to Arlington National Cemetery. At that time, his mother, sister and I went to see that interment at Arlington Cemetery, and then I went back twenty years later. That was my second visit; at that time we saw the grave of President Kennedy.

Letter from Clare to Herbert Johns
July 5, 1945
I just came back from walking in the rain. It seemed comforting when human tears fail. Today I received your letter, telling me you are in the hospital in Le Mans. I read the words a thousand times before they made any sense. Darling, I am so sorry. I am half crazy wondering what? How serious & how painful?

It was not too much of a shock before I just knew something was wrong. In your recent letters, you seemed to slow down so—no mention of news or activities.

Dear one, all this time you must spend lying there waiting and resting—think of me and of us together. You must get well and strong and come back to me.

Tell me, dear, can I write to you directly to the hospital or shall I keep on using the old address? Please advise!

If only I were there or could come to see you. But here I am so far away, when I would want to be only a kiss away from you. Write soon and give me some of the medical details.

The letter, postmarked nine days before Herbert died, was returned to Clare Johns, unopened.

MARION GURFEIN
World War II, Korean War; Interview
I went to Cooper-Union Art School, and that's where I met my husband. Joe was in the engineering school on scholarship. I was very lucky to get a full scholarship because my father died when I was only fifteen years old. Joe came from Brooklyn, I came from up in the Bronx. We were married six months before the war began—six very glamorous months. Joe was attached to the First Cavalry Division; we still had horses, we still had mules, believe it or not. And for six months we wore evening gowns every Saturday night. We were out in Fort Lewis, Texas, right on the Mexican border. That was very exciting for a girl who was

brought up in the Bronx. I mean all of a sudden there was Mexico and bullfights.

I was about four weeks pregnant when Joe left for war. I didn't know I was pregnant. My daughter was born while Joe was overseas, and he didn't come back for 32 months. She was born in December 1943, and he came back in 1945 and met a little girl who promptly said, "Hello, Daddy," and she pushed me away! So there was no question of her bonding with her father. I had to go back to New York to my mother, and we all lived in an apartment because my other sister, her husband had been drafted, and then I had a single sister, so we were all in one apartment. Let's see, that was four women and one baby. One baby to spoil. I was so self-conscious and so uncomfortable to think that I had a baby that would cry at night, living with my sisters and all.

But we all did our part. We flattened all the cans, we gave in every bit of rubber in the house. Even spatulas were thrown in. You did everything for the war effort. You wrote to your husband every single day. Joe tried to write to me, but his letters would have trouble coming through. I was in a terrible state, because he was a paratrooper when he went over and I didn't know if I would ever see him again. I'd sit in the park with the other girls, and the telegrams were coming constantly. This one's husband was killed, this one's husband was missing. It wasn't very pleasant. We'd all sit and console each other. We'd tell these girls whose husbands were missing in action, "Oh, you know he'll turn up." The Army never contacted us. There were too many people in the Army. Everyone was in the Army; there were no men around. It was an all-woman society.

One day, before Margie was born, I decided it would be fun to send him a little newspaper every month and call it "The Goofein Journal." I also started painting funny little cards. I did it to keep Joe's morale up and to keep my morale up. I remember someone saying to my mother-in-law, "Oh my daughter is crying, and your daughter-in-law is laughing." They didn't see me crying in private; in public, I just carried on. I felt that was part of the war effort. That's how you kept yourself going. I sent him pictures of the family; when we were on a ski holiday, I took pictures of my sisters. I did try to keep him amused, and the most wonderful thing was that I would do this every month, and he actually brought back all these "Goofein Journals."

Joe was all over the place. He started out in North Africa, and then he was up in Sicily and Italy and France and England, and finally Germany. He did not go in with the invasion. His letters would come in huge batches. In those days, we had three deliveries a day, so I would be downstairs at 8 o'clock in the morning, downstairs at 11 o'clock, and downstairs at 3 o'clock. Now either you would

Posters from the Library of Congress's collection demonstrate
World War II's unique call for sacrifice on the home front.
Ration cards, victory gardens, and civil defense jobs were
among the many ways America supported the war effort.

be delirious with joy or you'd have three different opportunities to say, "Oh God, there's nothing from him." Every now and then a telegram would come from Joe. They had little set phrases, like Number 19 would say, "I miss you," and Number 8 would say, "It's a beautiful day, I wish you were here." And he would send me these funny little messages.

It seemed I spent all my time in the park, because there was one across the street from my house, and it was a beautiful park. We'd sit there with our babies, and sometimes someone would say, "Marion, you got a telegram." And my heart would constrict: From the War Department? "No, it's from Joe, saying I love you and I miss you." Joe would write marvelous love letters. One of the girls in the park, her husband was a lawyer, and he was very careful about what he wrote, asked me to share Joe's love letters with her, because her husband was writing to her as though she was going to sue him.

Our park was Joyce Kilmer Park; it's still there, but it's been destroyed. The apartment house was on the Concourse, and that was very high-toned. There was a big hotel just opposite, the Concourse Plaza Hotel. The whole concourse had been planted with trees after World War I; every soldier that died in that war and was from the Bronx, there was a tree with his name. Joyce Kilmer Park had a magnificent fountain; it was all marble. It's near the Bronx County Courthouse and Yankee Stadium. There were lots of restaurants because people would gather after the baseball games. And all the big baseball players stayed at that hotel.

I was frightened to death; I used to dream at night about airplanes coming over. We'd see newsreels. There was no television. The radio was very important to us. I remember General Eisenhower telling us there was not enough rubber for tires and how we had to conserve everything. We couldn't get silk stockings; we painted our legs with orange makeup, and we'd draw a line up the back. All this makeup would come off inside your dress; we were constantly having to wash our dresses. Nylon stockings were just coming in. I entered a poetry contest and won a pair of nylons, and everybody envied me. So many things were disappearing, crazy things like spices, pepper; you couldn't get gum or soap. Now, we could have survived without all those things, but when meat and sugar started to disappear, and you couldn't get canned goods or shoes, that was when things were getting tight. I started to sew during the war, but of course it was hard to get material. Dresses were skimpy.

Of course, some people hoarded. When we moved into that nice apartment, we found pounds of sugar that had been hidden, and it was all packed down. Tempers were very high; we were all very nervous because we never knew if we would see our men again. We used to have all-vegetable meals; my mother would call it the Blue Plate Special. Whenever I could get some fancy canned goods, I would mail them to Joe.

We didn't have air-conditioning in those days, and we lived up on the top floor. It would go up to 90 degrees in that apartment. At one point, we took a tiny apartment near the beach. From there, in Far Rockaway, we could take a bus to the beach, and Margie could go in and out of the water, and I'd send pictures of her to Joe.

There was a black market. If you had the money, you could get anything you wanted. I heard a woman say once, "Steak, steak! I'm so sick of steak!" I remember I turned on her. We were getting on each other's nerves. For instance, there were some people whose sons and husbands were in certain industries. They didn't have to go to war, and they would brag about how much money they were making. Of course you resented that. You couldn't help resent it. So it wasn't all sweetness back home.

The war ended in stages. When the European war ended, I remember my mother said, "Go out," and we were running in the streets. We ended up in a little neighborhood pub, my sisters and I. When the Japanese war ended, I was out in that beach apartment with the baby. I remember we all went outside, and there was kissing. For several months, there was no sign of Joe coming home. Then one day I got a telegram, "Thirty days hath November and so do you and I." He came into Florida on a ship. My in-laws came, and we were sitting there waiting for him in the living room, trembling. I could hear the elevator come up—the elevator was near our apartment—and I ran out, and Joe stepped out of that elevator. We spent the night together at the hotel across the street—that was the treat. We could have stayed there several days; my mother said she would stay with the baby. But Joe wanted to meet his daughter, so he came back to the apartment. Somehow we all fit in.

And then a telegram came to Joe. Somebody had passed a bill that said that no man would have to go back; if he came home on leave, he could stay. And Joe called me into the bedroom and showed me that piece of paper. And I always cry when I'm happy, so I burst into tears. My sister passed by, and she thought Joe was telling me that he was going to divorce me.

He stayed and his orders came for Providence, Rhode Island. Three months later, Joe received orders to report to Harvard to study for his master's degree in engineering. By then, Marion was pregnant with their second child. After assignments to Fort Belvoir, Virginia, and Fort Knox, Kentucky, Joe was ordered to Okinawa when war broke out in Korea. He was told that after his first eight months there, he could bring Marion and the children. Marion went back to New York, but there was no room in her mother's apartment for her and two children. They lived with her in-laws and then spent the summer in Far Rockaway, staying on into the off-season.

By then Joe had been gone a whole year and a half. He had been up in the Chosin Reservoir, which was very, very bad. He had been surrounded and he did lead a battalion out; he's written up in several books on Korea. By then he had become a lieutenant colonel, and if he stayed, there was a good chance he could become a colonel and a general. But I wanted Joe home, and he wanted to get home. Other people he was with at this headquarters had their wives in Japan. See, they had been sent over to Korea from Japan, and they could fly back and see their families. Finally Joe said to the general, "Look, you are all going back and seeing your families, but I haven't seen my family in 18 months and they're way back in New York." I was real proud of him.

He came home the day after Valentine's Day. I bought a heart-shaped pan and baked a chocolate cake. So every February 15th after that, we had a home-baked chocolate cake, because that was the day that Daddy came home. And the kids and I would sing, "When Daddy comes marching home again, Hurray! Hurray!."

It sounds like I had a terrible life, but I didn't. I had a wonderful marriage. The three-year-old boy during the Korean War was terrible. He said, "My daddy doesn't want to be here." I had to pick up the "Goofein Journal" again.

And then when Vietnam came, Joe was in and out of Vietnam. Well, by then, we had a great life. Stationed in Bermuda and in Europe, in Arlington. I had a job by then. We were enjoying life very much, taking trips. He had to figure out how much equipment the Army needed in Vietnam, how many nails and like that. Eventually he went over with some general, and they were investigating about floating piers so they could unload the equipment on the docks in Vietnam. And he kept going and coming back and going and coming back. Finally I said to Joe—and I don't know if this was the reason he quit or he didn't believe in that Vietnam War—but I said to him, "Honey I can't sit out a third war." And Joe said, "Don't worry. I'm getting out." He got out and became a professor at George Mason University. He had 26 years in the Army and 26 years as a professor.

Joe said he loved everything he did in the Army and loved teaching, and if they hadn't paid him, he would have paid them. Three years before Joe retired from George Mason, they named a scholarship in his honor for the student in engineering who best exemplified Joe Gurfein.

{ ONE WOMAN'S STORY }

Meda Hallyburton Brendall

*"I made one or two understand I wasn't there to fool around.
I was there for the war effort."*

Some cities during wartime offer more possibilities for home front stories. Take Baltimore, which during World War II was a key port for shipping of both men and matériel. It was also home to shipyards and other industrial plants that were vital to the war effort.

Bethlehem-Fairfield Shipyards was working at full capacity and was in desperate need of qualified workers. In 1941, they accepted the application of a thirty-year-old single mother from Morgantown, North Carolina. When Meda Montana Hallyburton showed up for work in the mostly male preserve of the shipyard, her new bosses quickly found out that they were dealing with a woman who knew—and spoke—her mind.

Hallyburton could work in the yards, on the ships, or in the pipe shop, and she expressed a strong preference for the latter, a place where she could do her work and be left alone. "I made one or two understand I wasn't there to fool around," she later recalled in an interview. "I was there for the war effort and to weld for our boys overseas."

Hallyburton came to Baltimore after training to be a welder in her North Carolina hometown, but her story began in Nez Perce, Idaho, where she was born in 1911, the seventh of eight children. Her parents, both natives of Morgantown, had moved west when her father won a land grant. Meda Montana was given both her names by a local Indian woman who helped Mrs. Hallyburton with her growing brood of children.

The Hallyburtons returned to North Carolina when Meda was five. Family gatherings in the small town were plentiful, but among Meda's fondest

*Meda Hallyburton (right) and her co-workers Lula Barber and
Meta Kres, outside the Bethlehem-Fairfield Shipyards,
Baltimore, Maryland, 1942. During the war Meda was raising
a young son as a single parent and working seven days a week.*

memories were visits paid by a family friend, a local lawyer named Sam Ervin, who liked to sit on the family back porch with her father.

Meda married at the age of twenty-two, and her son Paul was born two years later. The marriage did not last; her husband was irresponsible with money, and they separated when she expressed a desire to go to college. She worked for Sam Ervin and for her father and rented out two rooms in her house to make ends meet during the Depression. But she found herself drawn to another kind of work, that of welding. "My dad encouraged me," she recalled, "and nobody in the world could be any better. He said, 'Sissy, they're giving lessons, why don't you take 'em? You like stuff like that.' So I did." Meda began to work with a local man, and she soon became aware of the social implications of her ambition.

"At that time, people had the idea that it wasn't a respectable job. I had my high school education, I was from a good family, I belonged to the best clubs in town. But some of my friends I played bridge with, they looked down their nose. They thought it was little degraded for a Hallyburton to do that."

With World War II threatening to draw in the United States, there was a growing need for welders, though not anywhere near Morgantown. With the help of her mentor, Meda applied for jobs in Baltimore, Spartanburg, South Carolina, and Portland, Oregon. Her first preference was Baltimore; she had visited an aunt there several times as a teenager and liked the town.

In Baltimore, Meda and her son Paul Steppe (he had kept his father's last name) rented an apartment; their landlady, an elderly woman, agreed to watch the young boy while his mother was at work. And that work schedule was grueling: 6 A.M. to 4 P.M. seven days a week. But she loved her work and took it very seriously. "You had something before you that meant a life. I didn't weld it right, maybe that was one that ruined the whole thing." She proved to be one of the most reliable workers in the shop; she can't remember ever having to do over a single piece of pipe. A few old timers in the shop liked her and gave her the affectionate nickname "Peanut."

Meda had a number of friends, including several other women, but she was also clear about behavior she wouldn't tolerate. Cursing was prohibited in the shop, but one woman flaunted her nasty language. "She kept saying things," Meda recalled, "and I said, 'I wish you wouldn't do that. It bothers me.' And she said, 'Do your work.' And I said, 'If you do that again, I'm gonna smack you.' She said, 'You haven't got the nerve.' About that time she hit the floor. She didn't call me any more bad names."

Work didn't leave Meda much time or energy for recreation. "You don't hunt for entertainment," she said. "You're tired when you get home, fix something to eat, don't want to take a bath, just fall right in bed." If she got off early, she and Paul would go to a movie. He had a little radio he listened to, and he loved to do art work. "He was good boy; I didn't worry about him," Meda remembered.

Even in a big city, she found people who just couldn't accept the idea of a working woman. She once boarded a streetcar in her welder's clothes and found a seat next to a woman who turned away, making her disgust clear. " I started to get off at my stop," Meda recalled, "and she said, 'Are you a welder?' And I said, 'Yes, ma'am, and proud of it. And I'm not contagious.' Well, the bus driver heard me, and he just laughed and laughed." A passenger got up and offered his seat to Meda, and she told him, "It's people like you that make the world go round."

When the intercom at the shipyard crackled with the announcement that the war was over, Meda recalled, "We shouted, but we cried, because that was our jobs. We cried when we said good-bye; we knew we would never see each other again." Her boss made sure she had another job right away, at the office of the Social Security Administration, where she worked for the next five years. Meda then bought a motel in suburban Laurel, Maryland, not far from a race track; she opened a restaurant nearby that served burgers and North Carolina-style barbecue and attracted a steady clientele of horse players and policemen.

In 1950, Paul Steppe enlisted in the Marines and went off to fight in Korea. His stories appear in several chapters of this book. Meda continued to stay in touch with family and friends in Morgantown, and in 1965 she was married for the second time, to her high school sweetheart, a minister with a congregation in her hometown. She sold her business, moved back south, and became Meda Brendall.

Meda's second husband died in 1996, and she decided to return to Baltimore to be near her five grandchildren. In her eighties, she kept busy with volunteer work at a senior center and for her church. In 2001, she took an ailing Paul home with her from a rehabilitation hospital where, in her opinion, he wasn't getting the best care. In remission from cancer and slowed by a lung ailment, Paul was given six months to live by one doctor when his mother picked him up. He lived with Meda until March 2004, when a heart attack ended his life at the age of seventy-two.

At ninety-two, Meda Brendall gave a no-nonsense and lengthy interview about her experiences as a single mother contributing to the war effort. "Don't call me Rosie the Riveter," she said defiantly. "I am not Rosie the Riveter, all respects to her job. I worked too hard to be called Rosie the Riveter."

{ CHAPTER SIX }

Coming Home

A V-J Day celebration, August 1945. After nearly four years of sacrifice and restraint, America cut loose upon hearing of the Japanese surrender.

October 17, 1945, New York Harbor. The aircraft carrier
Enterprise *docks at 7:20 A.M., with families and friends*
swarming the dock to greet its crew, finally home from
World War II. From the William Barr collection.

War is Over

"Strangely, my sympathy was quickly going to our former enemy, the German civilians."

The end of war was not an end of duty, but it was difficult for many GIs to accept that once the shooting stopped they were not free to return home. Demobilization was a painfully slow process, and at the end of the World Wars some were pressed into serving with the occupying forces. For those who had to live among the former enemy, the experience could be more than a little enlightening, and especially in Europe there were fringe benefits of leave in areas little touched by the war and rich in both history and culture.

JOHN WISTER

World War I; Army; Letter written November 15, 1918

Just as we were going to start back to dinner, the Cathedral bells started ringing as you never heard anything ring. We knew then, of course, that the Armistice had been signed; that is why I am likely to remember Orleans Cathedral as long as I live. The Liberty Bell in Independence Hall is all very well, but I wasn't there to hear it ring in 1776, and I have heard the bells of Orleans.

In the afternoon I visited with Mr. Turbat about six outlying farms where he had nursery stock growing. Got back into Orleans to find the streets filled with merrymakers, lots of French soldiers parading and singing "The Marseillaise," everything brilliantly lighted. After the darkness of the nights ever since arriving in France it was quite a contrast.

I went up to Paris on the 7 A.M. train Tuesday, and smiled on the M.P. long enough to persuade him to mark my pass good until Wednesday morning. He wanted to send me out Tuesday night, but I told him what a mean cold ride it was in the night, and he said, "Oh Hell, the war's over," and marked it OK.

Well I guess you read in the papers how Paris celebrated, and newspaper writers are better at description than I am; that's what they get paid for. Even at 10 in the morning the streets were filled with merrymakers, the chief merry-making consisting of kissing everyone in sight.

By noon all the important streets were a solid mass of people, and if you wanted to get anywhere you had to dodge into the side streets. At the Place de la Concorde, there were hundreds of light artillery guns captured from the Germans, and during the afternoon people started to go off with them. I thought someone would get hurt as they were pretty heavy, but the people were never rough the way they get at home when there's a big crowd, and there were prac-tically no drunks. The few there were, were mostly Americans, and they were only hilarious. The M.P.s were very smiling and didn't bother anybody. There wasn't a need to but you can never tell about an M.P.

SALLY HITCHCOCK PULLMAN

World War II; Army Nurse Corps; Letter August 14, 1945

Just before I went on night shift for the fourth time, I told the kids it was my luck in the Army to have something momentous happen. It did! Plunged into bed this morning and slept all day, staggered into the tent at 4:30 from the night nurses quarters.

"Anything happen today?" I asked.

"Oh nothing new. Of course you knew the war is over!"

That's how I knew. What a momentous event!!

Before I close, I have to tell you about a very momentous event. It's been nine months since I slept in a real bed in my tent, except for the first week when we came here. We've been on canvas cots. Tomorrow we get real beds again, which we gave up to the patients when our hospital was so overcrowded. So, back to civilization!

DENTON CROCKER

World War II; Army; Memoir

Crocker was a scientist stationed in the Philippines when the Japanese surrendered.

Letter to his fiancée, August 16, 1945

It would be wonderful to have the war end so soon, but until the air raids cease here, and until American & allied troops are well established in Japan, I am ready to believe nothing. (But I'm hoping my darling, and if hope could win the war, I'd have done so single-handed long ago.)

If the war ends now, I'm not sure I'll be home any sooner than I might otherwise—six months seems a logical figure, but at least it is absolutely sure that when I get there it will be for good.

You are probably quite right, dear, that we need a few weeks after I come home in order to make plans. It is hard for me out here to visualize how much planning must be done. A lot depends on the time of year I get back and how long it will be before school opens. This will determine where we set up our first real housekeeping I should think.

If we could be married by April it would be perfect because we'd be able to take a month or even two for a honeymoon, and then there is an awful lot of heavy and technical reading I must do to acquire the background in biological theories that I need for graduate work.

Crocker finally departed from Japan on November 26, 1945, according to his separation papers. He wrote this reminiscence in 1997.

Of the voyage, its great-circle route taking us northward toward the Aleutians, I remember the hold crammed with tiers of bunks, and water of condensation from the human cargo of many "sardines" streaming down the inside of the cold hull. I can also recall standing watch outside in the bow in a dense, cold mist, having been instructed to keep an eye out for mines, which were reported to have come loose from their moorings. We arrived in the US at San Pedro, CA. From there I was carried by troop train to Ft. Devens, MA. That trip too is largely a blank, but I do remember annoyance at not knowing most of the time where we were, even what state we were in. Somewhere in the plains a wheel of one of the train cars jumped off the track and it was some hours before we could continue. During the delay, I walked a mile or two away from the train along a dirt road, trying to get a feel of the place, but if I knew then where it was, I now have forgotten. It was my great good fortune to arrive home on Dec. 23 and so to be able to celebrate Christmas with my family and my wife-to-be. JM [Jean-Marie] and I were married on February 23.

VINCENT REED

World War I; Army; Memoir

While the message regarding the signing of the Armistice was received by the regiment about 9:30 P.M., the night before, we did not receive the word until the next morning. Happy? I was the happiest mortal in the world, I believe.

And now the daily talk was what we would do next. When would we go home, or if not where would we be sent?

Then came the news that we had been chosen as one of the divisions to become a part of the Army of Occupation, and that we would march into Germany. It did not seem like an honor to me, as I wanted to return home.

The band played as we marched through each town and the houses were hung with French and U.S. flags. We were cheered by the people as we marched.

On December 21, 1918, after marching through a half dozen or more towns, Reed's unit stopped in Gerolstein, its permanent posting for the remainder of the Occupation.

The mess room of one of the companies was in one of the rooms of a bottling works and this was used for our Christmas entertainment. We had a large tree decorated but not very elaborately. The program consisted of stunts by any one of the men who could sing, dance, or do anything special. We sang some Army songs, then the Y handed out chocolate and cigarettes. That was our Christmas Eve in Germany. That night we had a snow, so the next morning everything was covered with a beautiful mantle of white and it looked very fitting on a Christmas morning.

About the first of the year we moved our headquarters down the street to a private home. It was the home of Matthew Hurt, a very pleasant old gentleman. He had a wife, one son about fifteen years of age, and a daughter about twenty years of age. She was tall, dark-haired, and rather an attractive girl. All of us in the headquarters soon became very good friends to them. He had a son in the German army who had been all through the war without being injured, but after the Armistice was signed was on his way home when he took sick with the flu and died very suddenly. Mr. Hurt had a paper knife made from a German cartridge, which he gave to me while there.

After seeing so many of the German people and living in their homes, we came to have a different impression of them than we had had before. Everywhere the people treated us with the same respect that they would have treated their own soldiers. When we stopped overnight in any of the towns, the people would bring us hot dishes of food of some sort. In Gerolstein, I talked with so many of them, and they all had the same attitude of the war, namely that they were only in it because they had to be; in other words, the German government ordered them into the army, and they had to go.

VINCENT REED 1918

*Reed stayed in Europe for nearly six months after the
Armistice ended World War I. In Chambery, France, an artist
created this painting from a photograph Reed gave him.*

As the spring months came, we heard more rumors about going home. We could not depend upon them, however. My work in the headquarters gave me considerable time to myself. One of us had to be on duty until 11 P.M. in order to receive reports from the companies, which had to be consolidated and made ready to be sent to Regimental Headquarters early the next morning.

Later in April, the word came down.

We are preparing daily to leave Gerolstein for home. We have turned in all of our horses, wagons, and unnecessary equipment, and are issuing daily orders regarding our leaving.

A letter written to Jo and dated May 5th reads, "Sunday we had the finest dinner. We contributed five francs each and bought a lot of extras. We had fried ham, mashed taters, peas, corn, macaroni, cheese, jams, apple cobbler, bread, butter, and coffee. It was Mother's Day, so I walked in the woods and gathered some wildflowers and pressed them. I wrote one letter to the mother of one of the boys who was killed on the front.

The following Sunday we left our quarters, marched to the train, loading at 8 P.M. We backtracked through Germany and into France. In this warm, sunny month of May, France was at her best. All through the country were hedges of white flowers in full bloom, similar to our bridal wreath. It made a beautiful sight. Then all of the fields looked so pretty in their covering of green grass or crops.

Then finally came the day, embarkation, about May 28. What a different trip this was from the one coming over. Then we were in danger of torpedoes and mines, but this time all was at peace. And so we take one last look at France where we have fought together and lived together for a year.

My ticket took me to New Rochelle, Ill., where I changed to the Burlington, Chi. K.C. #55, good old Quincy train. I wired mother to meet me at midnight. My, it seemed like the train would not go fast enough. As the train passed the Soldiers Home, I was on the platform, waiting to be the first off the train. As the train stopped I was down the steps and into mother's arms. Dear, sweet mother, she was so happy to have me safely at home once more.

After a few days of visiting friends at home, we went to Rensselaer for that meeting with Jo, for which I had looked for so long. I thought sure I had told her I would be there on Thursday, but evidently I said Friday, for she was not at the station to meet us. However, we drove over to the farm in my cousin's buggy. Jo was gone to the woods to gather gooseberries. So I set down the road to meet her. As I was coming up one side of a hill, she was coming up the other side when her sister Carrie said, "Oh, there's a soldier coming." Jo's heart almost jumped out of her mouth, for she had planned to meet me dressed in such a pretty dress and looking very much like a lady, and instead she had on a pair of coveralls and overshoes, with an old sun hat. As if her clothes mattered to me.

I spent about a week with her, then came back to Quincy for a few days, then went back on the 5th of July with the marriage license. On July 6th at 8 P.M. we were married with members of our families there as our only guests. When I asked her mother for her, I told her how much I loved Jo, and she said, "Tell me that ten years from now, and I will believe you." Well, ten years have passed and gone. Before Mother Glasscock passed on to her heavenly home she said that now she believes me.

WILLIAM WHITING

World War II; Army; Memoir

At the end of the war in Europe, Whiting's battalion was assigned to the Ninth Army, which had taken over from the First Army, which in turn was being transferred for duty in the Pacific Theater.

I was the battalion military government officer. It was very easy duty with not much time or effort required, and we were living very comfortably. It was not pleasant duty, as we were not to permit the German civilians to migrate to the west, which many wished to do. We were in the area given over to the Russians by then President Franklin D. Roosevelt at Yalta. Many of the civilians were terrified of the soon to come Russians and were attempting to flee to the American or British zones. They were mostly elderly people with as much of their worldly possessions as they could load in old baby buggies, wheelbarrows, children's wagons, anything with wheels that they could pull or push. We did not permit them to pass our checkpoints on the roads, but as scared as they were, we were sure they bypassed us at night in the fields and woods.

Strangely, my sympathy was quickly going to our former enemy, the German civilians. They seemed to be victims of an evil government, little people who had lost everything and now were trying to save their lives. Some of the German troops had apparently been unbelievably savage in their treatment of Russian and Ukrainian people in 1941-1942, and there were reports of similar and perhaps reprisal treatment of the German people by the conquering Russian soldiers.

We all were living in German homes, undamaged and vacated by the owners. The girls and women came in during the daytime to clean and look after their things. One put a sheet in my bedroll. We were not allowed to have any but official dealings with civilians, the so-called non-fraternization policy. We were not so stupid not to realize that some of the men and German frauleins had struck up friendships on the quiet, but we did not look for trouble as long as such friendships were out of view.

We became friendly with our German family, the Gartners. We were friendly and were as easy as we could be on their furniture and possessions, and they in turn were friendly to us. The Germans were by nature respecters of law and order and authority, and we were representatives of that. We were glad the war was over and they were glad the war was over, and there was much incentive on both sides to be friends. An easy, friendly relationship developed after a few days. Sixteen-year-old Rose Marie acted as our interpreter as well as entering in on her own. Shortly after arriving I got an ETO (or Eisenhower) jacket, and it

GIs toast the end of World War II, August 1945, in this photo-
graph snapped by Robert Lee Olen. The relief for many was
underscored by fears that an invasion of Japan would have
cost many lives on both sides.

needed a little tailoring to make it fit just right. Momma (as Mrs. Gartner want-ed to be called) did some very expert work on it at her insistence. She also did our laundry and generally looked after us. Many evenings we sat around the kitchen table with them and talked for hours. They were as curious about Americans and the USA as we were about them and Germany. We had ample supplies of soap, candy, cigarettes, and many other things, in extremely short supply or non-existent in Germany for several years, which we shared with them in return for their many kindnesses to us. "Momma" teased me about being too thin and too young to be married and a father. One day I was wrapping some film I had appropriated to send home (where film was scarce). Momma and Rose Marie saw what I was doing and insisted on putting in something "for your little girl" and gave me one of Rose Marie's bracelets from her baby days. It was a strange but pleasant relationship, forced to a large degree by circumstances but nonetheless enjoyed by both sides. We did not talk much heavy politics, but we did discuss it somewhat.

In mid-August, Whiting and two buddies, Jack Dick and Doc Banish, got two weeks' leave and headed for the Riviera for some rest and relaxation.

We arrived back at the battalion just before supper on the 31st, and Doc and I told the others at mess what a great time we had. Immediately after supper Colonel Head called me into a private room and said he was sorry to be the one who had to tell me, but that my brother had been killed. He then gave me the telegram from home and left me alone. After 15 minutes or so I left and went to my quarters, trying to sort out my thoughts and grief, and read the mail that had arrived while I was away. It was a very sad and hard evening for me. I wrote my mother and father, and then Jeanie [his wife]. I was humbled by the fact that I had worried much about myself and not at all about my brother, or for that matter anyone at home.

He was an administrative officer in the Air Force and had never been sent overseas. I did not consider him at risk. Much later I learned that he and a friend had gone up in a rented two-seater plane that crashed on takeoff, and both were killed. He was killed on August 12th, after the atomic bombs had been dropped on Hiroshima and Nagasaki and just before the Japanese surrendered. At that time I am sure that my parents had begun to relax about their two sons in the service.

It turned out that the telegram arrived in the morning just before my group was to leave for the Riviera, and Colonel Head decided there was nothing I could do, no way I could get home, so he chose to withhold the news and let me go. He did what he thought was best for me. It was sad to learn later that my parents, my mother especially, thought the Army would fly me home immediately. Unfortunately, she believed the nonsense the government put in the newspapers during the war for civilian consumption, such as flying soldiers home when tragedy struck a family.

In October, Whiting was assigned to a town called Schwabisch-Gmund, about 25 miles east of Stuttgart.

At the end of October we were informed of another delay to the end of November. One of the popular songs that fall was "I'll Be Home for Christmas," and we hoped we would make it.

JOSEPH STEINBACHER

World War II; Army; Memoir
Steinbacher spent over a year in the infantry fighting the Japanese in New Guinea and the Philippines. He and his unit were slated to be part of the force invading Japan. After the end of the war, Steinbacher's unit was sent to Tokyo as part of the occupying force.

One day I am posted on guard duty in downtown Tokyo. This is the only time I ever walk a post while overseas. The Japanese civilians crowd around to stare at me and try out their English that a surprisingly large proportion of them can use pretty fluently. They are really friendly, which surprises me, as I figured the Japanese civilians would have been brainwashed into thinking the American troops would pillage and rape. Once the hostilities ended, the Japanese seemed to think it was time to get acquainted and learn to emulate their American conquerors.

You need 55 points to get out of the service and I, being a single man, even though I have been much longer in the South Pacific, only have 52 points. I will have to stay in Japan for several more months.

Most of our time is taken up with standing company formations and doing odd jobs such as policing the area. We also do a lot of close-order drill. Close order drill and calisthenics are on the program to keep us in good physical condition. Our afternoons are usually what is called free time, when the GIs can sit around, shoot the bull, play cards, or write letters. Our social life is about nil since the troops are restricted in so many ways. Some of the troopers do get permission to make a social call to a family in the area. These soldiers are often called Jap lovers by other troopers, and I have to keep breaking up some heated arguments.

Soon I will be heading home. I had a few hundred Japanese yen and wondered where to exchange them for U.S. dollars. A buddy told me there was a high-stakes poker game going on in one of the barracks. That's for me, I thought. I would either lose my little stake in a hurry or, if luck was with me, could win a good roll that would let me go home in style. Soon I was in the game, and for a change I had fantastic luck. Full houses, straights, and flushes seemed to gravitate my way, and soon I had most of the money on the table. Amid some good-natured joshing I checked out and headed for the division money changer.

I was set for a nice, quiet trip home but no luck. We no sooner sailed than I came down with a terrible case of malaria. They had only something called bismuth pills and absolutely nothing to help me, so I suffered the daily bout with the malaria all the way across the Pacific to Seattle. I checked into a hospital at Fort Lawton in Seattle, got dosed up well with quinine, and was okay in a few days.

One day, I was called in to a little office where a corporal sat behind a desk. He shoved a couple of documents in front of me and told me to sign one of them. I asked what the documents were and he said one set were reenlistment papers and the other discharge papers. If I would sign to reenlist, they would increase my rank to staff sergeant. The Army was still trying, but I wasn't buying. I didn't have any more lives to give to my country. I signed the discharge papers and was no longer a member of the armed forces. It was the month of January in this year of our Lord, 1946.

DONALD SPENCER
World War II; Army Air Corps; Memoir
Spencer was a gunner on a bomber that flew missions over Germany and Belgium. He was assigned to the Army of Occupation at an air base in Venlo, Holland, on the German border. His memoir combines letters with a narrative written by one of his sisters.

The ship sailed from Le Havre on November 4, 1945. The second day out, they ran into a very bad North Atlantic storm. Waves of fifty and sixty feet pounded them for three days and two nights. Ninety percent of troops and crew aboard were seasick. Don and a new friend did not get sick, despite the odors in their compartment.

They sailed into New York harbor on the morning of November 11, Armistice Day, 1945. They sailed by the Statue of Liberty with the decks jammed shoulder to shoulder, and all aboard cheering. Farther up the harbor with the skyscrapers of New York City in the background they were met by fireboats that were spouting water into the air.

Several motorized barges pulled up alongside the ship with bands aboard them playing, and on one of the barges the Rockette dancers were doing their famous dance kicks. It was quite an unexpected welcome. New York City was celebrating Armistice Day and the arrival of troop ships from Europe, and just by chance they became part of it.

Don boarded a train for Camp Chaffee, Arkansas, and arrived there on the night of November 12th. Don's father, brother Dick [who had just been released from four years' service with the Air Corps], and brother-in-law Joe Glaze drove from Tulsa to see Don that Sunday afternoon. Don had no tie on and his shirt open at the neck. Don's brother Dick said, "Look, Dad, he's a man now; he has hair on his chest."

FREDERICK STILSON

World War I; Army; Memoir

Several weeks after the Armistice of November 11, 1918, Stilson and his unit were stationed in Toul, France, knowing they were part of the Army of the Occupation.

We sat down to a real Thanksgiving dinner about 2 o'clock. After the meal was over, I was called upon for a speech, and so I got up and talked about going home, and how soon it would be. I predicted that we would be on our way in a couple of months and elaborated on that.

It was during this period that "Robbie" and I decided to take our leave and go gadding to Southern France. We arrived in Paris around noon. Three American officers on leave can do a lot of sightseeing in 24 hours or so. Our first stop was at the American "Bar" in the Place-de-la-Opera, or the opera square, right alongside of the Paris Opera House. Walsh had a favorite drink he wanted us to try called a "porto-flipp." It is made of port wine with an egg beaten up in it and spiced to taste. I had four of them, and when I got up I could hardly stand.

The trio boarded a train to Marseilles. Nice and Monte Carlo were among their destinations, with eating and drinking their main sources of amusement.

On our return to Pierrepont, we found several changes which were not to my liking. First, there was a general order came through that we had to start drilling the men an hour a day as infantrymen. We had to unpack, clean up the arms, and prepare them for an inspection, and I mean a real one. It fell upon my shoulders to get this done. I became very unpopular with the outfit.

One sergeant, an engineering graduate of an eastern university, was demoted to private, and all my pleading later couldn't get his rank restored. He was perhaps too easy on his platoon. Some of the new ones were tough "Hombres," and we didn't get along too well. The men wanted to go home, were dissatisfied with the set up, and usually took it out on the Skipper, if they could.

One night, a bunch came in drunk from a party and rousted out the men and the caretakers of the bathhouse, and a general free-for-all ensued. I knew we had to reassert discipline or there would be trouble. In the next village to us there had been an insurrection with some outfit, and someone had shot their captain, and he expired.

I strapped on my Sam Browne belt, leaving the .45 automatic off, as I wanted to be unarmed when I faced up to the company. I had decided before I went out not to punish anyone. I told them off and ordered the top sergeant to detail the men who had busted up the bathhouse to make repairs. That was done, and I called the incident closed. At least I obtained respect for not being armed.

In May 1919, Stilson and the rest of the First Battalion were ordered to Le Mans, the assembly point for final inspections before returning the U.S. Stilson again got leave and headed for Paris. He toured Versailles and Fontainebleau, saw the Paris catacombs, attended High Mass in the Cathedral of Notre Dame. He was also the victim of an assault.

I went to get on the train as it pulled into the station, when five or six big bruising Frenchmen pushed me back against the wall and started to work me over. Luckily there were a couple of gendarmes (police) nearby, and they quickly broke it up. I found out that the attackers were communists. With the date being near the First of May, decided I was a good bet for a beating. The "Yanks," as we were called, were beginning to get unpopular, because we had more "dough" than the French soldiers and civilians. So I got off after a few blows, which didn't do any harm.

After more sightseeing, Stilson returned to his regiment.

When I got there, all things had been changed. I had been relieved of duty as company commander, and my place had been taken by Captain Davey, who had originally commanded "C" Company until he was wounded and sent to a hospital in the rear. I was rather flustered at the change. A new company roster was made out, and I was completely omitted, not even mentioned.

While in this camp, the regiment was "paid off" in U.S. currency, and, as some outfits hadn't been paid for several months, they got a "bundle." The more crafty started card or crap games and relieved the innocent victims of their newly received 20 dollar bills. In officers' row, I was in one tent where a crap game was in progress. Looking on (no, I didn't play), I saw several thousand dollars change hands in a few hours.

President Wilson's *George Washington* was anchored in the harbor of Brest awaiting the settlement of the peace proposals and the organization of the League of Nations. This had been going on for several months. Meanwhile, a perfectly good transport, capacity 10,000 men, lay at anchor. I heard many a growl and gripe about this both from officers and men, who had been delayed too long waiting to get shipped back to the states. We were all volunteers and had to stay until the last and clean up the debris of war made by the others. That was the lot of most of the special engineer regiments like ours.

Finally our turn came, and we went aboard the S.S. *Winnifredian* of the Allen line (British). We sailed out of Brest on the 29th of May, 1919.

They arrived in Boston on June 9, and three days later, the company began breaking up. Stilson was assigned command of a troop train headed for the Midwest with 320 casual troops from many different companies. When the two officers who were to help him didn't show up, the train left anyway.

I had instructed the sergeants, "You will find me in the last car of this train in the last seat at the rear door with the conductor and brakeman, and you can reach me there." I was through being responsible now and had learned to pass the buck and quit worrying over the welfare of a bunch of guys I had never seen before.

WILLIAM FREDERICK NICE

World War I; Marine Corps; Interview

You can bet your bottom dollar that we were glad to get back to God's country again. There was only one unfortunate incident to mar the return voyage. No, there was not a submarine attack this time, but I lost a neat little sum of money in a poker game. There was over $900 in the pot and I was dealing. I dealt one card to Lieutenant W.M. Gore of Oklahoma and it was the jack of hearts, just the one he needed to complete a straight flush. Boy that was a sad blow. It hurt me as much as any of the wounds I got on the other side.

SALLY HITCHCOCK PULLMAN

World War II; Army Nurse Corps; Memoir

Sally Hitchcock was a nurse stationed in the Philippines at the end of the war. Her memoir is a collection of letters to her parents, bolstered by her memories.

Letter to her parents

August 28, 1945

Life goes on. There is less work for all of us. Carl left for home two days ago. He was a consistently good friend and took my buddies and me around the island many times. Always a gentleman. I hope he can repair his marriage. So many sad disruptions over here.

Guess what! I wore a dress the other night, the first time in a year! Orders came out we can wear dresses after duty. We all flew to our footlockers and delved deep into the moldy smelling footlockers and retrieved our dresses.

Went to Dick's quarters to meet Casey and Shirl before a dance. I was shocked. His is a segregated quartermaster unit. I was not aware of whole units of Negro men and it came as a shock. No wonder I never saw any Negroes in my hospital. I was overwhelmed with a feeling of terrible guilt and unease. I was glad when we left. It was not a good feeling. It is wrong!!

SALLY HITCHCOCK PULLMAN 1945

Sally Hitchcock (far right) and her nurse pals in Los Angeles on their way home from duty in the Pacific Theater. The president of the Union Pacific Railroad donated his private car so that they could ride to Chicago in style.

October 3, 1945

Everything is in a turmoil. Shirl's and my names have gone in to go home! What a dream. We know now some time in the near future we'll be on our way. We will NOT go to Japan. We will leave Leyte for San Francisco.

November 20, 1945

Still dreaming of the final word to go home. We know it is coming soon. In the meantime, we are all working very hard. This Officers' Ward is very busy and a lot of fun. We all laugh a lot on duty. Laughter is a great healer. These guys are sharp and educated and fun to be with. So if I must be here still, it's fun to be here!

When we get to the States, we go across country to Fort Dix in New Jersey. I'll be separated there and then have 45 days leave. Won't make Christmas, but

I'll love to be home, put on a dress, any dress, just to get rid of these uniform pants! I've worn these shirts and pants so long!

November 26, 1945

Yesterday was our day! We were relieved of duty after working all morning. It was funny yesterday morning when I woke up; the sky was red and the ocean beautiful. I had a feeling it would be that day and I told Shirl so. The night before, I had washed, starched, and ironed all my clothes. For the first time I ever have moved in this man's (and woman's) Army, I am ready!

Hitchcock and her nurse pals sailed from the Philippines on November 27.

December 12, 1945

Before we got to Pearl Harbor we had a water shortage, so en route we decided to throw our pants and shirts over the side when they were dirty. But we were called by the captain to his quarters and told not to do that any more because boats and Army planes seeing Army uniforms would feel a plane or ship had gone down and they would begin a search for survivors. No more heaving of clothes overboard. We now just pack them in the bottom of the suitcase for use at home!!

Telegram, December 12, 1945

LEAVING PEARL HARBOR FOR HOME TOMORROW DON'T EXPECT ME FOR CHRISTMAS LEAVE THE TREE AND SNOW

Story, Los Angeles Herald Express
December 22, 1945

"Tell the folks to keep the Christmas tree up."

"I'm going to sit in a tub and soak for hours—with nobody to tell me to hurry."

These were the typical reactions from 12 Army nurses en route today to Fort Dix, New Jersey, in the private car of William M. Jeffers, retiring Union Pacific President, whose gesture to the Army is making the car available to the Leyte returnees to be home for Christmas.

Attached to the *Los Angeles Limited*, the special car will pull into New York Monday, where the nurses, after spending Christmas with their parents and friends, will report to Fort Dix for separation.

Lieut. Sally Hitchcock's special request is to ski once more, while Lieut. Helen E. Gestwicki wants "oodles and oodles" of fresh vegetables and ice cream.

We didn't travel all the way to New York in that "plushy" car! In Chicago we were transferred to a troop train bound for Fort Dix.

The trip across to Chicago was unbelievable. We had our own porter and staff, all of whom spoiled us. We ate well, had cocktail hour, saw winter scenery. In a little town outside Laramie, Wyoming, three girls got off to buy something and the train left without them. They hired a taxi to drive them at high speed to Laramie where they reboarded. They were lucky!!

When I went through the front door of the house, all the lights were on. The tree was aglow and the long-dreamt-of scent of Christmas balsam greeted me. It was a joyous moment. We were all there, safe and sound, together. The war was finally, truly over.

CHUCK HAGEL
Vietnam War; Army; Interview
Chuck Hagel and his brother Tom were assigned to the same company in Vietnam.

My brother Tom had been wounded a third time. Getting into October, as I recall, we were starting to get a little attention from the commanders: two brothers, one wounded twice, the other a third time. And getting close to their date of departures. So they pulled Tom and me out of the field for a little bit and gave us some headquarters jobs. I knew in October I was getting close and I was pleased to be going home except for this problem. I didn't want to leave my brother here. I was bothered by that. I went to see if I could extend my time, because you could extend your time in those days. I asked about staying longer, about going home when Tom did, and I didn't tell Tom, but he heard about it through a sergeant. Tom was very, very upset about that with me. He said, "No, that's the wrong thing to do. Our mother is expecting you home. I'll be fine."

{ IMAGES FROM WARTIME }

Join the Army, See the World

War's end didn't always mean a quick conclusion to the obligations of service. And for some soldiers, a long postwar wait for orders to ship out turned into an excuse for cultural immersion. Some members of the Army of Occupation of World War I amused and educated themselves by touring France and Germany, visiting historical sites and enjoying the hospitality of the locals. Even the Germans seemed to harbor no bitterness about the hostilities just concluded. For veterans of World War II, opportunities lay in another part of the world. Those who served in the China-Burma-India Theater and in non-combat capacities in the Pacific saw the post-VJ Day months as a chance to pick up firsthand knowledge of exotic cultures. Though there was no lingering in Vietnam and very little after the Persian Gulf War, there were still moments during those conflicts when an inquisitive American could learn something about a little-known place and people. Soldiers open to the experience of travel had a chance to profit from it in ways they couldn't have imagined.

John Manger (left) served with an Army engineer battalion that saw plenty of Europe following the Normandy invasion. His caption: "Somewhere in Belgium, 28 Nov 1944."

Working away from the front lines, technical specialists had more opportunities to explore. Malaria expert Denton Crocker (above) in the Stanley-Owens Mountains of New Guinea. Oil analyst Patricia Seawalt (below) with an Arabian woman during the Persian Gulf War.

Following the Armistice of 1918, Frederick Stilson (opposite) spent eight largely glorious
months touring France. His one bad experience: getting mugged in a Paris railroad station by
men police identified as communists. Rhona Knox Prescott and a friend in the ruins of a village near Qui Nhon, Vietnam, 1967 (top). John Enman (above left, at left) and Frank
Feingerts, in Kashmir, India, June 1945. They are in a tourist boat called a shikara, about to
cross Dal Lake to the Shalimar Gardens. On the day in 1945 before his tank unit was to cross
the Rhine River, Bruce Fenchel and a local boy enjoyed a break from war (above right).

ROSALIND WESTFALL SELLMER 1945

As a trained flight nurse, Rosalind Westfall Sellmer accompanied many casualties out of the war zone and back to the U.S. In this 1945 photo, a wounded soldier disembarks from a plane in Bermuda.

Home on a Stretcher

"I figured if I went home halfway, I'd never make anything,
I'd never make it."

Then there were the soldiers who got to go home early, though unexpectedly. The journey for a wounded man (or a pregnant nurse) from the front back to the States never seemed to be easy, punctuated by long delays or transportation mishaps. The professionalism of the medical personnel was easily matched by the masters of armed forces red tape, who seemed determined to drag out the journey home.

MAX CLELAND
    Vietnam War; Army; Interview
Cleland was severely wounded when he picked up a live grenade, which he thought he had dropped. The explosion immediately blew off his right arm and leg, and his left leg was amputated within the hour.

Because it was Vietnam, they had chopper medevacs. It was a clear day in the middle of the day. To the division aid station. And within the hour I was in the air, medevaced maybe 40 miles away to a field hospital. A team of five doctors saved my life. I heard from one of the doctors, and he said I owed my life to the anesthesiologist because every time my blood pressure would go down, my breathing would stop, he would stop the operation, build up the blood pressure, and they could start up again. I went through 46 pints of blood in five hours. The surgeon who later wrote me and was working at a VA [Veterans Administration] hospital when I was head of the VA said he never dared come see me because he couldn't face me.

The shipping back was a hellish thing. I was moved very quickly from the field hospital to one right in Danang. I wanted to stay in the Navy hospital in

Danang, because I knew I was going to get better treatment there. But they said, "No, you're an Army guy," and they sent me down to some place northeast of Saigon that was a hellhole. I was there for seven days, and I almost died. They almost killed me. I was lucky to survive that place. Then one night in an Air Force hospital in Cam Ranh Bay, then a C-130 to Japan near Yokohama, the 106 General Hospital, which is no longer there. I went back to that ground about two years ago, and it's now a park. I had a little sense of serenity about that place because I had come back to life there. I'm glad that it's a park. It has a certain serenity to it. Hopefully that's a precursor of history in the 21st century, less war and more serenity.

And then medevaced after seven days in a C-141, one stop in Anchorage, Alaska, to Walter Reed to begin a whole life here. Eight months at Walter Reed— I was looked upon as a long-term case. I did not know if that was mental or physical. But I was a long-term case all right. The rehab thing was as much another war, a war ultimately with Walter Reed, which was really wonderful for me initially: the snake pit, the camaraderie of the guys. And then the devastation of being shipped out to the Veterans Administration hospital in Washington. I wanted to stay in Washington. I didn't want to go back home, because I figured if I went home halfway, I'd never make anything, I'd never make it. I wanted to go home in as good a shape as I would ever be. I battled the VA for another year trying to get my artificial limbs, trying to do my PT [Physical Therapy] every day. Finally got a decent set of limbs and I went home in December '69. I can remember sitting there in my mother and daddy's living room and saying, "Well, no job, no future, no girlfriend, no car, no apartment, no money—this is a great time to run for the state senate."

JEANNE URBIN MARKLE
Vietnam War; Army Nurse Corps; Interview
Markle, a nurse, and her husband Brian, a doctor, went to Vietnam together in December 1966.

I had gotten pregnant and was expecting our daughter, so I came home early, in August. I flew out of Ton Son Nhut [Air Force Base, in Saigon]. Brian drove me to Saigon. You looked at the back of the plane, and it opened up and there were all stretchers. There were about 20 seats up front behind the cockpit door. They told me at Ton Son Nhut that everyone had to be on a stretcher when they took off and landed. And I thought, How am I gonna lay on a stretcher for 22 hours? Nothing's wrong with me; I don't want to take the bed of a wounded soldier. I was told, "We already arranged to have one of the seats saved for you, so after takeoff you can go up and sit in a seat, but you have to come back to your stretcher for meals."

I was in the blue pajamas, with the seersucker housecoat; we were all dressed alike. The person across from me was a schoolteacher who had been drafted. I think he was from North or South Dakota, and he had lost his leg below the knee. He was very jovial, and we joked most of the way. I enjoyed talking to him.

As usual I was the only female on this plane, except for the nurses. To go home, soldiers were really injured; these were the injured that would never come back to the war. It was very depressing to look around and see all these injuries and the nurses talking to them, giving them their medication. There was a boy at the feet of the schoolteacher, and I guess this laid a fit of depression on me because it was so sad—he had lost both arms and was blind. I sat there as the nurse fed him, and I thought, If he was not blind, he could see the spoon coming to his mouth. Or if he had arms he could deal with himself getting food to his mouth. But he doesn't have either. That was a moment of despair. Nothing I had gone through was as bad as what that young man was going to face the rest of his life.

My orders hadn't come through to get out of the country. I was supposed to go home two months before. The orders got misplaced some place over the Pacific or the United States, and so I am lingering in Vietnam, getting more pregnant by the day. So it took an act of Congress to get me home. They told me they were going to get me home before the baby was born. When I finally complained, I went to the general. He understood that I was seven months pregnant and it was time for me to go home. He called Ton Son Nhut Air Force Base and arranged my flight; that took about 15 minutes.

At Ton Son Nhut, the doctor came in to examine me and he asked, "Where do you want to go?" (*The Air Force would drop her off at any stop the flight was making. Markle knew she would have to pay her own way back home from wherever the plane landed.*) I don't have much money and I don't have a credit card. If they dropped me off in San Francisco, then I got to get all the way home to Indiana, and how much is that airplane gonna cost? I got a friend in Washington, D.C., that I can stay with until I get mustered out. I'll stay with her, and that's only a hop, skip, and a jump from Indiana.

Her plane landed at Andrews Air Force Base in Maryland, and she was taken by ambulance to Walter Reed Medical Center in Washington.

I hadn't been over 15 miles an hour in a jeep for a long, long time. So this ambulance is flying down the interstate at about 65 miles an hour, and I just couldn't believe it. He let me sit up front with him, and that feeling—like you're coming back to the world and you're coming to it like a bullet.

I discovered that I was a patient at Walter Reed. I said, "Oh, I don't need to be a patient. I'm just here to go home. I just need to go to the office tomorrow and get my papers and get booted out." "Oh no, you have to become a patient and be released from the hospital. We'll put you up on the ward." My mother didn't know. I was calling her all this time, but she did not know that I was seven months pregnant or that I was coming home. I didn't tell her, because she would have been calling the president. I didn't want that, so I was surprising her, you might say.

They took me up to this ward with pregnant women who had been hospitalized for some reason. And I'm in the shower, and I remember the nurse coming in and saying, "Lieutenant, you've been in here for over an hour. I think you ought to come out." Cause it's hot water! And the dirt's just imbedded in your skin. And it took an hour just to make me feel like I was clean.

It was Sunday, and the doctors did not come in until Monday. When one did come in, he told her that she needed tests.

So I borrowed a dime and I went out to the hall telephone and I called the surgeon general. I get this secretary, and she says she will check on my papers and call me back. She does, and she says, "Lieutenant Markle, what are you doing in Washington, D.C.? You were supposed to be in San Francisco and get discharged. None of this would have happened." I said, "Well, you need to tell the Air Force that."

Her orders came the next day, hand-delivered by the secretary.

I just walked out of the hospital; I was never discharged. I just went down and gave them my medical records and kept on walking right out the door.

She flew to Chicago, where her family met her.

My mother and my father cried, and my sister and her little girl came from Indiana. I still fit in my uniform; I had lost over 28 pounds. At Ton Son Nhut they told us not to wear our uniforms. The minute you get out of where you are going, you get into your civilian clothes. You are not a popular person in the United States at this time. It might be easy for you if people ask you where you've been, not to tell them.

JEANNE URBIN MARKLE 1967

Jeanne Markle and her husband Brian served in Vietnam
together, but she came home early to complete her pregnancy.
She shot this picture from inside a transport plane as it was
loading at Ton Son Nhut Air Force Base in Saigon.

CATHERINE NEVILLE 1944

Catherine Neville served as a nurse in World War II and the Korean War. She noticed an enormous difference in the reception veterans of each war received when they returned to the United States.

No Parades

*"I just ducked into a restroom and took off my uniform
and threw it in the trash and 'became' a civilian."*

*When veterans returned from Korea, they were greeted with what James Walsh calls
a "collective grunt for ingratitude." Korea was hardly the crusade that the two
World Wars had been, and moreover, its uncertain conclusion didn't lend itself to
victory celebrations. The reception many Vietnam veterans got was even worse,
especially as the war dragged on and increasingly divided the country.*

CATHERINE NEVILLE

    Korean War; Army Nurse Corps; Interview
*Neville was a nurse who served both in World War II, when she was stationed in
England, and in the Korean War, when she served in hospitals in Korea and Japan.*

    There were no parades. Well you see you came out as an individual, and I
think that's what happened to the Korean veterans as well as the Vietnam veterans. They came home to nothing, but it was because they weren't a unit. They
were by themselves, or maybe a half dozen, and they went through some separation center, and that's all. They went back to their homes. It was like there was
no end to it. I'm sure it must have been a letdown for them, they were just glad
to get out. But there was no recognition, which we didn't have.

CHUCK HAGEL

    Vietnam War; Army; Interview
The outprocessing was terrible. Now for me, wanting just to get the hell out, it
was the greatest thing that could have happened. The last thing I wanted was
to hear a bunch of majors or sergeant majors tell me about anything. But when

you think, when you let somebody get out on that street in San Francisco, or wherever they're gonna go to, with a full wallet, new class A's, and "Thank you for your service, young man, now go have a good life," considering what they had just been through [there is] no transition, no kind of bringing it down a little bit, no adjustment. I mean, you had your physical and you had your chaplain talk to you and a couple of psychiatrists talk to you, and that whole thing was about an hour.

That just wasn't a good way to do it, because in those days, in '68, you had those draftees in there, many of them not suited to be there for a variety of reasons, and they needed some counseling out of this. Now some guys were going to be headed for trouble no matter what. Some guys went in with trouble, and they came out with trouble. Maybe Vietnam made it worse for some guys. In some cases it wouldn't have mattered if they had gone to Vietnam or not.

When I was deputy administrator of the Veterans Administration during the first Reagan Administration, I had many Vietnam veterans say to me the same thing I'm saying to you: "If I would have had maybe a week or ten days to think about things and get myself together…." In some cases these kids didn't go home to their mother or their wives for a month. They did it on the basis of, "Well, I deserve it. All I've been through and I survived, I paid my debt."

How did the public receive you when you walked out of that gate into civilian life?

I didn't ever experience any difficult time. I suppose I got out at the right time, about December '68. I know as you move forward the intensity of the anti-war movement is kind of rough. And I went back to the Midwest where it was a different world. I was brought back to the bosom of veterans and service to your country. I had great experiences with the veterans of World War II and Korea— very encouraging, very helpful.

Rod Hinsch
Vietnam War; Army; Interview
Finally all of a sudden the day is there and you get on the plane and everybody's talking and the plane starts up and everyone gets quiet. It's real quiet. And then you can hear the plane's wheels as they jump and they're off the ground and everybody starts yelling and screaming, "That's it! We're out of here! We're not in Vietnam anymore!" And so from then on, it's a party. Finally getting back home and getting on the ground is pretty anticlimactic.

When I came back I wanted to look up some of my friends, and this was the

CHUCK HAGEL 1968

After a year's tour of duty in Vietnam, Chuck Hagel (right)
came home to a rural Nebraska community whose citizens
embraced him and supported his service.

part where I was kind of disillusioned. You see, it was a very unpopular war. You take part in something tremendous, right or wrong, you did things that you normally would never have an opportunity to do. You feel good about a lot of things that you did, and you want to talk about it. But your own generation doesn't want to hear it; as a matter of fact, your own generation feels that you are something less than admirable for doing any of it. I really wanted to talk to my friends, but they didn't want to hear it. So basically I just hung the uniform back in the closet and tried to fit in with my own generation.

RONALD WINTER
Vietnam War; Marine Corps; Interview

I got home about midnight, and my family picked me up at the airport. It was all very nice, everyone was happy, but no one asked me about Vietnam ever. Not then, not now. Ever. The next night, I went out to a night spot up the road— they always had good food, they always had good bands. Went out to get a couple beers. I was sitting on a stool with my back to the wall talking to my sister. And a guy with long hair and love beads and a peace sign snuck up and punched me in the face. Sucker punched me. I couldn't believe that. That was my welcome home.

We were told when we got to Travis Air Force Base in California, "When you finish getting home, don't wear your uniform out in public." That's a horrible thing to tell American servicemen: Don't wear your uniform in public. You'll be drawing attention to yourself of a kind you don't want. It wasn't a good home-coming. It wasn't fun, it wasn't nice. It made me wonder why I'd gone in the first place.

RHONA KNOX PRESCOTT
Vietnam War; Army Nurse Corps; Interview
When I came back, I was the only woman on the plane. We came into McCord Air Force Base in Washington State on a military flight, and then we had to somehow get down to San Francisco to a civilian airport. In uniform. When I got to San Francisco, everybody was just yelling and looking mad and calling us names. Since I was a woman, I just ducked into a restroom and took off my uniform and threw it in the trash and "became" a civilian.

I went across country to visit my dad and his wife (my stepmother was a nurse in the Korean conflict), thinking, "Oh, this is safe haven. Now I can just blab and yell and scream and get it all out of my system and they are going to understand." They didn't understand, either. My dad paced; he seemed embarrassed. He didn't say anything, but he wasn't with me. My stepmother actually yelled at me and told me that it couldn't possibly have been like that. She said, "The news says this, you say that." She wanted me to keep my voice lowered and stop my ranting and raving because the neighbors would be concerned. There was just no understanding or support in this place at all.

So I just became a "little woman" who didn't talk about the military or Vietnam. I just kind of kept it all inside. From what I understand, that is pretty much what the guys did, too. It was easier for me because I could hide; there were hardly any women in the military at that time. That is what we all did. Nobody would talk about it because it fell on deaf ears. There was so much emotion pent up.

JAMES WALSH
Korean War; Army; Memoir
I rotated back to the good old USA in May 1952, an alive, very bright, single-rocker U.S. Army staff sergeant.

It took two weeks for the troop ship to cross the Pacific Ocean. When it docked at San Francisco's Presidio, it nearly keeled over, every GI who could crowding the rails dockside. We looked for the welcoming committee, a band, the Red Cross with coffee and donuts.

There was no crowd, no band, no Red Cross, no coffee or donuts, nothing to welcome America's fighting men home from Korea in late May 1952. There was a collective grunt for ingratitude.

The ship's unloading ramp hit the landing, and GIs, thrilled to be back on American soil while irritated they'd been forgotten, filed cheerfully toward the reception building. From out of nowhere, three civilians, a beautiful young woman dressed prettier than a fashion model and an older pretty woman, as sharply dressed holding the hand of an older handsome man in a black serge suit and red tie, rushed onto the landing. A GI broke ranks and ran from the ramp into the arms of his sweetheart, his parents. They hugged and kissed, kissed and hugged, hugged and kissed.

There wasn't a dry GI eye aboard the ship or on the landing.

I had in mind a reception of my own. After I'd arrived at Fort Sheridan, Illinois, and got my orders for leave, I was going to catch a Chicago bus, get off in front of St. Juliana School, pull my kid brother out of grade school, and march two blocks of Oketo Street to home and a surprise on Mom and Dad.

It was me that was surprised. At the gates of Fort Sheridan, there were Mom, Dad, sister Kay, and brothers Jack, Ed, and Denny.

There wasn't a dry GI eye.

The war changed anyone who was off to serve in it, from those who never made it out of the States to the front line soldiers. Their assumption—and fervent hope—was that they could return to a home front unaltered since they left. Inevitably, some would be disappointed or worse.

BRUCE FENCHEL
World War II; Army; Interview
Fenchel was 18 years old when he left Strawberry Point, Iowa, in 1943 to serve in a tank battalion in Europe under the command of General Patton. He fought in several major battles, and his unit helped to liberate the Ohrdruf Concentration Camp.

I arrived home at twenty years old. My father had died while I was overseas, and that was a crushing blow to me. I just didn't know what to expect when I got home. My mother was only about forty-seven years old, and the one thing that shocked me was that she had gone from brown hair to gray hair in that length of time that her boys were overseas. I wanted to surprise her, so I took a train all the way to Manchester, Iowa, which was 16 miles from Strawberry Point. I hitchhiked home with my duffel bag on my back. The first car that came along was the sister of a friend I had graduated high school with, and she took me right to my doorstep.

After I got settled in, it might have been the next day or the following day, my mother said, "You know, there's a phone call for you. Cliff Huntley's Meat Market wants to interview you for a job, to learn the meat cutting business." I guess I had been in the meat-cutting business for the last year or so, and I didn't want any part of it, but I agreed to go and talk to him. On my way up, a car passed me and it backfired and I just lost it. I was face down in the dirt clawing with both hands. I got up, brushed myself off, and acted like I had tripped.

It was only within minutes that I met a high school classmate that had served in the Navy and been released. I told him about my experience, and he said, "Well, you've got to do something to get that off your mind. I'm hitchhiking down to Iowa City to see about going to college, on the GI Bill." I said, "Well, I guess I'll go along with you," with no intention of ever enrolling, because I didn't think I'd be able to afford to go to college. So the two of us thumbed our way down to Iowa City, which was more than a hundred miles, and when I left Iowa City, I was enrolled in liberal arts and hopefully trying to get into dental school. We hitchhiked home. I got home late that evening and walked into the house, and my mother said, "That was one long interview."

CORBIN WILLIS
World War II; Army Air Corps, Air Force; Memoir
Willis was aboard a bomber that was shot down in November 1944 over Germany, and it was reported as presumed destroyed. He spent five months as a prisoner of war and was never able to contact his wife or family before being released at the end of the war. He finally began his long trip home in the summer of 1945.

We were assigned to a German luxury liner that operated out of South America. It was converted to a military troop transport, and all the portholes were covered and welded shut. We had forty officers to a room and were far more crowded than in our POW barracks. If you slept on your side your elbows hit the bunk above you. The ship was so crowded that only one-third of the passengers were allowed on deck at a time to prevent capsizing. This was fine until we encountered rough seas. Only two or three of us did not get sick from the pitching and yawing action, and the room was one mass of vomit and odors.

We arrived in New York harbor with a fanfare of fireboats and harbor tugs spraying water into the air. They had a huge sign painted on the warehouse at the wharf where we docked that read, "Welcome Home POWs." We were all a batch of weak sisters. Our emotions ran rampant. We could hardly wait to debark, but waited for the band to strike up their music—"Don't Fence Me In" and "Candy" were both hit songs while I was in POW camps, but they were appropriate for the occasion. We were taken to Camp Kilmer, New Jersey, and we all headed for telephones to call our loved ones. They had set up telephone booths about as far as the eye could see, and each one had a line in front of it. I remember they handed us cartons of milk while I was standing there waiting, and it tasted like ambrosia—wonderful stuff.

I finally got a telephone and tried to call my wife in Washington, D.C., but our telephone had been disconnected. I was unable to locate her through the locator files, so I called my parents in Denver and got my mother. She did not believe it was me, so the operator in New Jersey who placed our calls for us finally convinced her it was not a hoax. My mother proceeded to cry for about eleven long minutes before I could get a question in edgewise. I asked about my wife, but she lied and told me she was not sure of her location, so I would have to go to Colorado and, when I arrived, she would have the location.

I then boarded a train after getting uniforms. I now weighed 121, down from 165, so the uniforms issued lasted only a few weeks before I outgrew them. I arrived in Denver in about three days. At the train my mother told me that my wife had remarried in my absence and had started a family. That was the most painful experience I had as a POW. I accepted all the experience of combat and being a POW but was not prepared for that shock!!

My mother and father hovered over me day and night to try to make me happy, and finally I accepted the fact of the situation and set my course for my future. I filed for divorce from my wife under the only statute of law allowed in Colorado—"Adultery." When the baby was born, it was born in my name, because the other marriage was null and void. The father upon remarriage had to adopt his own son. These are some of the tragedies of war that take a definite bite out of personal emotions.

{ ONE MAN'S STORY }

Paul Steppe

"Sure enough, someone had kissed me and I missed it."

Steppe was a marine serving in Korea. On Christmas Eve, 1951, he was crouched in a bunker when he was wounded by a grenade. His wounds, in one foot and his buttocks, were serious enough for him to be evacuated. Following are excerpts from his memoir.

As I was being lifted off the floor I woke up and saw six South Korean workers that were attached to our company, preparing to carry me to the battalion aid station. They carried me outside and proceeded down the reverse clip to the base of the hill we occupied.

Due to the bouncing around, almost falling off the stretcher head first, I remained fully awake. Several times the stretcher-bearers slipped and went down on their knees and I almost slid off the stretcher. It eventually happened! On another slip I fell off the stretcher face down in about two feet of snow. From the tone of their language I knew the Koreans were cursing each other out for dropping me. I wasn't injured and the blanket still covered my face.

Ultimately we arrived at what looked to be the battalion aid station. I no more than shut my eyes when a chaplain came by and touched my shoulder and asked me if I was comfortable, was I warm, did I want anything? "Would you like a miniature?" He was holding about five small whiskey miniatures as he swayed back and forth himself, obviously from his Christmas Eve celebration. I told him no thanks and he prayed for me. I shut my eyes in disbelief. The padre was ready for hospitalization himself.

The next time I awoke, a female American Army nurse was asking me some questions. I don't remember what I said because I had not seen an American

Paul Steppe outside a two-man bunker, where he spent much of his time in Korea on what he would call an "everlasting watch." He was wounded in such a structure and began his eventful journey back to the United States.

female in a long time. I couldn't take my eyes from her. It was almost a shock!

I noticed I had a bandage over each breast. Before I laid my head back on the pillow I asked the nurse why those bandages, because I was not injured there. She remarked that the doctors were joking around and made a "bra" to hold some shrapnel "you may want to keep." I told her that I didn't want the shrapnel, and she removed the bandages and walked away.

I slept most of the day and upon waking overheard other servicemen talking about the movie star Paul Douglas coming through the tent with a troupe of dancers and singers. They greeted everyone, shook their hands, and the guys got kisses on their cheeks from the girls. My cheeks were covered with beard. I mentioned this to one of the fellows, who informed me that I got kissed on the forehead. I didn't believe him until he dug out a metal mirror and I was able to see for myself. Sure enough, someone had kissed me and I missed it.

The time came for me to leave the hospital tent. I was carried outside to a waiting helicopter. Another Marine was placed on the other side of the helicopter,

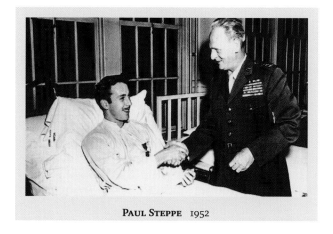

PAUL STEPPE 1952

Paul Steppe receives a Purple Heart from Lt. Gen. Franklin H. Hart, in Yokosuka, Japan. His injuries required that he return to the States, but he almost didn't make it.

but it took six men to carry him, he was so large. After he was secured, the pilot tried to start the helicopter, but the engine kept spitting and sputtering. In the meantime I kept thinking about that huge fellow on the other side. Flying low and somewhat lopsided, due to the giant strapped in on the other side of the craft, prevented me from seeing the hospital ship as we approached it.

The sea was extremely rough on the ship, rocking it back and forth, with dark clouds moving swiftly. Suddenly there was a loud boom, sounding like an explosion. I heard bells ring and the public address system was sounding off codes and numbers. This meant nothing to me. I just wanted to know if we were sinking! A corpsman in my ward looked out of a porthole and said there had been a collision. A destroyer had difficulty coming alongside the hospital ship due to the waves and crashed into her right side. It was learned that the destroyer had some bodies they wanted transferred off their ship. There was no serious damage to either ship.

Steppe was transferred to an Air Force base in Tokyo and then to the U.S. Naval Hospital in Yokosuka, Japan.

The doctor appeared at my bunk as I was writing more letters home. He informed me that I was going home by the end of the week and would eventually and probably end up at the closest Naval facility to my home. My injury was healing well, but I would have to undergo therapy for a period of time. For a while I felt somewhat guilty about going home, but then I reasoned that if I was still on the front lines with my buddies I would probably be rotated back to the States anyway. This diminished the guilt feeling.

The next afternoon I was given an hour's notice to pack up my gear and to stay in my bunk. A stretcher was brought into the ward that was placed on a four-wheel cart. I was loaded onto the stretcher. I could have walked, but this was the way I had to be transported.

The bus was loaded to capacity quickly, and the driver drove into areas unknown. While we were driving through Tokyo, a streetcar rammed our hospital bus from the rear. One person that had a seat and was sitting upright was knocked to the floor but not injured. Almost an hour later we got underway again for our intended destination, a US Air Force base on the other side of Tokyo.

The bus drove onto the airstrip, where a huge four-engine Military Air Transport Service (MATS) plane was awaiting our arrival. We were carried up a ramp near the tail of the plane and again strapped onto hanging loops that secured the stretchers. There were more delays. It seemed that some injured civilian workers had not showed up yet. When they did show up, everyone applauded.

The huge plane maneuvered its way onto the end of the runway facing Tokyo Bay. At that end of the runway the elevation of the ground was only seven feet from the water. The plane's engines were roaring, the brakes were released, and the plane began moving at high speed down the runway. I noticed that ambulances and fire apparatus were on the sides of the runway, following the trail of the plane.

About ten to twelve seconds after the brakes had been released and the plane was moving at high speed down the runway, the right landing gear broke from the fuselage, causing the right side of the plane and its wing with two engines to hit the pavement of the runway. The plane skidded right off the runway into the soil, which blackened the plane's windows, then veered left and right for a considerable distance, then spun around several times before it came to a stop at the end of the runway at the water's edge. As soon as the plane did stop, a corpsman opened the left side emergency door and was hit in the face and body with foam from one of the firefighting trucks.

Only one person was injured in the crash. In less than two hours, another plane was found and rigged up to handle the stretchers.

With my eyes shut I listened as the plane roared down the runway and lifted up, kept climbing, and finally reached an altitude where the plane leveled off. We were on our way to Guam, I thought. A corpsman told me later that the stopover in Guam had been cancelled and we were flying direct to Hawaii for a few days' rest. I did sleep many hours and woke up to see a bright sun shining through the windows. I saw a ship in the Pacific Ocean that looked to be about an inch long and was fascinated with the view.

Conclusion.

And so endeth the memoirs which I began before I started for home and to which I have added comments now and then until now, 15 yrs afterward, I have brought it to a close.

Looking back over my service in France, I might later think of dozens of incidents I might have included in the narrative but it has been impossible to remember all the little events in sequence.

I was eager to go to France if it became necessary, and since I was there I made the best of the situation. Conditions were pretty bad at times but I managed to bear with them.

We were honored by being sent to the Army of Occupation

CHAPTER SEVEN

Reflections

The conclusion to Vincent Reed's memoir. Reed began writing in a diary while serving in World War I, added other recollections over the years, and finished the document in 1933.

WILLIAM ARNETT CA 1941

*Arnett operated a tank destroyer, was on the beach at
Normandy on D-Day, and saw some of the worst fighting in
Europe in the last year of the war. Fifty-seven years later, he
was still having nightmares about the war.*

Aftermath

"There is not enough gold in Fort Knox to make me do it again, but I am glad I did it."

WILLIAM ARNETT

Army

Arnett was in a tank destroyer unit in Europe following the Normandy Invasion.

After about a week in combat, you're old. I don't care if you're nineteen years old or what. It's not like when you're drunk and drive; nobody thinks they're going to have an accident. When you're in combat, you know you can be killed or hurt.

After the war I was outside at the factory where I worked and there was a noise that sounded very much like a shell coming in, and although the war had been over for about nine or ten months, I still hit the dirt. Just an automatic thing. I had recurring bad dreams where your wife kicks you to wake you up because you're moanin' and groanin' and everything. That went on very heavy for about 15 or 20 years. Even today [2001] about once a year I'll have one of those dreams. Anybody's that in combat long enough will crack up. No doubt about it.

MAX CLELAND

Army

Cleland was an Army officer in Vietnam when he was severely wounded.

I came home feeling very guilty, feeling very embarrassed. You know: If I'm such a great military leader, why did I get wounded, why did I get wounded this way? A million questions. You replay the tape in your mind. With no answer. Same ending. It was well over 30 years later that one of the men who first got to me,

David Lloyd, called me after seeing a documentary on The History Channel about combat medics on which I told my story. He said, "It wasn't your grenade," and I said, "How do you know?" And he said, "Because I was first to you."

It set me reeling for a while. For days I didn't sleep all that well, because you arrange the furniture of your experience in your mind, and for 35 years the furniture is just like that. And there's a certain security about it. All of a sudden somebody comes in and rearranges the furniture of your experience. And so it took a while to adjust to the new reality. And the new reality was, it wasn't my grenade. It was the grenade of a guy behind me who'd been in country a day or two and been convinced by himself or somebody else that he should lengthen the pins on the grenades he was carrying to make them easier to pull out in combat. That made him a walking time bomb.

I look back now at my young troops, and I love them more now than I did then. I wish I could put my arms around all of them. We went through something unique, the camaraderie of the battlefield, the camaraderie of the trenches. I think Vietnam veterans try to embrace each other because we were isolated and pretty much left alone and abandoned by the country.

ISABELLE CEDAR COOK
Army Nurse Corps
Cook served in North Africa, Italy, and France.

I keep thinking about the children that will soon only know World War II as a chapter in the history books. I wanted very much to share my experiences with them, so I decided to write a book. I called it *In Times of War,* because in times of war, things are very different from other times. Relationships don't last very long. Sometimes you go with a soldier for several weeks or months, and then they go into combat and you never hear from them again. And you don't know whether they were killed in action, whether they were wounded, or what happened to them. So you're always left with that feeling, what could have been but wasn't. We tried to act as sisters or mothers; some of these men were so young, seventeen years old; you just had to be there to comfort them, hold their hand.

I've joined the Third General Hospital World War II Association. We meet every two years for reunions; they always have a newsletter full of pictures, and everyone contributes their stories. I also have a photo album of the Third General Hospital, all the members of the hospital: There were approximately 50 doctors, 100 nurses, 500 enlisted men, Red Cross workers, physiotherapists, dieticians, and administrative staff. I am a charter member of the Women's

Memorial in Washington, D.C. I have been going to the schools to talk with children about what it was like to be a nurse during those times.

VINCENT REED

Army

Reed was an infantryman during some of the fiercest fighting during World War I, and after the Armistice he served for six months in the occupying Allied forces.

We were honored by being sent to Germany as a part of the Army of Occupation, but it did not seem an honor to me, as I was anxious to return home. However, I was there, so I endeavored to see everything possible, took advantage of every opportunity to go on leaves of absence and see the country. There were days when I longed to return to my loved ones and it seemed as though we would never reach the time to return. However, as the time for our departure drew near, we became so busy in finishing our records and paperwork that the last few weeks sped like lightning. But as there is an end to everything, so my army service came to an end, and I again took my place in the ranks of the workers.

Would I go again? I should hate to have to go again under the same conditions. I appreciated all of the good times in France and Germany and all the trips I made, but I should hate to have to go through another war to have those enjoyments. May God speed the day when all war will be outlawed. I certainly hope my boys will never have to go through such a war. And so I repeat, may God speed the day when men and nations may be able to settle their difficulties without having to resort to armed force and the destruction of life and property.

ALVIN DICKSON

Army

Dickson served in the Army during the Battle of the Bulge.

In the early days after I got out of the service I was having a lot of nightmares. I didn't talk to anybody about it. I just wanted to put it out of my mind. The horror of war was fresh in my mind. Some of the things carry over. When I was in a house at night I would close all the drapes, because just like on the battlefield, if they can see you and you can't see them, you're at a disadvantage. I don't think I could have talked like this some years ago.

I got this job, and I was restless. I couldn't stay at my desk; I was walking back and forth. Eventually they fired me, and I don't blame them. I got a job at a small newspaper in Cleveland as an advertising manager. That didn't work out. I had to do something; I had a family. So I went into the insurance business and became somewhat successful at that, came to Toledo as a general agent, and from that time on I did well.

JOHN ENMAN

Army

Enman was an Army photographer who served in the China-Burma-India Theater of World War II.

World War II took three years of my life, but looking back, it was a worthwhile swap. I matured faster, becoming wiser sooner in the ways of the world than had I remained at home; had, obviously, unforgettable experiences that were mostly pleasant and frequently funny; saw a world not yet overrun by tourists and exploding populations; made lasting friendships; and got enough financial help from the GI Bill to see me through graduate schools and into an enjoyable academic career I probably would not otherwise have experienced.

BRUCE FENCHEL

Army

Fenchel was in a tank company that landed on Utah Beach on D-Day. He saw action at several battles and helped to liberate a concentration camp.

My problems really developed after I retired. Then the garbage started coming back, so realistic it would be in dreams some 50 years later. I would scream out in a nightmare. So I went back to work for a few years part-time.

My one brother that was in the Marines has never been able to talk about the war. He went into Nagasaki on the day after it was bombed. We didn't share too many military stories; I guess we just wanted to get away from it. Another brother, being in the Air Force, had horrific stories, but he would tell me and no one else. I think that's why I'm glad for this opportunity, to encourage more and more people who do remember their stories to get them on paper for their children, their grandchildren, their great-grandchildren, so that we never forget that this horrible thing did take place.

I did keep in touch with my gunner for a number of years. He would call me every Christmas morning. I had thought he was killed in action, but he was captured by the Germans and spent the rest of his time in a German prisoner of war camp.

The military experience taught you forgiveness. It's kind of like a sentence that has been placed on you; you may get out of jail but you never get over the sentence. You take it to your grave with you.

BRUCE FENCHEL 1943

Fenchel's tank company landed on Normandy on D-Day. His brother served in the Army Air Corps, and for years, they would share their stories of the war only with each other. Being in the military, he says, "taught you forgiveness."

VIOLET ASKINS HILL GORDON

Women's Army Corps

Gordon was one of the first African-American women to serve in the new Women's Army Auxiliary Corps during World War II.

I doubt that I would have gone into social work if I had not had the interpersonal experience with a couple of people who were also in the service and were moving in that direction. It drew my attention to a profession that I had really not considered up until that time. So, once having decided on that, I knew where I was headed.

The other thing of value is that right after high school I had worked as a clerk for A. Philip Randolph. He organized the Brotherhood of Sleeping Car Porters, the first black labor union. He was ahead of the Martin Luther King era in that the first march on Washington was organized by him. The point of all this is that it enabled me to really see group activism and to see that there could be a role in that for me if this was something that I wanted to pursue. It really formed my political and social point of view. I went from having gone to a school in Batavia, Illinois, which is a suburb of Chicago, a town of five thousand people, to experiences with the labor union movement, followed by movement into the WAC, which moved me into an administrative as well as a command level. It enabled me to move away from being a somewhat shy, introspective person.

CHUCK HAGEL

Army

Hagel served a one-year tour of duty in Vietnam, where he was twice wounded. In his first year out of the Army he was working as a reporter and was drawn to covering a Veterans Day ceremony.

I think anyone who has served their country in uniform and has experienced what no one else has experienced, poignantly out of this country, even more poignantly than that in a war, all of that will always be a part of you that can never be taken away or be decoupled from the whole person that you are. And then your recognition of all the other people who have served and have been through what you have been through, just to be near somebody and know that he knows that you know. I think that's why the Vietnam Veterans Memorial is so powerful—you don't even have to say a word.

So I wanted to be near those other veterans. I didn't expect any recognition. I just wanted to be part of a group of people who had done something special. It didn't mean they were any better or smarter. But we'd done something that most people will never do.

There's not a day goes by that you don't at least pull back on some little thing—life's not about big things every day—and you don't recall an experience you had in the service, in Vietnam: a tolerance, an understanding, reaching beyond to understand more than the obvious.

ROD HINSCH

Army

Hinsch volunteered for the Army out of high school and became a member of the Special Forces in Vietnam. After five years of not talking about his experiences, Hinsch began opening up.

I decided I just gotta talk about this. I wrote about just what I'd seen, not about what anyone had said. I had always been a history buff, so when I went to college on the GI Bill, that was my major. Later on, people wanted to know, so I started working with schools and different organizations, telling people what this was all about.

At that time, and we're in the '80s, kids wanted to know just what it was that upset their parents so much when they watched television. They had no idea what it was, but we were going to tell them. And now people are still interested, and that's good, that's great.

I think anybody who went to Vietnam thinks about it every day. Not in a bad way. It's just that once a Vietnam veteran, always a Vietnam veteran. Because of a lot of social and cultural things that were different from the Korean or the Second World War, we tend to be impacted in a different way.

THOMAS HODGE
Marine Corps
Hodge was a truck driver for the Marines in Vietnam.

I still have friends today, Vietnam has really messed them up. I think about Vietnam; it's almost an everyday thing.

I started in a job when I got back, and somebody asked me if I'd been in the military and I said I was in the Marines in Vietnam. The guy said, "Oh, you were one of Uncle Sam's hired assassins." I took offense to that. I said, "We didn't ask to go to that war. We were sent there because we had a uniform on."

I've been down to the Vietnam Veterans Memorial in Washington several times. I've taken my children and explained just what this Wall is for. I had to explain a lot to them about Vietnam. I feel the Wall is great for the men who died in Vietnam, but there are lots of guys who have died since then from their wounds, and they're not recognized.

Most times if I go to public events, I have to stand at the back of the event because I can keep an eye on everybody else. No one else has got my back. When I was in Vietnam, if you were three or ninety-three, I didn't trust you.

WILLIAM LONCARIC
Army
Loncaric was on the beach on D-Day and later helped to liberate the death camp at Dachau. He answers an interviewer's question about what his service in the military taught him.

You're never afraid of a situation. You just face up to any situation you had; you face it straight ahead. And nothing bothered me. My philosophy is, Whatever happens, happens for the best. The first few days of Normandy, I didn't

Lasting Memories

 Out of the war experience, so many survivors look for something beyond their luck: when they didn't catch the bullet that downed the soldier next to them, or when they were too sick to board a troop ship that later was torpedoed and took all passengers down with it. Again and again, veterans have told interviewers or written in their memoirs and letters about the camaraderie they enjoyed in wartime. It begins with barracks life, where it's understood that you have surrendered your rights to basic privacy and it's important to find a core group, or at least one buddy, you can get along with. But it's in the field, whether on the front lines or working in support of those who are under fire, that you learn to watch out not just for yourself but also for those around you. The shared experience of facing danger is a powerful bonding agent. The friendships forged under these special circumstances can last a lifetime. At the very least, the memories of them do.

Patricia Seawalt with unidentified soldier, Saudi Arabia, 1990. In her collection, she recalls pulling a practical joke on Halloween night that helped to lighten the mood.

On patrol in Vietnam, from the Robert Bendl collection. Bendl
served in the Army infantry for two years, doing one tour of
duty in the late 1960s. Ben Snyder (below, front row, right)
and the crew of his World War II bomber, Short Run.

In this photo from the Frederick Stilson collection (above), a trio of GIs perch on a German 6-inch naval gun in post-World War I France. James Walsh took this photo of his pals Carroll Truscott and Dean Warren (below) in Korea.

Donald Finn (above, at right) in Hawaii with two buddies, 1940. Finn was still stationed in Pearl Harbor a year later, on December 7. Isabelle Cedar Cook (below, kneeling, second from left) and her fellow nurses prepare to depart Africa for Italy, 1944.

think I was going to make it. And now I'm eighty years of age, and I can't believe I'm still alive.

JEANNE URBIN MARKLE
Army Nurse Corps
Markle was a nurse who went to Vietnam with husband Brian, a doctor.

Nobody asked me anything about Vietnam. It was just like it was a great big secret: Don't talk about it. My mom and dad, it was hard for them to vocalize the questions they would like to ask me. And my mother was really kind of honest when she said, "Your letters were all happy. You talked about this and that and the people and what they were doing. Every letter you wrote me, there was not a mention of the war." A few years ago, I let my best friend read my letters— because my mother saved every one of them, and I think there were 200 of them, and I still have them and I've got the ones she sent me—and my friend came back and said, "You really didn't tell your mother anything about the war." And I said, "How could you? Nobody understands what you've gone through."

The only way I could get on with my life was to kind of encapsulate that and say it was this chapter in a book and I've gotta close that. And it got easier and easier every day to not talk about it, because nobody talked about it. So maybe it was a good thing. I don't know, but there were times where I'd wake up and be crying because I was having dreams, and there was nobody to ask, "What's wrong?" "Oh, nothing."

I didn't really feel like that piece of me was put back until the dedication of the Vietnam Women's Memorial. Brian and I flew to Washington, D.C., with all the other women veterans. We were recognized for our service. A little bit too late, but better than never. It was very, very touching. We were marching down the street and there were veterans lining the streets and the sidewalks, and we had the 24th banner [for their hospital], and you could hear, "I was there, I was there, thank you, ma'am! You saved my life!" It was so touching. It was probably one of the best experiences of my life. We were able to talk to each other. Seven of my Quonset hut roommates were there, so after 25, 30 years it was great to be able to sit and talk.

WALTER MORRIS
Army
Morris helped to form the first African-American paratroop company during World War II.

I was scared to death to get out of the service, because I went in as a kid and, you know, the Army was always there.

He moved to Seattle to pick up his prewar occupation as an apprentice brick-layer, working for his father. Because he was a veteran, the union made him a full bricklayer.

That upset my father and all the other bricklayers because now my father had to pay me the union scale. The other bricklayers had to work next to me and I didn't know what the hell I was doing, and I was making the same wages as they were making. So they wouldn't help me. But finally they came around and everything worked out all right.

We have a 555 Parachute Association for ex-troopers, ex-airborne men, and we have around 1,100 members. We have chapters from California to Chicago to New York, and we have one here in Palm Coast [Florida]. We meet every three months; there's not much to talk about—we tell the same lies over and over again. Of the original 20 soldiers who started out as a test platoon, there are only six of us alive today.

Basic training that one gets as a soldier or sailor follows them throughout their life. For example: punctuality. It teaches you to be on time; there's no excuse. They say, 10 o'clock—you have to be there. A lot of people who don't go through that training, it's 10:00, 10:10, no big deal. I think what the Army did was instill in me good habits that's carried me through for the last 60 years.

JOANNE PALELLA

Army

Palella enlisted in the Army in 1980 at the age of eighteen and served during the Persian Gulf War as a truck driver and ammunition specialist.

I don't ever want to see war again. I'll fight a war when it's in my own back-yard on my own land. Otherwise, I won't go. When I left Saudi Arabia after all the dead I saw and smelled and all the destruction, I realized how easy life was to take. We made a joke: hamburger meat, because that's what it looked like when the corpses were open and bloated for three days. It was the only thing we could do, though I vomited the first time I was there. I don't want to think of people as hamburger meat ever, ever again.

The military did a great thing for me, the war at least. It allowed me to real-ize that it's actually not the big things that matter, like getting a car or a house. Those are very important things in life. But it's the little things, like talking to your mother and sharing a meal with a friend and before you go letting them know you love them even if you're fighting with them—because you never know where your life or their life is going to go, and the last words you want them to know is that there was love.

The military is great for some people; it was great for me. I've seen it ruin others. I think it's a great structure in life, but so are a lot of other things. If it's for you, do it; if not, don't. I would encourage children or family members to go into the military if I saw it inclined in their personality.

Women are a lot more accepted in the military. It's more accepted by mothers who have raised their young sons to learn that women are equal. Just like what African Americans went through in World War II. They fought for their country, came back, and were treated as second-rate citizens again. In the '60s that was revolted against and justly so. Women are better off, though there is some way to go.

SALLY HITCHCOCK PULLMAN
Army Nurse Corps
Sally Hitchcock was a nurse during World War II, serving in the Pacific Theater.

All this happened a long time ago. It was a terrible time, an inspiring time, a sad and wonderful time, a time which molded all of us into people different from the person we had been before.

When the war ended, life went on. Many of the deep friendships we formed then have continued to the present. Sadly I have lost track of many wonderful Army friends. The good side for me is that the memory of these friends is frozen in time. Their faces remain forever young, their bodies straight and slim, their smiles bright.

NATHANIEL RALEY
Army Air Corps
Raley was a fighter pilot who was shot down over Anzio, Italy, and spent over 14 months as a prisoner of war in various camps in Italy and Germany.

When I was in combat, in the prison, I never had any nightmares. I got home, and my bedroom was next to my mother's bedroom, and I started having screaming nightmares about being a prisoner, about combat. Mother would come in and shake me to get me out of it. Then when I got into college, my roommate, it scared him. He would shake me to get me out of that nightmare. Eventually I met the girl I married, and I told her about having screaming nightmares. She said, "Oh, sure, sure." She passed it off. The first night I had one I scared the poor girl out of her wits. She said I was never violent; all I would do is lie there and scream. The nightmares continued, but they've tapered off. But I've had dreams; one dream my daughter was being tortured in front of me to make me talk. And she wasn't even born until the 1950s, so I dreamed about things that were not real.

I have the highest respect for the American military, and sometimes I choke up on that. I think everybody needs to have some military experience. And I have no sympathy for anyone who is afraid. I was afraid. If you're not afraid, you don't know what's going on around you. Fear is a healthy thing—but controlled fear, not absolutely frightened.

I wouldn't take anything for the experience. There's not enough gold in Fort Knox to make me do it again, but I am glad I did it.

SIDNEY RICHES
Army

Riches served in the Army infantry in the Pacific Theater of World War II, worked at various jobs after the war, and then reenlisted and served during the Korean War as well.

My gradual adjustment to civilian life was fairly smooth in comparison with some returnees who had a difficult period of mental adjustment of being "alone" in a broad spectrum of seemingly uncaring humanity. Being an integral part of a cohesive military unit, one enjoyed comradeship and togetherness not at first evident on the outside, thus enforcing the illogical notion in one's receptive mind that this new environment was going to take some getting used to. My better period of therapy was in Imperial Valley where the work was hard, rugged, tedious, and long hours. My days (and nights) included operating and maintaining farm equipment, plowing, irrigating, discing, etc., besides tending a herd of livestock, all of which took much of my energies and helped immeasurably to bring me to a leveled balance of stability.

DONALD SPENCER
Army Air Corps

Spencer was a gunner whose bomber flew missions over France, Belgium, and Germany during World War II. The following is from a July 2, 1945, letter to his sister.

It's hard to think what good you could have derived from your combat experiences, but all one's life seems to work together for the good if you let it. When you look back at many things you could change, if you could, you wouldn't

Clare Morrison Crane's first husband, Herbert Johns, was stationed in England in World War II. He was diagnosed with leukemia and was on his way back to the U.S. in July 1945 when he died in Newfoundland. Flight Officer Louie Bronzy (right) visits his grave in the military cemetery there. In 1947, that cemetery was closed, and Johns's remains were moved to Arlington Cemetery, where he was buried a second time (above).

really. Most of our experiences, good and bad, are for our good. Each setback & knock makes you that much better and more ready for the next ones. I talk, I mean write, like a preacher or something worse. I just want you to realize this one thing. If you welcome life whatever it brings you, make the most of it, know with all your heart that it is working for your good, you will find happiness through the long days and months ahead.

PAUL STEPPE

Marine Corps

Steppe served as a combat marine during the Korean War; he was injured by a grenade in December 1951 and evacuated to the United States.

I had a little leather binder that had all the addresses of my buddies. When I got hurt, that was lost. I didn't have any addresses, and when I wanted to get in touch with them, I'd forgotten their last names. I contacted one from Maryland, and he didn't even want to talk to me. He wanted to forget it. And there are probably a lot of people out there like that that don't want to talk about what we're talking about today.

For a short time I became a police officer, and my experiences carried over because I didn't take anything from anybody. I was able to take physical control of myself. And I thought I did a good job.

I'm very thankful that I've been allowed to live and relate this story. Would I do it again? Without hesitation. I wasn't a hero. I know I used a flamethrower in attacking bunkers and killed people. The first time I shot a man over there, I was reluctant to do it, but I knew if I didn't, he might shoot me. After the first kill, it becomes a little bit easier. I wasn't the only one who shot him; I think four or five hit him at the same time, so I could always say, "I helped kill him."

The smell of the bodies always stays with you. One time I was running over a hill and a machine gun was following me, and I thought, I'm sure he's gonna get me. So I stopped. And he stopped. And then I started running different paces, slow and fast; he couldn't keep up with me. I was grateful that he was a bad shot. I jumped into this big hole and the hole was full of dead body pieces. I had to stay there all night by myself. I had dropped my flamethrower before I went over this ridge.

War brings out the worst and the best in us. Sometimes you're arrogant and you don't wish to be arrogant. Sometimes you're nasty and you don't wish to be nasty. A lot of veterans turned to alcohol because they couldn't make those decisions.

At my age now, I look back on the war as a necessary thing at the time. I look back and I know I've found peace with God, and he has accepted me for who I am.

That Korean time was the most fabulous time of America. America was trying to get back on its feet from a four-year war, and all of a sudden we're hit with this invasion of South Korea, and troops came to the call. So that was a fine, fine moment for America right then.

MALCOLM STILSON

Army Air Corps

Stilson served in the U.S. Army during World War II; after two years of Stateside duty, he was shipped out to India, where he played piano for a troupe in the Entertainment Production Unit of Special Services.

As I look back in retrospect at my travels in India, I begin to see the great pleasures I missed in not learning more about its history and peoples. The chance that I had while there to learn its languages, to view its great men (Gandhi was there and a vibrant force in 1945), and to appreciate its arts, was one I should not have missed. However, I did not take advantage of my opportunities. Perhaps this is the main idiosyncrasy of the American traveler, whether civilian or soldier. He races through a foreign country in order to get home and tell his neighbors he has been there. All I could think about during my enforced sojourn in India was the number of interesting stories I would have to tell when I arrived back in the United States. And, in the process, I lost the opportunity to make my stay more interesting and to really learn something worthwhile about the country.

TRACY SUGARMAN

Navy

Sugarman was a naval officer in command of a group of small support craft during the Normandy invasion.

One of the most remarkable things that made an impression on me that has lasted over all these years was learning about the productivity of this country, seeing it demonstrated. On our little beach, Utah Beach, those first weeks of the invasion, 30 landing ship tanks would pull up on the beach and just disgorge. And they'd pull off, and another 30 would be in there the next day. And another 30. And another 30. This was one beach in one theater of operations. You know, there was Omaha Beach, there were the three Canadian and British beaches, there was the Pacific, there were the Aleutians, there was the

Caribbean. I was just floored and I thought, My God, where is this coming from? And the whole country was in on it. It was a total effort. It had to be a total effort, because we were starting from scratch.

I don't think my experience is actually very different from most men and women who have actually seen combat. When you have actually dealt with death and young people dying, and you're also dealing with the bureaucracy that's attendant to any military function, you're dealing with orders that come from somewhere out there that have not a hell of a lot to do with the reality in which you've got to carry them out. You have responsibilities for your men, for their safety, to see how many survive. You see how many needless deaths are caused in a war by screw-ups, SNAFU, bad orders, ignorance, prejudice, and you realize that this is the worst possible way of solving a problem. It may be necessary, and I certainly do believe that it was necessary to fight World War II.

It's one of the reasons that when I got out of the service, I became very committed to organizing internationally to make better mechanisms for solving these problems. A lot of our problems I think are caused by prejudice, by racial prejudice, religious prejudice. And what I saw in my limited time in Normandy is that when you are really on-site when people are fighting and dying there's no prejudice involved, that it's nonsense, it's really irrelevant, it's an invention, it's a luxury of feeling superior when you're in a comfortable position somewhere. And I swore that I would take those positions when I got home, and it has been a compass for me and for my kids.

JAMES WALSH
Army
Walsh quit the seminary, against his Irish Catholic parents' wishes, to join the Army and fight in the Korean War.

The time for my active duty enlistment had run out on November 11, 1952. I was now in the inactive reserve, back home in Chicago and looking around for a college to attend, or failing mid-semester admission, a full-time job. Was it to be Northwestern, Notre Dame, or Lawter Chemical?

Dad had an answer. "I've the papers, Jim, commissioning you a lieutenant in the Irish Republican Army. Your ticket to Ireland is in the mail. You'll train the lads in the north in combat techniques."

I'd slugged too many beers. It must have affected my hearing. "What?"

"We've got weapons in the hands of Catholic lads in the six counties of the north, lads willing to use them to drive Protestants out of the Province of Ulster.

312 | VOICES OF WAR

You'll teach the lads tactics."

"Tactics? Drive Protestants out of Ulster!" By the look on his face, this wasn't a joke. I reacted indignantly. "Fight Protestants? Dad, who do you think was beside me those months of combat in Korea? What religion do you think my section sergeant, squad leader, assistant gunner, 1st ammo bearer, and on and on and on and on were? They were Protestants! Only I and Norb Gzregorek were Catholic. Whatever our religious beliefs on the front line, there wasn't separation of church and state, especially when we moved out on attack and dug in. We were buddies. We took care of one another. I'm not now about to go over to the north of Ireland to teach Catholics to kill Protestants." I paused for effect. "Dad, I'm an American!"

His limestone face turned red, lips curled, drawn as they were around cutting teeth.

I wasn't unnerved, though I'd committed an act of ancestral treason.

RONALD WINTER

Marine Corps

Winter was a Marine who worked as mechanic on helicopters and flew over 300 missions on them as a machine gunner during the Vietnam War.

I had been in college when I decided to go into the service, and when I got back I went back to college and got an associate's degree in electrical engineering and a bachelor's degree in English. I went to work as a reporter, and the media at that time were portraying all Vietnam vets—I can remember the phrase—as walking time bombs, that somehow or another we were supposed to be waiting for that moment when something would go off in our heads and we would lay waste to the countryside. The actual number of people who live the stereotype is very small. A lot of the people whom the media portrayed as the long-haired person with the drug problem and the vacant stare—it turned out a lot of them were never even in Vietnam or a lot of them were never even in the service.

A lot of the editors I worked with were active in the antiwar movement when I was in Vietnam, and I guess people like me were a reminder to them that it might not have been all that they thought it was. I can remember sitting in a newsroom one day when something came up about Vietnam veterans and it was all negative, and I finally just stopped and said, "You know, I served in Vietnam." And the place went dead quiet. "You?" "Well yeah, me." I didn't fit the stereotype. As it turned out, there were about 20 of us there. Most of the Vietnam veterans did not know the other guys were Vietnam veterans, because it wasn't a good career move to talk about it.

I think it started changing when the Wall [the Vietnam Veterans Memorial] was dedicated in Washington in '82. When the hostages came home from Iran, people realized, Well, we gave them a parade, but we never did anything for the Vietnam vets. Well, Vietnam vets had a parade in Washington in '82, but we put it on ourselves. I think that began changing people's perceptions.

Overall, time's a great healer, and it has brought out the truth.

Max Cleland
Army

We felt like we had to take our place in the line. That fundamental feeling is epitomized in Stephen Ambrose's story, *Citizen Soldiers*. In American history, each time you go to war, you have some commitment from just basic Americans who just feel that in their gut that they have a duty and obligation to take their place in the line. Whatever that place is. And that's really, I think, the strength of American defense. We need the professionals. We need the weapons systems. But after six years on the Armed Services Committee, my view is still the same as it was when I was a young lieutenant in Vietnam with those kids in the foxhole. Their sheer willingness to do their duty, to take their place in the line, is the strength of American defense.

{ ONE WOMAN'S STORY }

Rhona Knox Prescott

"As I was healing…I realized that I could help with others that seemed to come to me."

"I thought I was fine," Rhona Knox Prescott told an interviewer in 2002. She was speaking of her first days back from service as an Army nurse. She served in the U.S. Army from December 1961 to May 1968, the last year of her hitch spent in Vietnam. But in looking back at her experience, during which her best friend was killed in the crash of a plane that Rhona would have been on (see Chapter Four), she realized that this was no ordinary time for her.

"I was extremely high-strung, take no prisoners, extremely high-energy, and so goal-oriented that I think my normal personality disappeared in that year," she recalled. "I became a real tyrannical kind of a driven person, simply to keep myself from dealing with all the stuff that was going on inside." After she left the Army, she tried her hand at civilian nursing. "I realized driving back and forth to work that if there was an ambulance or accident I would literally freeze and I would have to pull over, not to help the person but because I couldn't see straight to drive. I realized something had changed in me and I wasn't right and I really couldn't ethically do nursing because I could not render first aid. I would just stand there, stunned."

What really confirmed her intuition was a home accident involving her husband. "He fell off a ladder and he cut the bottom of his foot. Somehow he managed to get down to an artery; he had a gusher going. He was screaming, he was on the floor, he was bleeding rapidly. I ran upstairs and got a clamp. I had my own little cabinet of surgical instruments. I came down, dug around in the foot, clamped off the artery just like I had been doing for the last year. No big deal. Of course, since he was awake, he felt the soft tissue that I also clamped

Rhona Knox, with two medical corpsmen near An Khe, 1967. Her experiences as an Army nurse in Vietnam have reverberated through her life. Coming to terms with what the war did to her and to her first husband, also a Vietnam veteran, took many years.

and he shrieked like a banshee. Reacting to his screams, irrationally, I took the clamp off, let him bleed, and called 911. Now, this is so diametrically opposed to what I had been doing for a year and how I had functioned in crisis for a year that I realized: This is a different person, no longer a nurse. That was the end of nursing for me."

By then she had children, so "I was able to hide out at home for a couple of years." Her husband, also a Vietnam veteran, was still in the service, so "I went through all the motions of being a military wife, going to the social things, the tea parties, and what not." They were stationed for a time in Germany, which she enjoyed. "I kind of lived on the surface and didn't think much, had no goals except to just raise the kids." Back in the States, her husband processed out of the military, "and then we had to make some decisions because his earning capacity wasn't as great." She wound up going to school on the GI Bill and getting into social work. "I couldn't tell you how. I guess the people that I met thought that it would be good to be away from the blood and guts nursing, but still into the psychiatric field (which I really had a lot of background in from Vietnam from dealing with my staff)." Ultimately she got a master's degree in social work, getting her bachelor's and master's in two and a half years. "And raising the kids and cooking for my husband and cleaning the house. Talk about your 'type A,' driven, take no prisoners personality," she added, laughing.

She became a licensed clinical social worker. "I wound up healing on a different level, no blood and guts but the mental aspect of it, and was very good at it." She worked at several Veterans Administration hospitals. Meanwhile, her husband had died nine years into their marriage, so "I was out in the marketplace again, dating." Through a friend she met a Vietnam vet who was single, and they began seeing each other regularly. He took her to a vet center to meet some Vietnam nurses, and "I went with him because I was dating him and I trusted him." The nurses had formed a therapy group, and they asked her to join them. "Once I got there I realized that I was 'home' and I needed to be there. That started my personal treatment, being in therapy."

At the VA hospital where she worked, she began allowing the Vietnam vets "who just sort of 'sniffed me out' " to come into her office and talk about their war experiences. "As I was healing, I realized that I could help with some of these others that seemed to come to me. So this opened a whole new track and led to my employment at the vet center, where I became an official therapist for 'Nam vets with PTSD [post-traumatic stress disorder]."

Even after the work of her group therapy was over, she kept in touch with some of her nurse friends, getting together once a month for coffee. "Somewhere in those meetings one of the gals said, 'You know, when I was in Vietnam I used to write these letters home, and I have them. Would you like to see them?' So she passed the letters around. They were pretty poignant, and somebody said, jokingly, 'Gee, you ought to publish that!' Then somebody else said, 'Hey, when I was in Vietnam, the war was winding down and I had time to keep a diary. Anybody want to see it?' So we passed that around. That was kind of heavy duty, but it was worthwhile to read." Rhona had been writing poetry and offered her work—"I have some of these bizarre, dark poems, do you want to see them?"—to the group. "As it turned out, all of us had written from Vietnam on."

They edited their material and looked for a publisher to put it into a book. But they had no luck: "The war was still very unpopular and writings about it were not marketable." A teacher in charge of a printing program at a vocational high school offered to print the material for the group for a fee. "We all chipped in money to pay for it, and we just figured it was part of our therapy to unload the stuff into a tangible form and maybe somebody would read it some day."

They managed to sell out the first printing by standing on street corners or when one of them gave a speech at a school. "A side thing is that we had pledged any profits we had achieved (tongue in cheek) to the Vietnam Women's Memorial, which is actually the nurses' statue. We sold the books, and the money we made from them after we got our money back that we put in, we gave it to the Women's Memorial." The book has been reprinted, and Rhona and her friends are once again selling copies.

"My children grew up hard," Rhona Knox Prescott admitted. "They were raised by a single parent because their dad was a Vietnam vet. He was one of those Vietnam vets that didn't get into therapy and indirectly took himself out. There are fifty-eight thousand, two hundred and some names on the wall, killed in action. There are at least twice that many who have either committed suicide or have managed to get themselves killed who are not on that wall. My husband was one of them. The children were very young when that happened, so they grew up with a single parent who was a very take-no-prisoners type of personality. It was hard for them. Now they are all adults and have children of their own, and we have talked, and they have been to the Wall. In fact, my son was the one that took me to the Wall when he was thirteen. He took it upon himself to get me there."

Volunteers conduct an interview during the World War II
Reunion in Washington, D.C., in May 2004.
The Veterans History Project urges grassroots participation
in its efforts to record the stories of wartime veterans.

Tell Us Your Story

Every veteran has a story to tell, and the mission of the Library of Congress Veterans History Project is to collect and preserve those stories from men and women who served in all branches of military service: the Air Force, Army, Coast Guard, Marine Corps, Navy, and Merchant Marine, with an emphasis on World War I, World War II, and the Korean, Vietnam, and Persian Gulf Wars. The project also documents the contributions of civilians, such as war industry workers and medical volunteers, who served in support of the armed forces.

All over the country, communities are honoring our veterans. With its heavy reliance on volunteers, the Veterans History Project is a wonderful way for communities to get involved in recording history and to share in our collective appreciation for the sacrifices of our armed services in wartime. We are particularly eager to capture the memories of World War II veterans of all ranks. Most of them are now in their 80s, and their stories must be recorded soon. We want to urge veterans and families of deceased veterans of that war, World War I, Korea, Vietnam, and the Persian Gulf to share their stories and ensure that the human experiences in these conflicts are recorded in this significant archive.

A visit to the Veterans History Project's Web site, at www.loc.gov/vets, will provide you with all the information you need to conduct interviews of your own and help contribute to this national effort. As the moving stories in this volume make clear, the contributions of millions of ordinary Americans helped preserve this country's ideals. Without donning a uniform or shipping out to a foreign land, you can now make your own contribution to honoring their sacrifice and patriotism. Few things have been more rewarding to me as Librarian of Congress than my own experience of interviewing veterans for this project, and I know this is true of many others here at the nation's library.

The focus of the project is on audio and video recordings of personal wartime experiences, but written memoirs and diaries, as well as collections of letters and photographs that tell the veteran's or civilian's story are also welcome. Maps, home movies, drawings, and other documents may be included as well. The Veterans History Project does not collect or accept objects such as medals, uniforms, or other memorabilia.

How to Participate

The Veterans History Project encourages contributions from ordinary citizens. You may be a veteran, be related to one, or know one with an existing collection of written materials that fit our criteria. Or you may want to record the memories of a veteran, either on videotape or audiotape. The VHP can help you with guidelines and tips. We will send you the necessary forms for donating materials to the project.

What Happens to Your Materials

After you submit the interview, with the required Biographical Data and Release Forms, the interview and other documents will be preserved according to professional archival standards. Certain information from the participants' Biographical Data Forms will be presented to the public in the project's National Registry of Service on the Web site. The materials will be available to researchers, educators, family members, and others at the American Folklife Center in the Library of Congress.

For more information about the Veterans History Project , please contact:

The Veterans History Project
American Folklife Center
Library of Congress
101 Independence Ave., SE
Washington, DC 20540-4615
www.loc.gov/vets

—James H. Billington
The Librarian of Congress

{ RESOURCES }

MILITARY HISTORY CENTERS

Each of the service branches maintains a history center containing a reference collection of books, documents, published unit histories, photographs, medals, and artifacts. The addresses and Web sites for these centers are listed below.

United States Air Force
Air Force History Support Office
AFHSO/HOS
Reference and Analysis Division
200 McChord Street, Box 94
Bolling AFB, DC 20332-1111
Telephone: (202) 404-2261
Web site: http://www.airforcehistory.hq.af.mil/

U.S. Air Force Historical Research Agency
600 Chennault Circle
Building 1405
Maxwell AFB, AL 36112-6424
Telephone: (334) 953-2395
Web site: http://www.au.af.mil/au/afhra/

U.S. Air Force Museum
1100 Spaatz Street
Wright-Patterson AFB, OH 45433-7102
Telephone: (937) 255-3286
Web site: http://www.wpafb.af.mil/museum/
United States Army
U.S. Army Center of Military History Building 35
102 Fourth Avenue
Ft. McNair, DC 20319-5058
Telephone: (202) 685-2733
Web site: http://www.army.mil/cmh-pg/default.htm

U.S. Army Military History Institute
Carlisle Barracks, PA 17013-5008
Telephone: (717) 245-3611
Web site: http://carlisle-www.army.mil/usamhi/

United States Coast Guard
U.S. Coast Guard Historian's Office
United States Coast Guard Headquarters
Room B-717
2100 Second St., SW
Washington, DC 20953
Telephone: (202) 267-2596
Web site:
http://www.uscg.mil/hq/g-cp/history/collect.html

Coast Guard Museum
U.S. Coast Guard Academy
15 Mohegan Avenue
New London, CT 06320-8511
Telephone: (860) 444-8511

Web site:
http://www.uscg.mil/hq/g-cp/museum/MuseumInfo.html

United States Marine Corps
Marine Corps Historical Center Washington Navy Yard
Building 58
1254 Charles Morris Street, SE
Washington Navy Yard, DC 20374-5040
Telephone: (202) 433-3483
Web site:
http://hqinet001.hqmc.usmc.mil/HD/Home_Page.htm

Marine Corps Air-Ground Museum
Marine Corps Combat Development Command
2014 Anderson Avenue
Quantico, VA 22134-5002
Telephone: (703) 784-2607
Web site:
http://hqinet001.hqmc.usmc.mil/HD/Home_Page.htm

United States Navy
Naval Historical Center
Washington Navy Yard
Building 57
805 Kidder Breese Street, SE
Washington Navy Yard, DC 20374-5060
Telephone: (202) 433-3634
Web site: http://www.history.navy.mil/

LOCATING MILITARY SERVICE RECORDS

Individual Personnel Files

The National Archives and Records Administration (NARA) is the official repository for records of military personnel who have been discharged from the U.S. Air Force, Army, Marine Corps, Navy, and Coast Guard.

A veteran (or next of kin) may request his or her individual military personnel file (201 file) by sending a request to the National Personnel Records Center, Military Records Facility, 9700 Page Boulevard, St. Louis, MO 63132-5100.

Additional information about the contents of these personnel files, instructions for submitting a request, and a downloadable PDF copy of the request form may be found on the National Personnel Records Center home page of the National Archives and Records Administration Web site (http://www.archives.gov/facilities/mo/st_louis/military_personnel_records.html).

Personnel records of civilians who worked for the various branches of the military are also held by the National Personnel Records Center. The address to write for these records is National Personnel Records Center, Civilian Records Facility, 111 Winnebago Street, St. Louis, MO 63118-4199.

{ AFTERWORD }

Embracing History

WHEN THE VETERANS HISTORY PROJECT at the Library of Congress became law on October 27, 2000, the Veterans History Project began archiving oral histories, memoirs, letters, photographs and journals from veterans and civilians who served in every war or conflict from World War I to the present. History holds no clear road map for the future, but the Veterans History Project continues to help us understand war and its impact on society through its collection of oral histories. It serves as a resource to help educate future generations on the meaning of service and the importance of global cooperation.

The Project's interviews are archived and become a permanent record of the courage and sacrifices of thousands of men and women who served our country during times of war. Americans have much to learn from those who served. The more we understand about war, duty and sacrifice, the more ardently we will pursue peace.

This Project serves as a dynamic way of educating those who have never experienced war. One can never underestimate the power of role models— whether they are family, friends or figures one only reads about. The Veterans History Project is a treasure-trove for discovering quiet heroes and humble warriors who serve as role models to us all. It is through their stories that Americans can begin to appreciate the extraordinary sacrifices made by so many to ensure America's freedom.

Two years ago, I was interviewed for the Veterans History Project about my service in the Vietnam War as an Army sergeant with my brother, Tom. My interview was one thread woven into the fabric of Veterans History Project interviews that I hope will help to contribute to a wider understanding of war. I am proud to have been a part of the creation of the Veterans History Project and honored to have my story included in the Project's collection.

Everyone who served in the military or civilian support has an important story to share. I encourage all war veterans to share their stories with the Veterans History Project. If you know war veterans, help them record their histories and thank them for their service. Visit the Veterans History Project website at www.loc.gov/vets to find information and forms for participation.

Abraham Lincoln remarked in his annual message to Congress on December 1, 1862 that "we cannot escape history...no personal significance or insignificance can spare one or another of us." The Veterans History Project allows us to embrace American history through the voices of those who have lived it. It is through their stories that we find strength in the American spirit and hope for a better future.

U.S. Sen. Chuck Hagel
Washington, D.C., 2004

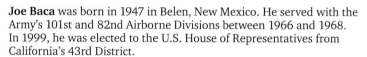

{ CONTRIBUTORS }

To read the full stories of the contributors, visit www.loc.gov/vets

Jay Adams was born in 1922 in Painesville, Ohio. From 1942 to 1945 he served with the Army in an engineer battalion in the European Theater. He lives in Ohio.

William Arnett was born in 1917 in Clarksburg, West Virginia. He served in the Army infantry from 1941 to 1945, operating a tank destroyer in the European Theater of World War II. He lives in West Virginia.

BACA

Joe Baca was born in 1947 in Belen, New Mexico. He served with the Army's 101st and 82nd Airborne Divisions between 1966 and 1968. In 1999, he was elected to the U.S. House of Representatives from California's 43rd District.

James Baross was born in 1923 in Greenlawn, New York. From 1942 to 1945 he served with the Army Air Corps in the Pacific Theater of World War II.

William Barr was born in 1919 in Hamilton, Ontario, Canada.He served in the Navy from 1942 to 1945 in the Pacific Theater as a Photographer's Mate 1st Class. He lives in Michigan.

Robert Bendl was born in 1949 in Midlothian, Virginia. He served with the Army infantry between 1967 and 1969, doing one tour of duty in Vietnam. He lives in Virginia.

Samuel Boylston was born in 1923 in Springfield, South Carolina. He served with the Army Air Corps between 1943 and 1945 in the Pacific Theater of World War II. He died in 2001.

Meda Hallyburton Brendall was born in 1911 in Nez Perce, Idaho. During World War II, she worked as a civilian welder in the Bethlehem-Fairfield Shipyards in Baltimore, Maryland. Her son, Paul Steppe, is also featured in this book.

John Butler was born in 1945 in Rockford, Illinois. Between 1967 and 1970, he served in the Marine Corps, doing one tour of duty in Vietnam. He lives in Virginia.

Steve Buyer was born in 1958 in Rensselaer, Indiana. His Army Reserve unit was called to duty for the Persian Gulf War in November 1990; he served in the JAG Corps. In 1992, he was elected to represent the 4th District of Indiana in the U.S. House of Representatives.

Max Cleland was born in 1942 in Lithonia, Georgia. He began his active service with the Army with the Signal Corps in 1965; in 1968

{ CONTRIBUTORS }

he was severely wounded while serving in Vietnam and subsequently received an honorable discharge. He has been Administrator of the Veterans Administration and has represented Georgia in the U.S. Senate.

Isabelle Cedar Cook was born in 1918 in Amityville, New York. In the Army Nurse Corps from 1942 to 1945, she served in North Africa, Italy, and France. She lives in California.

Clare Morrison Crane was born in 1921 in Cleveland, Ohio. In 1943, she married Army officer Herbert Johns. She worked in one of Cleveland's USO clubs while her husband was stationed in Europe. Herbert Johns died in July 1945, en route back to the United States for medical treatment. She later remarried and now lives in Ohio.

Denton Crocker was born in 1919 in Salem, Massachusetts. He served in the Army in their Malaria Survey Unit in the Pacific Theater between 1942 and 1945. He lives in New York.

DIERKES

Alvin Dickson was born in 1918 in Canton, Ohio. From 1942 to 1945 he served with the Army's 11th Armored Division in the European Theater of World War II. He lives in Ohio.

Raymond Dierkes was born in 1923 in St. Louis, Missouri. From 1943 to 1945 he served in two Navy construction battalions, seeing action in both the European and Pacific Theaters. He lives in Missouri.

SPENCER

John Earle was born in 1916 in Dryden, New York. He served from 1942 to 1946 with the Army's Special Services Unit in the European Theater of World War II. He lives in California.

John Enman was born in 1921 in Newton, Massachusetts. From 1943 to 1946 he served in the Army Air Corps with the 2nd Photo Procurement Detail; he was stationed in India. He lives in Pennsylvania.

Bruce Fenchel was born in 1925 in Strawberry Point, Iowa. He served in a tank battalion in the European Theater of World War II. He lives in Iowa.

Donald Finn was born in 1915 in Expanse, Saskatchewan, and grew up in Idaho. He served in the U.S. Navy from 1939 to 1945, was stationed at Pearl Harbor on December 7, 1941, and saw action in the Pacific Theater. He lives in Illinois.

Margaret (Peggy) Henry Fleming was born in 1920 in Milwaukee, Wisconsin. She was a Red Cross worker during World War II, serving in the European Theater. She lives in Ohio.

{ CONTRIBUTORS }

HINSCH

Mary Sheldon Gill was born in 1921 in Albany, New York. She joined the Women's Army Corps in 1942 and did clerical work at an Army hospital in Asheville, North Carolina, until her discharge in 1944. She lives in Florida.

Violet Askins Hill Gordon was born in 1916 in Talihina, Oklahoma. She served in the Women's Army Auxiliary Corps from 1942 to 1946. She lives in Florida.

Marion Reh Gurfein was born in 1920 in New York, New York. She married Joseph Gurfein, an Army officer, in 1941. He served in both World War II and the Korean War, while Marion cared for their daughter (born during World War II) and son (born between the wars) in New York City. She lives in Virginia.

Chuck Hagel was born in 1946 in North Platte, Nebraska. He served in the Army infantry from 1967 to 1968, doing one tour of duty in Vietnam. In 1996, he was elected to represent Nebraska in the U.S. Senate.

Rod Hinsch was born in 1946 in Beech Grove, Indiana. Between 1964 and 1970 he served with the Army's Special Forces unit, doing one tour of duty in Vietnam. He lives in Indiana.

Rafael Hirtz was born in 1921 in Buenos Aires. He became a naturalized citizen when his family moved to California in the 1930s. From 1940 to 1946 he served with the Army in the Signal Corps and with the Office of Strategic Services. He died in 2003.

Thomas Hodge was born in 1949 in Springfield, Massachusetts. He served with the Marine Corps's Truck Division from 1968 to 1971, doing one tour of duty in Vietnam. He currently lives in Massachusetts.

Jeanne Holm was born in 1921 in Portland, Oregon. From 1942 to 1975 she served in the military, first in the Women's Army Corps and later in the Air Force, achieving the rank of Major General before her retirement. She lives in Maryland.

Theodore Kohls was born in 1902 in Watertown, Wisconsin. From 1917 to 1919 he served in the Army infantry, seeing combat action in World War I. He died in 1948.

Robert Krishef was born in 1931 in Minneapolis, Minnesota. He served in the Army infantry from 1952 to 1954 and fought in the Korean War. He lives in Minnesota.

{ CONTRIBUTORS }

MORRIS

NEVILLE

Kevin Roy Lee was born in 1964 in Bethesda, Maryland. He enlisted in the Army in 1983, serving in the Persian Gulf War in a transportation battalion. He lives in Tennessee.

William Loncaric was born in 1921 in St. Louis, Missouri. He served from 1942 to 1981 in the Army, and in World War II he was a member of the 250th Field Artillery Battalion, seeing action in the European Theater. He lives in Florida.

Bill McGlynn served with the Army Air Corps in the European Theater of World War II. He lives in New York.

John Manger was born in 1916 in Laurium, Michigan. Between 1942 and 1946 he served with the Army's 164th Engineer Battalion in the European Theater of World War II. He lives in Texas.

Jeanne Urbin Markle was born in 1943 in Logansport, Indiana. She served in the Army Nurse Corps from 1964 to 1967 and did one tour of duty in Vietnam. She lives in Indiana.

Helen Minor was born in 1921 in Batavia, New York. From 1944 to 1947 she served in the Women's Army Corps, working as an occupational therapist in a number of hospitals around the U.S. She lives in Michigan.

Walter Morris was born in 1921 in Waynesboro, Georgia. He served in the Army from 1941 to 1946 and helped organize the 555 Parachute Infantry Battalion. He lives in Florida.

Catherine Neville was born in 1916 in Bedford, Massachusetts. From 1943 to 1966, she served in the Army Nurse Corps. She was stationed in England, Korea, Japan, and various locations in the United States during World War II and the Korean War. She lives in Massachusetts.

William Frederick Nice was born in 1882 in Philadelphia. He served in the Marine Corps from 1905 to 1919; he saw duty in Haiti, Santo Domingo, Nicaragua, Mexico, and Cuba before he shipped out in 1917 to France to fight in World War I. He died in 1965.

Irving Oblas was born in 1912 in New York, New York. From 1943 to 1946, he served in the Navy; his main duties were as a court reporter. He died in 1997.

Robert Lee Olen was born in 1923 in Brooklyn, New York. He served with the Army's 10th Mountain Division in the European Theater of World War II between 1943 and 1945. He died in 2001.

{ CONTRIBUTORS }

Joanne Palella was born in 1962 in Chicago, Illinois. She served in the Army from 1981 to 1993 and saw action in the Persian Gulf War. She lives in Wisconsin.

Rhona Knox Prescott was born in 1941 on Staten Island, New York. From 1961 to 1968 she served in the Army Nurse Corps, doing one tour of duty in Vietnam. She lives in Florida.

Sally Hitchcock Pullman was born in 1919 in Bristol, Connecticut. She served with the Army Nurse Corps from 1944 to 1946 in the Pacific Theater of World War II. She lives in Connecticut.

RALEY

Nathaniel Raley was born in 1922 in Demopolis, Alabama. From 1942 to 1945 he was a pilot in the Army Air Force, flying missions in the European Theater of World War II. He lives in Alabama.

Vincent Reed was born in 1889 in New London, Missouri. From 1918 to 1919 he served in the Army infantry, fighting in France during World War I. He died in 1976.

Charles Restifo was born in 1917 in New York, New York. Between 1942 and 1945 he served in the Pacific Theater of World War II with the Army's 161st Photographic Company. He died in 1995.

Sidney Riches was born in 1914 in Superior, Wisconsin. He served with the Army from 1940 to 1946 and from 1948 to 1968. He fought with the infantry in the Pacific Theater of World War II. He lives in California.

Arnold Robbins was born in 1920 in Cleveland, Ohio. He served in the Army from 1941 to 1945 and was stationed in Iceland, England, and France during World War II. He died in 1998.

SCHROCK

Edward Schrock was born in 1941 in Middletown, Ohio. He served in the Navy from 1964 to 1988, doing two tours of duty in Vietnam. In 2000, he was elected to represent Virginia's Second District in the U.S. House of Representatives.

Patricia Seawalt was born in 1947 in Beardstown, Illinois. She had completed 13 years of service with the Air Force and Army Reserves when the Persian Gulf War began. She reenlisted and served with the Army's Oil Analysis Program during that conflict. She lives in Illinois.

{ CONTRIBUTORS }

F. Rosalind Westfall Sellmer was born in 1920 in Dunbar, West Virginia. Between 1942 and 1947, she served as an Army Air Corps nurse, stationed in Baton Rouge, Louisiana; Newfoundland; the Azores; and Paris. She lives in Indiana.

Ben Snyder was born in 1920 in Philadelphia, Pennsylvania. From 1943 to 1945, he served with the Army Air Corps in the Pacific Theater of World War II. He lives in Michigan.

Donald Spencer was born in 1924 in Colorado Springs, Colorado. He served with the Army Air Corps from 1943 to 1945 in the European Theater of World War II. He lives in Oregon.

Joseph Steinbacher was born in 1923 in Foley, Alabama. From 1943 to 1945, he served in the Army infantry, fighting in the Pacific Theater of World War II. He lives in Washington.

Paul Steppe was born in 1932 in Morgantown, North Carolina. He served in the Marine Corps from 1950 to 1952, seeing action in the Korean War. He died in 2004. The story of his mother, Meda Brendall, is also featured in this book.

Frederick Stilson was born in 1889 in Galesburg, Illinois. From 1917 to 1919, he served in the Army Corps of Engineers and was stationed in France and Germany during World War I. He died in 1974. The story of his son Malcolm Stilson is also featured in this book.

M. STILSON

Malcolm Stilson was born in 1923 in Los Angeles, California. He served in the Army Air Corps from 1942 to 1946; in the China-Burma-India Theater he worked with the Entertainment Production Unit. His father, Frederick Stilson, is also featured in this book.

Tracy Sugarman was born in 1921 in Syracuse, New York. He served from 1942 to 1945 in the Navy as an officer in charge of small landing craft; he was involved with the Normandy invasion and subsequent operations. He lives in Connecticut.

Patty Thomas was born in 1922 in Erie, Pennsylvania. From 1944 to 1945, she worked as a dancer in the USO, performing in shows in the Pacific Theater of World War II. She lives in Florida.

SUGARMAN

Ernest Thorp was born in 1921 in Clinton, Illinois. He served in the Army Air Corps from 1942 to 1945, flying missions in the European Theater of World War II. He lives in Illinois.

{ CONTRIBUTORS }

TSUNEISHI

Warren Tsuneishi was born in 1921 in Monrovia, California. He served from 1943 to 1946 with the Army, translating captured enemy documents in the Pacific Theater of World War II. He lives in Maryland.

Bill Vicars was born in 1940 in Paris, Illinois. Between 1959 and 1980, he served in the Army and did two tours of duty in Vietnam as a member of the infantry. He lives in Texas.

Marie Brand Voltzke was born in 1918 in Wolf Summit, West Virginia. From 1943 to 1945, she served in the WAVEs; her duty station was Washington, D.C. She lives in California.

VOLTZKE

R. James Walsh was born in 1931 in Chicago, Illinois. He served in the Korean War with the Army infantry from 1951 to 1952. He lives in Indiana.

William Whiting was born in 1920 in Mayville, Wisconsin. He served in an artillery battalion of the Army in the European Theater of World War II. He lives in New Hampshire.

WILAYTO

Henry Wilayto was born in 1917 in Nashua, New Hampshire. He served in the Army from 1940 to 1948; between 1942 and 1945 he was a prisoner of war of the Japanese. He lives in Massachusetts.

Corbin Willis was born in 1922 in Fort Morgan, Colorado. He served in the military between 1941 and 1961. He was in the Army Air Corps in the European Theater of World War II and in the Air Force during the Korean War. He lives in Oregon.

Ron Winter was born in 1947 in Troy, New York. From 1966 to 1970 he served in the Marine Corps, doing one tour of duty in Vietnam. He lives in Connecticut.

John Wister was born in 1887 in Philadelphia, Pennsylvania. He served in the Army between 1917 and 1919, running an ordnance depot in France in World War I. He died in 1982.

YOUNGINER

Janice Bickerstaff Yeoman was born in 1950 in Pawtucket, Rhode Island. She worked for the USO from 1963 to 1968, entertaining the troops during the Vietnam War era. She lives in Indiana.

Jacob Younginer was born in 1942 in Lexington, South Carolina. He served in the Air Force from 1964 to 1992, doing one tour of duty in Vietnam. He lives in Georgia.

{ PHOTO CREDITS }

{ INDEX }

{ ACKNOWLEDGMENTS }

Special thanks to the staff of the Veterans History Project, especially Sarah Rouse, Eileen Simon, Ellen McCulloch-Lovell, Bev Lindsey, Diane Kresh, David Albee, Peter Bartis, Anneliesa Clump Behrend, Clare Denk, Sheila Dyer, Megan Harris, Neil Huntley, Jason Lee, Rachel Mears, Christine Middleton, Nancy Mitchell, Judy Ng, Tim Roberts, Sandra Savage, Tim Schurtter, Jonathan Setliff, Virginia Sorkin, Taru Spiegel, and Lee Woodman. I am grateful to Betsy Miller and Moryma Aydelott, plus Morgan Cundiff, Glenn Gardner, and Corey Keith, all of the Library of Congress's Network Development team. Also thanks to Betsy Dunford of Congressman Ron Kind's office, Nathan Mick of Senator Chuck Hagel's office, and Elaine Iler of Max Cleland's office. My wife, Barbara Humphrys, informs and inspires me, as always. I would like to dedicate my work on this book to the memory of my parents, Sanford and Marie Wiener, who served in World War II and married in Italy in February 1945. I only wish I'd asked them about their own stories of war.
—Tom Wiener

PUBLISHED BY THE NATIONAL GEOGRAPHIC SOCIETY
John M. Fahey, Jr., *President and Chief Executive Officer*
Gilbert M. Grosvenor, *Chairman of the Board*
Nina D. Hoffman, *Executive Vice President*

PREPARED BY THE BOOK DIVISION
Kevin Mulroy, *Vice President and Editor-in-Chief*
Charles Kogod, *Illustrations Director*
Marianne R. Koszorus, *Design Director*

STAFF FOR THIS BOOK
Lisa Krause Thomas, *Editor*
Walton Rawls, *Text Editor*
Paula Dailey, *Illustrations Editor*
Bill Marr, *Art Director*
Gary Colbert, *Production Director*
Richard Wain, *Production Project Manager*
Sharon Berry, *Illustrations Assistant*
Rebecca Hale, *Contributing Photographer*
Emily McCarthy, *Editorial Intern*

MANUFACTURING AND QUALITY CONTROL
Christopher A. Liedel, *Chief Financial Officer*
Phillip L. Schlosser, *Managing Director*
John T. Dunn, *Technical Director*
Vincent P. Ryan, *Manager*
Clifton M. Brown, *Manager*

STAFF FOR THE LIBRARY OF CONGRESS
W. Ralph Eubanks, *Director of Publishing*
Tom Wiener, *Writer and Editor*
Aimee Hess, *Editorial Assistant*
Eileen Simon, *Researcher*

One of the world's largest non-profit scientific and educational organizations, the National Geographic Society was founded in 1888 "for the increase and diffusion of geographic knowledge." Fulfilling this mission, the Society educates and inspires millions every day through its magazines, books, television programs, videos, maps and atlases, research grants, the National Geographic Bee, teacher workshops, and innovative classroom materials. The Society is supported through membership dues, charitable gifts, and income from the sale of its educational products. This support is vital to National Geographic's mission to increase global understanding and promote conservation of our planet through exploration, research, and education.

For more information, please call 1-800-NGS LINE (647-5463) or write to the following address:
National Geographic Society
1145 17th Street N.W.
Washington, D.C. 20036-4688
U.S.A.
Visit the Society's Web site at www.nationalgeographic.com.